THE EMPIRICAL ARCHITECTURE OF WEALTH

THE EMPIRICAL ARCHITECTURE OF WEALTH

A Quantitative Analysis of Global Development

Hugo M. Montesinos-Yufa

MONTESINOS
PRESS

Collegeville, Pennsylvania, 2026

The Empirical Architecture of Wealth
A Quantitative Analysis of Global Development

First Edition: January 2026

Published by **MONTESINOS** PRESS, Collegeville, Pennsylvania

Cover Design by **MONTESINOS** PRESS

Book Layout by **MONTESINOS** PRESS

Hardcover ISBN: 978-1-971413-00-6

To the memory of my parents, Hugo and Raquel.
And to my daughter, Olguita Raquel, who carries the future they dreamed of.

FREE DIGITAL COMPANION

FOR SCHOLARS & RESEARCHERS

www.hugomontesinos.com/WealthData

This volume contains detailed econometric models and regression tables that are designed to be studied in high resolution.

Scan the code above to download the free **Empirical Architecture Research Pack**, which includes:

- High-Resolution PDF of all Tables & Figures.
- The Complete Poverty Dataset.
- Replication Data for Researchers.

FOREWORD TO THE 2025 EDITION

The text you are about to read was my doctoral dissertation at Florida State University, written during 2018-2019, and defended in the summer of 2019. In the years since, the global economic landscape has shifted, but the fundamental questions of prosperity—why some nations rise while others stagnate—remain as urgent as ever. The answers, rooted in the deep structure of institutions, have not changed.

I am publishing this work in its original, rigorous form for a specific reason. Too often, economic insights are stripped of their empirical foundations when presented to the public. We are told what to think, but rarely shown the raw architecture of the evidence. This volume is that architecture. It contains econometric models, detailed regression tables, and rigorous technical arguments that link the interplay of geography, institutions, and human capital.

This work also marks the beginning of a methodological journey for me. During the writing of this dissertation, I had the privilege of being supervised by Professor James D. Gwartney. As many know, Jim was blind for the latter part of his career. This reality forced a unique discipline upon our work. We could not rely on standard visual crutches. Every graph, every table, and every statistical relationship had to be translated into a logical narrative that could be "seen" with the mind's eye.

That training helped me learn to visualize the invisible architecture of the data, and it implicitly shaped every page of this analysis. While this volume presents the data in standard visual tables for the academic reader, the logic behind them was forged almost entirely during verbal sessions.

For the general reader seeking a narrative exploration of these concepts, I am currently preparing a companion volume, **The Invisible Architecture of Wealth**, which focuses on the stories and mental models behind these numbers. But for the scholar, the student, and the skeptic who demands rigorous empirical models, proofs, and detailed arguments: this book is for you.

Hugo M. Montesinos-Yufa
Collegeville, Pennsylvania, December 2025

FLORIDA STATE UNIVERSITY

COLLEGE OF SOCIAL SCIENCES AND PUBLIC POLICY

ON GEOGRAPHY, INSTITUTIONS, HUMAN CAPITAL, AND ECONOMIC DEVELOPMENT

By

HUGO MOISES MONTESINOS YUFA

A Dissertation submitted to the
Department of Economics
in partial fulfillment of the
requirements for the degree of
Doctor of Philosophy

2019

Hugo Moises Montesinos Yufa defended this dissertation on August 19, 2019.

The members of the supervisory committee were:

James D. Gwartney
Professor Co-Directing Dissertation

Randall G. Holcombe
Professor Co-Directing Dissertation

Patricia Born
University Representative

Keith Ihlanfeldt
Committee Member

Anastasia Semykina
Committee Member

The Graduate School has verified and approved the above-named committee members, and certifies that the dissertation has been approved in accordance with university requirements.

To Olga

ACKNOWLEDGMENTS

To God, for giving me so much grace and so many blessings throughout my life, including my wonderful wife, Olga, and our potentially growing family; my biological parents, Hugo Jesus and Gladys Raquel; my sister Mariana Alicia Esther and brother-in-law Jonathan, my amazing niece Melissa Victoria and nephew Sebastian Abraham. My parents in law Pavel and Galina and my new sisters Natalia and Corina, and our extended families. You are all the most beautiful gift I could have ever imagined, and I feel fortunate and grateful to have you in my life.

To Jim and Amy Gwartney, for being the most amazing advisors for life that anyone could dream of. You are role models for my wife and me! Thank you so much for giving me your time, your love, and for being available every moment I needed it, particularly the most crucial times when I was arriving from Venezuela. Thank you also for so many lunches, dinners, breakfasts, blueberry muffins, and Starbucks coffee in the mornings, and for never letting me pay for anything. I will never be able to repay you, but I promise that I will pass the ball of kindness.

Dr. Gwartney, thank you so much for reading this dissertation entirely and for providing me with such fantastic and priceless advice. Learning from you was illuminating and humbling. Being your TA and RA was a big privilege. You taught me and helped me from day one; and you let me co-teach your graduate development class twice, the most enjoyable class in my life. That class set the stage for this dissertation and for other ongoing projects. Everything has been a life-changing experience. I have no words to thank you enough for everything! Thank you SO much!

To my committee members, professors Patty Born, James Gwartney, Randall Holcombe, Keith Idlanfeldt, and Anastasia Semykina. Thank you for being so willing to read my dissertation, participate in my defense, and advising me in the process. Dr. Semykina, special thanks to you for being so sweet and helpful all the time, and for providing me with words of wisdom and reassurance when I needed it the most. Thank you SO much!

Special thanks to Patty and Paul Schriefer for being a super couple role model for me. Patty, in particular, for being an academic mother in the realm of risk management and insurance.

To the FSU department of economics, I am greatly indebted for a fantastic academic atmosphere, including hosting several seminars/workshops per week. Especially the Quant and Regulation workshops were really helpful to foster an excellent academic environment. The following professors and friends were especially helpful during my doctoral studies: Amid Ardakani, Manoj Atolia, Paul Beaumont, Luque Boosey, Joe Calhoun, Gary Fournier, Lora Holcombe, Marc Isaac, Shawn Kantor, Carl Kitchens, Carrie Lee, Lora Holcombe, Randall Holcombe, Doug Norton, Dimitry Ryvkin, Katie Sherron, Cynthia Yang, and Thomas Zuehlke. Special thanks to Dr. Zuehlke, for being so helpful all the time, and for being an exceptional professor. In addition, I am thankful to all other econ Ph.D. students at FSU in my cohort and in other cohorts. I cannot name you all, but I am fortunate and grateful for having many productive intellectual interactions with you.

I am also greatly indebted to the following staff members at FSU: Jennifer Kirkland, Elizabeth Kistner, Laura Kitchens, June Bozeman, Wanda Michell, and Tonja Guilford. Without your help and support, this would not be possible! Thank you SO much!

To the Gus A. Stavros Center and all its members (current and past), thank you! These include Brandon Brice, Joab Corey, Joe Calhoun, Jeff Conley, Joe Connors, Jim Gwartney, Jennifer Kirkland, and Signe Thomas. It has been amazing to be part of the Stavros Center family. You are all not only phenomenal teachers but also remarkable human beings. I have learned so much from you! Especial thanks to Jennifer and Signe for always being good friends of mine, and to Dr. Calhoun and Joe Connors for facilitating my transition to FSU and being angels in my life. I will never be able to thank you enough.

To all my Table Tennis family, but especially to Willy, Shelly, and Mia Leparulo! Meeting you was a life-changing experience. You are also role models for me. Without you, I would not be in the FSU Table Tennis family. Thank you SO much!

To my extended biological families of Arlette, Raimundo, Mariana, and Daniela; and Tia Negra y Tio Rafael, thank you SO much for your love and support all the time. Also, to my non-biological families of Gianfranco, Susan, Domenica, Daniella, and Mia; Hugo Joaquin Faria and Maria Eugenia Zubillaga, my non-biological parents; and Daniel Morales, Carlos Navarro, and Hugo Faria, my Venezuelan research family team; thank you all SO much for your support.

To Alex Utzvisky and Dan Le, for being my best friends in Tallahassee. Alex, thanks for so many lunches and interesting conversations in the last five years. Dan, thanks for so many running adventures, for pushing me to run especially when I was stressed, and for taking care of the music at my wedding.

To father Tim and all the members of the Catholic Student Union at FSU, and to all the members of other students organizations in which I have participated in the last five years. These include Tango, Salsa (Azucar), Swing dancing, Ultimate Frisbee, and of course Table Tennis. Thank you for all the support and warm welcoming.

To all other individuals, families, and organizations that have supported me, and that I have interacted with over the last 5 years, thanks for so much!

I love you all, SO much!

TABLE OF CONTENTS

LIST OF TABLES

LIST OF FIGURES

ABSTRACT

Following the neoclassical model of Robert Solow, several theories have been proposed to explain the fundamental causes of growth and economic development. This dissertation analyzes three of the main hypotheses. Chapter 2 explores the hypothesis that geographic conditions associated with climate and location impact development adversely, and how this impact, if any, may have changed over time. The hypothesis that institutions are the main cause of economic development is analyzed in Chapter 3 with an emphasis on disentangling the roles of economic and political institutions. A causal link supporting the institutional hypothesis is established using ancestral instrumental variables as an exogenous source of variation in economic institutions. Chapter 4 turns the attention to human capital and its potential dual role as both a cause and a consequence of development. This dissertation finds evidence consistent with all three theories using an integrated approach and better quality data than previously used in the literature. Moreover, Appendix A builds a novel balanced poverty dataset covering 176 countries from 1970 to 2015, and Chapters 2 and 3 utilize these new data as an alternative measure of development.

Chapter 2 constructs an index of geographic disadvantage based on climate and location variables and identifies the most geographically disadvantaged countries according to this index. Geographic conditions are found to affect development adversely, both directly and indirectly through the quality of institutions, mainly through economic institutions and international trade. Even though the adverse impact of geography has declined over time, in part due to technological innovations, there remains a substantial geographic handicap on the relative levels of per capita GDP, poverty rate, and trade. Evidence of this is the differential impact on developing economies of the transportation and communication revolution (TCR): the volume of international trade is smaller, and it increased less, in geographically disadvantaged countries than in other countries. Nevertheless, the TCR has positively impacted a much broader share of the world's population (about 70 percent) than did the Industrial Revolution (about 15 percent) two centuries ago. The digital revolution of recent decades, in turn, is potentially impacting all countries, including the most geographically disadvantaged.

Chapter 3 shows that institutions, particularly economic institutions, are strongly associated with increases in per capita GDP and reductions in poverty rates. The distinction between economic and political institutions is crucial for economic development, and the usage of good-quality and comprehensive measures (as opposed to crude measures) of institutions is also essential to quantify the merits of the institutional hypothesis correctly.

Instrumental variable analysis indicates that the usual colonial instruments for political institutions, such as settler mortality rate and early disease environment, are invalid instruments for political institutions in part because they work through economic institutions and potentially other channels such as human capital. Falsification tests suggest that these instruments impact development directly even after controlling for political institutions. In contrast, ancestral instruments for economic institutions, including migratory distance from Ethiopia, are shown to pass the falsification tests, suggesting that their impact on development is only through economic institutions. A theory is provided linking ancestral migratory distance with pre-colonial culture, and through this channel, exogenously affecting current economic institutions. The results of the analysis indicate that institutions consistent with economic freedom significantly cause prosperity.

Chapter three also explores the relationship between political and economic institutions. Reforms towards inclusive political institutions typically occur first, followed by reforms towards inclusive economic institutions. The findings are consistent with the view that economic institutions are, at least partially, an outcome of the political process.

Chapter four focuses on human capital. The evidence indicates an important dual role of human capital in the development process, as both input and output. The findings suggest that there is a virtuous cycle of growth and human capital accumulation: levels and increases in human capital lead to growth and, in turn, growth leads to improvements in human capital. Recent large-scale international assessment tests provide better measures of human capital than those available in the past. Educational achievement outperforms educational attainment in income regressions, suggesting that the former is a more accurate measure of human capital than the latter and that schooling does not necessarily imply learning. Indeed, an essential part of human capital occurs at home. This research finds that the education of the parents and grandparents, the family size, the number of books at home, the expected occupational status at age 30, and the teaching environment at the school, are all key determinants of learning, explaining almost 40 percent of the variation in individual-level achievement scores.

CHAPTER 1

INTRODUCTION

"The consequences for human welfare involved in questions like these are simply staggering: once one starts to think about them, it is hard to think about anything else."
Robert Lucas.

It is not easy to fully quantify the importance of long-run economic growth in terms of the extent of its impact on human lives. Consider the U.S. economy in the last two centuries. The real per capita gross domestic product (GDP) in the United States increased by a factor of over 25 from $2,080 in 1820 to $52,591 in 2015. This increase in per capita GDP corresponds to an annual growth rate of approximately 1.7 percent.

Had the United States grown at 0.7 percent starting from the same level of $2,080 in 1820, its 2015 per capita GDP would be $8,106. This figure is similar to the 2015 per capita GDP of El Salvador and Cuba, and about half the 2015 per capita GDP of Venezuela. This hypothetical 2015 figure is also similar to the U.S. per capita GDP during 1932-1933, at the bottom of the great depression. In turn, if the U.S. had grown at 2.7 percent per year starting from the same level of $2,080 in 1820, its 2015 per capita GDP would be an astonishing $375,231. Such a figure seems almost unimaginable, but according to the data it is similar to the per capita GDP of Qatar in 1980, at the all-time peak of oil prices, when the population of Qatar was about 0.2 million.[1]

In the 1820 years AD, the per capita GDP of the world increased 42.6 percent (or 0.019 percent annually), from $803 in 1 to $1,145 in 1820. In 2016, the per capita GDP for the world was $14,934, more than 13 times the level in 1820, corresponding to an annual growth rate of 1.3 percent. This average figure, however, is slightly deceiving. Only a few countries having about 15 percent of the world's population, were directly impacted by the Industrial Revolution. It took over a century, and a huge reduction in transportation and communication costs, for the wave of modern economic development to reach out to enough countries to cover more than half of the world's population.

The facts mentioned above highlight the paramount importance of having annual growth rates of one additional percentage point over extended periods. Looking at these facts, it is not

[1] These figures are from the most recent release of the Maddison Project Database (2018) and are expressed in 2011 PPP dollars.

difficult to understand why Lucas (1988) wrote the quote at the beginning of this chapter and the paramount importance of questions like why some countries grow and prosper while others stagnate. Explaining the determinants of economic growth and the cross-country disparities in economic prosperity and well-being has been one of the most fundamental questions and challenges in the economic profession since Adam Smith published his seminal treatise *The Wealth of Nations* in 1776.

Several theories and explanations have been proposed to answer the questions above and to explain the remarkable economic development of the past 200 years. Prior to 1990, the dominating explanation was provided by Robert Solow. In the neoclassical model of Solow (1956), increases in the factors of production such as physical capital, human capital, labor, and technological progress, are the drivers of growth. The Solow model played a crucial role in the profession by identifying proximate causes of growth and their theoretical linkage in a mathematical model that can be solved for a steady-state equilibrium.

There are, however, at least two major drawbacks to the Solow model. First, it does not address the fundamental causes of growth (such as geography, institutions, or culture), but only proximate causes of growth (such as human capital, capital accumulation, and technological progress). That is, the Solow model does not explain what really drives prosperity, but it merely redescribes what it means to be prosperous. In other words, the factors of production can be better viewed as outcomes, rather than inputs, of the development process. North and Thomas (1976) pointed this out very clearly when they said: "The factors we have listed (innovation, economies of scale, education, capital accumulation, etc.) are not causes of growth; they are growth." North and Thomas (1976), p2.

Second, as pointed out by Hall and Jones (1999), the Solow model was unable to explain certain observable empirical facts. For example, given the law of diminishing returns, one would expect under the Solow model that capital would flow from capital-abundant countries to capital-poor countries, and that poorer countries would grow faster than more prosperous countries. But the complete opposite was happening, particularly prior to 2000. Developing countries were falling back rather than catching up, the predicted capital flows were not occurring, and foreign direct investment was going toward high-income countries, not toward low-income countries. In other words, convergence was not happening, suggesting that the Solow model was, at best, incomplete.

With this background, the pioneering work of Knack and Keefer (1995) and Keefer and Knack (1997) provided a key explanation of why convergence was not occurring. They explain that the divergence is due to a heterogeneous quality of institutions across countries. They were able to use a crude measure of institutional quality, such as rule of law or risk of expropriation, which they derived from the International Country Risk Guide for a limited sample of countries. After adjusting for differences in the quality of institution in their model, they observed (conditional) convergence. Their findings imply that institutions are a key left-out variable in the original formulation of the Solow model.

The recognition of the importance of institutions was advanced early on by many important scholars including Ronald Coase, Milton Friedman, Douglas North, James Buchanan, Elinor Ostrom, Armen Alchian, Mancur Olson, and Oliver Williamson. But it was not until after the empirical contributions of Stephen Knack and Philip Keefer, and the subsequent series of papers by Daron Acemoglu, Simon Johnson, and James Robinson, that empirical articles using relatively crude measures of institutions became a central part of the comparative economic development literature.

The difficulty associated with measuring economic institutions, which are inherently complex and multidimensional, and the lack of institutional data of good quality, has reduced the impact of the institutional approach. Following the initial contributions of Acemoglu and his collaborators, however, an abundance of political measures and crude measures of economic institutions have been widely utilized. But there is room for improvement in at least two clearly defined ways. First, by disentangling the effects of economic and political institutions. Second, by using better data, including better measures of institutions. Data of better quality reduces measurement error, increases precision in the estimation, and helps reduce potential endogeneity biases.

In a series of papers, Jeffrey Sachs advanced an alternative explanation for the systematic cross-country disparities in income levels and living standards. He argues that geographic factors such as climate and location affect institutions and have an independent effect on development. Specifically, Sachs (2003) argues that limited access to coastal trade, distance to major world markets, and tropical disease burdens (malaria ecology in particular) are major geographic disadvantages that explain income disparities among countries and the cross-country divergence observed prior to 2000. Sachs' point of view has led to a series of papers and ongoing debates competing over the relative roles and merits of geography and institutions for economic development.

Finally, an additional hypothesis is advanced independently by Glaeser et al. (2004). They argue that during the colonization process, the Europeans brought with them not only their institutions but their human capital, and it is the latter that explains the cross-country differences in per capita GDP. Similarly, Engerman and Sokoloff (2002), argue that factor endowments had a profound effect on the initial distribution of wealth, human capital, and political power and that the initial inequality has persisted over time.

These advances have led to several new unanswered questions. First, do Sachs' geographic disadvantages have a direct impact on development or merely an indirect effect, through institutions? Moreover, do these geographic effects change over time? Second, which institutions (economic institutions or political institutions) matter more for economic development, and how would the results of prior research be altered by the use of a more comprehensive and better-constructed set of institutional measures? Finally, what is the role of human capital in the growth process? Is it an input, an output, or both?

This research will utilize the level and growth rate of per capita GDP as the primary indicator of development. The level will be measured in 2011 dollars adjusted for purchasing power parity (PPP). This variable is primarily from the most recent release of the Maddison Project Database (2018). However, if additional data are available in the Penn World Table and the World Bank, these data will also be used to supplement analysis based on the Maddison dataset. Further, the extreme poverty rate will also be used as an alternative measure of economic development in chapters 2 and 3. The methodology for the construction of this variable, which is similar to that of Connors and Montesinos (2018), is described in Appendix A.

The remainder of the dissertation is organized as follows: Chapter two explores the geography hypothesis advanced by Sachs and provides new evidence on the Sachs-Acemoglu Debate. Chapter three examines the relative merits of economic versus political institutions for economic development. Chapter four analyzes the role of human capital in the development process, and Chapter 5 offers concluding remarks.

CHAPTER 2

GEOGRAPHY AND ECONOMIC DEVELOPMENT

"Division of labor is limited by the extent of the market."
Adam Smith.

2.1 Introduction

The potential impact of geography on economic development is a fundamental issue that has generated considerable attention and debate in the literature. Jeffrey Sachs, one of the strongest proponents of the geography hypothesis, argues that climate, geographical location, and distance to major markets significantly affect economic development even after controlling for the quality of institutions (Gallup, Sachs, and Mellinger, 1999; Sachs, 2003; and Sachs, 2012). Sachs and other proponents of the geography theory believe that because of geographic disadvantages, several countries have stagnating, low levels of per capita income.

The claim that geography matters for economic development is not new. Among others, Jones (1981), Diamond (1999), Landes (1998), and Pomeranz (2000) stress the importance of geography from a historical perspective. For example, Diamond (1997) argues that the east-west axis of Eurasia provided a natural geographic advantage over the north-south axes of Africa and the Americas.

Centuries ago, Machiavelli (1519) and Montesquieu (1748) believed that climate and tropical location directly affected the work and productivity of human beings. Moreover, Adam Smith (1776) also stressed the gains from expansion in the size of the market and division of labor resulting from geographic locations with access to a sea-coast and banks of navigable rivers. In the *Wealth of Nations*, Smith stated:

> *As by means of water-carriage a more extensive market is opened to every sort of industry than what land-carriage alone can afford it, so it is upon the sea coast, and along the banks of navigable rivers, that industry of every kind naturally begins to subdivide and improve itself, and it is frequently not till a long time after that those improvements extend themselves to the inland parts of the country… Six or eight men, therefore, by the help of water-carriage, can carry and bring back in the same time the same quantity of goods between London and Edinburgh, as fifty broad-wheeled waggons, attended by a hundred men, and drawn by four hundred horses.* (Smith, 1904, Ch. 3, P.20).

Smith went on to explain that because of this advantage the first improvements in art and industry occurred near the sea-coast or navigable rivers and that this same pattern was present in North America, along the Mediterranean coast, and in Egypt.

The critics of the geographic view, argue that the observed linkage between geographic factors and economic development is largely spurious because it fails to consider the importance of other factors, particularly, institutions, in the development process. The proponents of the institutional theory argue that institutional factors are the driving force of development, and once these factors are accounted for, the contemporary impact of geography on economic growth is minimal (Acemoglu, Johnson, and Robinson, 2001; Easterly and Levine 2003; Rodrik, Subramanian, and Trebbi 2004; Acemoglu and Robinson 2012). While the institutionalists acknowledge that geography has exerted a historical impact on economic development, they believe that its current impact on the development process is relatively minor.

It is important to clarify the meaning of "geography" as utilized in this chapter relative to other literature that also examines geography and the development process, such as the new economic geography. Paul Krugman (1991) makes the distinction between first-nature geography and second-nature geography. First-nature geography refers to fundamentally exogenous geographic characteristics such as climate and location. Weather conditions, temperature, humidity, access to coasts, disease environment, natural endowments, and terrain ruggedness are examples of first-nature geography. In contrast, second-nature geography refers to how people locate geographically relative to one another and how they interact based on their spatial distribution. Under second-nature geography, different spatial patterns of agglomeration can emerge endogenously as a result of people's choices and their initial geographic distribution.

This chapter focuses on first-nature geography in the context of the ongoing debate regarding the roles of geography versus institutions in the comparative economic development literature. Within the framework of the geography-institutions debate, this research will examine the following central question: Is unfavorable geography, including both climate and location, the primary cause of the stagnation and absence of development of the low-income countries of the world? Additional related questions will also be addressed: What are the countries that are most geographically disadvantaged? After considering the impact of institutions, does geography exert an independent impact on economic development? Has the adverse impact of geographic disadvantages changed in recent years? If so, why? In addressing these questions, this research will rely heavily on the three major indicators of geographic disadvantage used by Jeffery Sachs: distance to major markets, malaria ecology, and coastal population. While these measures are not the only potential geographic factors adversely affecting growth and development, they are clearly important factors and they have played a central role in the geography-institutional debate of recent decades.

The chapter is organized as follows. The next section 2.2 describes the primary database, key variables, and data sources of this research. Section 2.3 explains how geographic disadvantages are measured, identifies the 40 most disadvantaged countries, and examines their institutional and performance characteristics during 1970-2015. Section 2.4 uses regression analysis to investigate the impact of geography, institutions, and various control variables on per capita GDP and economic growth across countries and periods. Section 2.5 analyzes how the changes in transportation and communication costs and accompanying expansion in international trade has affected both the speed and pattern of economic growth. Section 2.6 examines the impact of geography on international trade, poverty rates, and child mortality in recent decades. Section 2.7 summarizes the key points.

2.2. Description of the Data

Several data sources were merged to explore the crucial questions of this chapter. The key variables are described below.

2.2.1. Geographic Variables

The fundamental geographic variables are from Gallup, Sachs, and Mellinger (1999); and Sachs (2003). These data are publicly available from the Web page of John Luke Gallup. The three key geographic variables are malaria ecology, distance to major markets, and the proportion of the population near an ice-free coastline.

Malaria ecology is a purely climatological variable indicating the ecological conditions for the prevalence of malaria. This variable comes from a highly disaggregated sub-national level index constructed by Kiszewski et al. (2004). The measure was then aggregated by Sachs (2003) to develop a country-level measure.[2] The basic formula for malaria ecology includes temperature, mosquito species abundance, and specificity of mosquito vector types (especially the human-biting and deadly ones). Sachs originally devised the malaria ecology index as an instrument for malaria risk arguing

[2] At the time that Sachs and his colleagues at the Harvard Center for International Development constructed the malaria ecology variable (between 2002 and 2003), the paper by Kiszewski et al. (2004) was still a work in progress.

that it is exogenous to public health interventions and economic outcomes due to its ecological/climatological foundation. The index is designed to capture variations in the disease environment across countries. The malaria ecology index ranges from 0 (least-favorable environment for malaria) to 31 (most-favorable environment for malaria). That is, higher numbers of this variable indicate a higher geographic (climatological) disadvantage for economic development. Others have used latitude, tropical or temperate locations, or distance from the equator to measure variations in climate. Sachs argues that these variables measure the climate factors relevant to development less accurately than malaria ecology.

The distance to major markets variable is the minimum air distance, in thousands of kilometers, from the capital city of each country to New York, Rotterdam, or Tokyo. Higher values of this variable are indicative of a more considerable geographic disadvantage. Location near the major markets of North America, Europe, or Asia will reduce transportation costs and facilitate integration with the world market network. This will enhance the attractiveness of the location for business and productive activities. In contrast, geographic remoteness acts as a natural barrier to market integration and economic development.

Coastal population indicates the proportion of the population of each country that resides within 100 kilometers from ice-free coastlines. Location near an ocean coastline will increase access to ocean shipping and thereby reduce transportation costs to the world's major markets. Therefore, a larger share of a country's population near an ocean coast will enhance the attractiveness of the country as a location for productive activity. Following Sachs, this factor is measured by the fraction of a country's population in 1994 living within 100 kilometers of an ocean coastline. This variable ranges from 0 to 1.

2.2.2. Institutional Variables

Measures of both economic and political institutions will be employed. The 2018 Economic Freedom of the World (EFW) index from Gwartney, Lawson, Hall, and Murphy (2018) will be the primary measure of economic institutional quality. Economic freedom facilitates and encourages gains from trade, entrepreneurship, innovation, and capital formation: all of which are essential sources of economic growth and development. The EFW index provides a comprehensive measure of the degree to which the institutions of a country are supportive of personal choice, voluntary exchange, market allocation of goods and services, free trade, and protection of individuals and their property from aggression by others. The summary index is based on ratings ranging from zero to ten for the 42 different components of the index. Higher summary EFW ratings are indicative of more economic freedom. The Economic Freedom of the World data also provide ratings for five areas. This research uses the following three areas of the EFW index: (1) the legal system and protection of property rights, (2) access to money of sound value, and (3) freedom of international exchange.

This chapter uses two measures of political institutions: (1) the Polity IV measure of democracy developed by Marshall, Gurr, and Jaggers (2016) and (2) the Freedom House (2019) index of civil liberties and political rights. The Polity IV database provides a measure of the degree of democracy ranging from -10 (strongly autocratic) to +10 (strongly democratic). Thus, higher ratings for this variable are indicative of more democratic political institutions.

Freedom House (2019) provides ratings for both civil liberties and political rights annually back to 1972. The civil liberties variable measures the freedom of expression and belief, associational and organizational rights, the rule of law, and personal autonomy without interference from the state. The political rights variable measures the degree to which people are free to participate in the political process, including the right to vote freely for distinct alternatives in legitimate elections, compete for public office, join political parties and organizations, and elect representatives who have a decisive impact on public policies and are accountable to the electorate. Both variables range from 1 (most free) to 7 (least free). The two measures were averaged and the original scale reversed so that higher ratings indicate more political freedom.

This chapter also utilized the rule of law variable from the World Bank's Governance Indicators (Kauffman, Kraay, and Mastruzzi, 2018) as an alternative institutional measure. This variable captures the "perceptions to the extent to which agents have confidence in and abide by the rules of society, and in particular the quality of contract enforcement, property rights, the police, and the courts, as well as the likelihood of crime and violence." The variable is standardized and ranges from minus 2.5 to plus 2.5. Higher numbers reflect closer adherence to the rule of law. This dataset is only available since 1996.

2.2.3. Per Capita GDP

This chapter uses per capita GDP in 2011 dollars adjusted for purchasing power parity (PPP). The per capita GDP data are primarily from the Maddison Project Database (MPD), which was recently updated by Bolt, Inklaar, de Jong, and van Zanden (2018). A few missing values were filled in using

Penn World Table (PWT) and the World Bank's World Development Indicators (WB).[3] The MPD distinguishes between measuring real GDP per capita at a point in time versus measuring it over time. The first measure is more suitable for comparisons across countries as it uses multiple-year price benchmarks in their PPP comparisons. The second measure is more suitable for comparisons within a country as it uses a single-year benchmark (2011) for the PPP price comparison and uses national accounts to derive the growth rates. Accordingly, the first measure will be used in regressions involving the level of per capita GDP at a point in time while the second measure will be used in regressions involving growth rates.

Nevertheless, no measure is ideal for simultaneously comparing per capita GDP both across countries and over time. For example, there are situations in which the per capita GDP for a set of countries is to be analyzed over time, and the result is to be compared to a different set of countries. Many attempts including Bolt et al. (2018), Deaton and Aten (2017), and Inklaar and Rao (2017) have been unsuccessful at reconciling the two GDP measures suggesting that measurement error in the variables is the best explanation for the discrepancies between the two[4]. To reduce measurement error, in situations involving the simultaneous comparison of per capita GDP both across countries and over time, the average of the two series may be superior and will also be utilized.

2.2.4. Poverty Rate

Appendix A explains the methodology and presents poverty rates for 1970-2015 derived for 176 countries from the World Bank *World Development Indicators* (2019) poverty rate data set. The World Bank defines extreme poverty as the percent of the population living on $1.90 or less (in 2011 PPP dollars) per day.

The World Bank poverty dataset is based on surveys that are conducted irregularly across time and countries. Therefore, this dataset has several missing values. As Appendix A explains, the missing values in the newest release of the World Bank (2019) poverty dataset were estimated using

---

[3] If data were missing from MPD, it was completed giving preference to PWT first, and WB second, ensuring comparability with MPD data which is in 2011 PPP dollars. Data for Bahamas, Belize, Brunei, Bhutan, Fiji, and Suriname are from PWT. Data for Angola, Kuwait, and Qatar prior to 1975 and from United Arab Emirates prior to 1990 also are from PWT. Finally, the data for Georgia prior to 1980 are from WB.

[4] According to Bolt et al. (2018), even after correcting for biases introduced in the measurement of prices adjusted for PPP in the 2005 International Comparison Program (ICP) and for shifts in the bundles of products across time and across countries, the differences between the two GDP series remained substantial, suggesting therefore that the best explanation for the discrepancies is measurement error.

an iterative algorithm similar to the one developed by Connors and Montesinos (2018). The methodology of Connors and Montesinos (2018) relies on two fundamental ideas: (1) that the best predictor of the poverty rate in one year is the observed poverty rate in adjacent years (either the year before or the year after), and (2) that the under-five child mortality rate is highly correlated with the extreme poverty rate and it has far fewer missing values. Using these two basic ideas, Connors and Montesinos (2018) developed an autoregressive and iterative algorithm to produce a weakly balanced annual poverty dataset that spans over 176 countries for the period 1970-2015.

The methodology used to derive the estimates of Appendix A differs from that of Connors and Montesinos (2018) in two main ways: First, a non-linear logistic transformation was used in each iteration. After the last iteration, the results were transformed back using the inverse logistic function to obtain the estimated poverty rate. Second, linear interpolation in the natural logarithm of the poverty rate odds ratio was used whenever possible. For example, if the poverty rate for a country is 50 percent in 1999 and 53 percent in 2002, but it is missing in the intermediate years, the model would predict a poverty rate of approximately 51 percent in 2000 and 52 percent in 2001. The interpolation is linear in the transformed space and approximately linear in the original space when the poverty rates are in a mid-range around 50 percent. But when the poverty rate approaches zero or 100 percent, the interpolation in the original space is non-linear according to the logistic function. The two models predict similar poverty rates except near the extremes (zero or 100 percent) where the iterative logistic model appears to deliver superior results. A more detailed description of the methodology is provided in Appendix A.

2.2.5. Demographics

The demographic variables employed are originally from the World Population Prospects (2017) developed by the United Nations' Population Division. Most of these data, however, are now available and more easily accessible from The World Bank's World Development Indicators.

The demographic measures are generally employed as control variables. The primary demographic variables of this research are the natural logarithm of the population of the country (in millions), and the percentage of the population in the prime working-age 25-59 group. The total population is expected to be positively associated with economic development because transaction costs are higher for trade across national boundaries, particularly when trade barriers are present, and the trading partners utilize different currencies and/or speak different languages. Therefore, other things constant, larger countries (and integrated market areas) are expected to derive more gains from trade, allowing them to grow more rapidly.

The percentage of the total population in the prime working-age 25-59 group is expected to affect economic development in several ways. Individuals in the prime working-age category will generally have higher skill levels, greater commitment to the labor market, and therefore higher productivity, enhancing growth. In addition, the share of the total population in the prime working-age group may reflect the phase or level of development of a country, and the changes in the share of the population in the prime working-age category over time may reflect movements across phases of the development process. See Gwartney, Montesinos, and Connors (2018) for further details. Both levels and increases in this variable are expected to be positively correlated with economic development.

2.2.6. Other Controls

Net fuel exports: This variable comes from The World Bank's World Development Indicators. Net fuel exports refer to the total fuel exports minus fuel imports as a percentage of GDP. Other things constant, the larger this variable, the larger the net revenues derived from fuel exports (including oil, natural gas, lubricants, and mineral fuels), reflecting a combination of both fuel prices and units sold. This variable also proxies for the degree of reliance on fuels, particularly when averaged over extended periods. In growth equations, this variable is expected to have a positive sign in periods when fuel prices are increasing and a negative sign in periods of decreasing fuel prices (and it is expected to be insignificant when fuel prices remain approximately constant). This is because in periods of increasing fuel prices, the additional revenues from exports will enhance growth for net fuel exporters while larger expenditures on fuel imports will slow growth for net fuel importers. In contrast, in periods of decreasing fuel prices, net fuel-exporters will derive lower revenues from the declining fuel prices (and potentially fewer units sold) while net fuel-importing countries will experience an additional disposable income.

Trade sector: This variable comes from the Penn World Table (version 9.0). The size of the trade sector is calculated as the total amount of merchandise imports plus merchandise exports as a percentage of GDP. Alternatively, the average dollar amount of merchandise exports plus imports per person is calculated. This variable is used in this chapter to explore channels through which geographic conditions might have affected economic development. Other things constant, if transportation and communication costs decline, world trade will rise. Moreover, the incentives to enact free-market trade policies will increase. Further, the pattern of the increase of the geographically disadvantaged countries and other economies may cast light on how unfavorable geographic conditions impact economic development and how this impact may have changed through time.

War on soil dummy: One crucial variable affecting economic development is the presence of bloody conflicts inside the country. In growth equations, a dummy variable for having a war on the soil will be utilized. This variable is equal to one if the country participated in a war on its soil involving annual war-related deaths of more than 0.1 percent of the population during the last 5 years of the period, and zero otherwise. In the period 1985-2000, four countries met this criterion: Angola, Burundi, Chad, and Rwanda. In the period 2000-2015, only Syria met this criterion. This dummy was constructed based on the dataset collected by Brandon Brice (2018), which builds and expands upon the Correlates of War project (COW) previously developed by Sarkees, Reid, and Wayman (2010).

Dummy for six small Middle-Eastern oil-exporting countries: This variable equals one for the countries Bahrain, Kuwait, Oman, Qatar, Saudi Arabia, and the United Arab Emirates. In contrast with other oil exporters, when the oil export revenues of these small countries rise, there is generally a substantial increase in emigration of workers with below-average earnings, which paradoxically tends to reduce per capita GDP. Thus, in growth equations, this variable is expected to have either an insignificant or negative sign.

2.2.7. Base Sample

There are 135 countries for which the per capita GDP data are available continuously since 1970 from Maddison (2018) and Penn World Table and for which the EFW data were also available in 2015. This set of 135 countries constitutes the primary database of this study. Demographic data on population by age groups are also available for these 135 countries for 1960-2015. The economic freedom data are unavailable for some of these countries for earlier years. However, the EFW data are available for approximately 100 countries back to 1980. Thus, cross-country analyses will generally involve between 100 and 135 countries.

2.3. Characteristics of Geographically Disadvantaged Countries

This section will focus on the identification and examination of the world's most geographically disadvantaged countries, their historical performance, and their institutional characteristics.

2.3.1 Measuring Geographic Disadvantages

In order to examine the key questions of this research, geographic disadvantages must be identified and measured. In order to achieve this objective, the three key geographic disadvantage variables of Sachs were standardized and aggregated into a single unidimensional measure. Table 2.1 presents a single standardized measure of geographic disadvantage. This measure was constructed by first standardizing, and then adding, the three key Sachs variables (population within 100 km of an ocean coastline, distance to major markets, and malaria ecology) in such a way that higher numbers indicate a higher geographic disadvantage for each of the variables. The final sum was then standardized to have a zero mean and a standard deviation of 1.

Table 2.1 presents the disadvantage standardized rating and ranking for the 40 most geographically disadvantaged countries among the 135 countries of our primary database, along with the variables used in its construction (malaria ecology, distance to major markets, and coastal population) in their original units. The five most geographically disadvantaged countries with their standardized geographic disadvantage score are Burkina Faso (2.79), Mali (2.68), Niger (2.06), Chad (2.04), and the Central African Republic (1.96). These five countries have high malaria ecology (approximately 20 or above) and are located approximately 5 thousand kilometers (about 3 thousand miles) from the closest major market center of the world (Rotterdam, New York, or Tokyo). Moreover, all five are landlocked with zero percent of their population living near 100 kilometers of an ocean coastline. With these conditions, the standardized geographic disadvantage measure indicates that these countries are between 1.96 and 2.79 standard deviations away from the world sample mean in terms of their unfavorable geographic conditions.

From the list of 40 most geographically disadvantaged countries, 36 are Sub-Saharan African countries. The four exceptions are Latin American countries: Brazil (0.77), Bolivia (0.90), Argentina (1.00), and Paraguay (1.21). Further, these four exceptions are in the bottom half of the 40 most disadvantaged countries. Paraguay is the only non-African country that makes the list of the 30 most geographically disadvantaged countries. Clearly, Sub-Saharan African countries dominate the list of countries with the most unfavorable geographic conditions for economic development.

Table 2.1 also presents the simple average of the three main Sachs variables in their original units as well as the standardized geographic disadvantage measure for the group of 40 and two additional groups: A group of 21 high-income countries[5], and the 74 other developing economies that comprise our primary database. As expected, relative to the 40 most geographically disadvantaged countries, the high-income countries and the other 74 developing economies have much lower malaria ecology, are located much closer to major world markets and have a much larger share of their population living near the coasts. The average standardized score for the group of 40 most geographically disadvantaged countries is +1.39, while it is -0.95 for the 21 high-income countries, and -0.44 for the group of 74 other developing economies.

2.3.2 Performance and the Institutional Characteristics of the Geographically Disadvantaged Countries

Once the most geographically disadvantaged countries have been identified including both their climate and location disadvantages, the next question is whether these unfavorable geographic conditions are the primary reason for the stagnation and absence of development of these countries. Have any of these countries achieved significant growth and development in recent decades? Table 2.2 takes an initial look at these questions.

Table 2.2 shows the per capita GDP (in 2011 PPP dollars) for the 40 most geographically disadvantaged countries in 1970, 1985, 2000, and 2015, as well as the growth rates for the periods 1970-1985, 1985-2000, and 2000-2015. Twenty-eight of these 40 countries had a 2015 per capita GDP figure of less than $5,000. The 2015 per capita GDP for eleven of these countries was less than $1,461 (or $4 per day), which was the average per capita GDP of the high-income countries in 1820.

During the first 15-year period — 1970-1985, Botswana was the only one of the 40 geographically disadvantaged countries with an annual growth rate of per capita GDP higher than 5 percent. Five others (Republic of Congo, Cameroon, Paraguay, Eswatini[6], and Brazil) grew at annual rates between 3 percent and 5 percent. For the group as a whole, the population-weighted annual

[5] The 21 high-income countries that constitute the West plus Japan are: Australia, Austria, Belgium, Canada, Switzerland, Germany, Denmark, Spain, Finland, France, United Kingdom, Ireland, Iceland, Italy, Japan, Luxembourg, Netherlands, Norway, New Zealand, Sweden, and the United States.

[6] The Kingdom of Eswatini, formerly Swaziland, recently changed its name.

growth rate of per capita GDP of the 40 most disadvantaged countries was only 1.16 during 1970-1985, well below the parallel figures of 2.29 percent and 2.78 percent of the 21 high-income and the 74 other developing countries during the same 15-year period.

During 1985-2000, once again, Botswana was the fastest growing country in the disadvantaged group with a 4.5 percent annual growth rate. Only one additional country, Mozambique, achieved a growth rate higher than 3 percent during 1985-2000. Interestingly, Mozambique's growth rate during this time frame was elevated as the result of a civil war that depressed its per capita GDP during the early part of this period. As a group, the annual growth rate of the population-weighted per capita GDP of the 40 most disadvantaged countries was negative (minus 0.5 percent) during 1985-2000. In contrast, both the 21 high-income and 74 other developing countries grew at annual rates of 2.15 percent and 2.72 percent, respectively.

There were some positive signs of economic development during the final 15 year period – 2000-2015. Five countries (Chad, Mozambique, Angola, Rwanda, and Ethiopia) grew at annual rates of 5 percent or more. Three additional countries (Nigeria, Ghana, and Sierra Leone) achieved annual growth rates of between 4 percent and 5 percent, and six more countries (Zambia, Lesotho, Tanzania, Uganda, Paraguay, and Liberia) grew at annual rates higher than 3 percent. The annual growth rate of the population-weighted per capita GDP for the 40 most geographically disadvantaged countries during 2000-2015 was 1.82 percent. This growth rate appears modestly large when compared with the rate for this group during the three prior decades. However, it is unimpressive when compared with the 4.74 percent annual growth rate of the 74 other developing economies during the same 15-year period.

During the entire 45-year period 1970-2015, the five countries with the most rapid growth in this group and their annual growth rates are Botswana (5.2 percent), Lesotho (3.1 percent), Eswatini (2.5 percent), Paraguay (2.3 percent), and Brazil (2.2 percent). The other 35 countries of this group had growth rates of 1.8 percent or less. Except for Botswana, the growth rates of the most geographically disadvantaged countries were either similar or substantially lower than the parallel rates of the 21 high-income countries and the 74 other developing economies during the full 1970-2015 period. During 1970-2000, almost without exception, the geographically disadvantaged countries lagged well behind. Encouraging signs began to appear only during the first 15 years of this century.

Interestingly, the population-weighted per capita GDP of the 40 most geographically disadvantaged countries was higher ($4,048) in 1970 than the parallel figure ($2,523) for the 74 other developing countries. However, the situation was reversed dramatically by 2015. During 2015, the population-weighted per capita GDP of the group of 40 geographically disadvantaged countries was ($6,286) compared to $11,500 for the other developing countries. Of course, this reversal reflects the substantially higher growth rate of per capita GDP of the latter compared to the former.

How about the institutional quality of the 40 most geographically disadvantaged countries? Table 2.3 presents the Economic Freedom of the World (EFW) summary rating and world ranking (when available) for these countries in the years 1985, 2000, and 2015. Among these 40 most geographically disadvantaged countries, Botswana had the highest average EFW rating during 1985-2015. Botswana also had the second highest EFW rating (5.4) in 1985, the highest EFW rating (7.2) in 2000, and the second highest EFW rating (7.4) in 2015 — behind Rwanda which substantially improved its rating from 6.00 in 2000 to 7.6 in 2015.

It is useful to compare the economic freedom ratings of Botswana and Rwanda with other sets of countries. The EFW rating of Botswana (5.4 in 1985, 7.2 in 2000, and 7.4 in 2015) was always substantially higher than the average EFW rating of the 40 most geographically disadvantaged countries (4.30 in 1985, 5.77 in 2000, and 6.14 in 2015). Botswana's summary EFW rating has also been at least modestly larger than the average EFW rating for the 74 other developing economies (5.23 in 1985, 6.58 in 2000, and 6.89 in 2015) but it was always lower than the average EFW rating of the 21 high-income countries (6.68 in 1985, 7.90 in 2000, and 7.74 in 2015). In recent years, however, the summary EFW ratings of Rwanda and Botswana are approaching those of the 21 high-income countries. By 2015, for example, the EFW rating of Rwanda (7.56) was slightly higher than 7 of the 21 high-income countries: Iceland (7.25), Italy (7.32), France (7.34), Belgium (7.42), Japan (7.46), and Spain (7.5). Unsurprisingly, Rwanda's annual growth rate of per capita GDP was strong (5.5 percent) during 2000-2015.

The poverty and under 5 mortality rates were also high for the most geographically disadvantaged countries. Table 2.4 presents the estimated extreme poverty rates ($1.90 per day) for these countries and their under-5 mortality rates (deaths per 1,000) for the years 1970, 1985, 2000, and 2015.

Several remarkable patterns are visible in the poverty rate data. First, the lowest poverty rates in this group of most geographically disadvantaged countries were achieved by the four non-African countries (Paraguay, Argentina, Bolivia, and Brazil). Except for Ivory Coast and Gabon, the estimated poverty rates for all of the African countries of the group were above 50 percent in 1970. Second, the poverty rates of the developing countries have substantially declined in recent decades. Third, the reductions in poverty rates have been substantially more rapid for the group of 74 other developing economies than for the geographically disadvantaged group. The population-weighted average poverty rate for the 40 disadvantaged countries was 58.7 percent in 1970 and 32.4 percent in 2015, a reduction of 44 percent. However, the average extreme poverty rate for the 74 other developing economies was even higher; it declined from 62.3 percent in 1970 to 6.5 percent in 2015, a reduction of almost 90 percent.

China and India contributed to the huge decline of the 74 other developing countries, but even without these two populous countries, the reduction in the poverty rates of the other developing countries was substantially greater than those of the disadvantaged group. For example, when China is excluded from the other developing group, the reduction in the poverty rate of the remaining countries was 82 percent. Similarly, when both China and India are excluded, the remaining countries achieved a reduction in the poverty rate of 87 percent. In general, the reductions in the poverty rates experienced by the 74 other developing economies were much more substantial than the corresponding reductions of the 40 geographically disadvantaged group.

The under-five mortality rates, expressed in deaths per thousand, followed a similar pattern, but the relative size of the reductions was smaller. The average under-five mortality rates for the group of 40 most geographically disadvantaged countries showed a 68 percent reduction during the entire period, declining from 200.7 in 1970 to 64.1 in 2015. Excluding the 4 Latin American countries the figures are higher but show a similar decline of 67 percent, from 236.3 in 1970 to 78.2 in 2015. Again, the other 74 developing economies experienced even more rapid reductions in the under-five mortality rates, falling from 147.2 in 1970 to 27.1 in 2015, a reduction of almost 82 percent. As in the case of the decline in the poverty rate, the reduction in the child mortality rate of the other developing group is not driven solely by China or India. Excluding them from the calculation the figures change slightly from 140.3 in 1970 to 27.56 in 2016, representing a smaller reduction of 80 percent, but still much more substantial than the percent reduction of the 40 most geographically disadvantaged countries.

Tables 2, 3, and 4 provide strong evidence that the economic performance of the geographically disadvantaged countries has been weak, substantially weaker than both the high-income and other developing countries. However, as Table 2.3 indicates, the geographically disadvantaged countries also have extremely weak economic institutions. As a result, it is difficult to disentangle whether the poor performance of these economies is because of their geographic disadvantages or poor quality of their economic institutions. The following section will explore this issue.

2.4 Geography, Institutions, and Economic Performance: Regression Analysis

This section will utilize regression analysis to examine the impact of geography and institutions on per capita GDP and economic growth. The determinants of income levels and growth rates will be examined across both countries and time. The goal is to provide insight concerning the importance of both geography and institutions on the performance of economies and how their impact may have changed through time.

2.4.1 Geography, Institutions, and Per Capita GDP

This section takes a closer look at the question of whether geography has exerted an impact on institutional quality. As Acemoglu, Johnson, and Robinson (2001) stressed, incentives matter. European colonizers sought to set up protective institutions when they planned on settling permanently in an area. This was the case in Canada, the United States, Australia, and New Zealand. In contrast, when settlement conditions were unfavorable as the result of climate, disease, or density of the domestic population, the Europeans were more interested in the extraction of various resources. Thus, extractive institutions generally emerged in areas unfavorable for settlement.

The structure of incentives resulting from climate and location will influence the choices of not only Europeans but also others. As a result, climate and location will impact institutional development more broadly. Consider how location impacts the development of institutions supportive of freedom of international trade. If a country is located close to major markets, the potential gains from international exchange will be greater. These potential gains will lead business owners and entrepreneurs to bring additional pressure for trade liberalization. In contrast, a remote location will mean that potential gains from trade liberalization will be minimal, and the incentive to promote a liberal trade policy will be weak. For example, the incentive to follow a liberal trade policy in countries like Ireland, Singapore, and Hong Kong is strong because these countries are located near major markets and the potential gains from trade liberalization are large. In contrast, the incentive to promote trade liberalization in countries like Burundi, Central African Republic, or Papua New Guinea is weak because the location of these countries is remote and distant from major markets. Thus, the potential gains from trade liberalization are small.

Climate may also influence the incentive to support a legal structure protective of property rights and enforcement of contracts. A hot and humid climate prone to malaria, for example, will be a relatively unattractive place to conduct business or locate the productive activity. When this is the case, the potential gains from additional capital formation or trade with foreigners associated with more secure property rights will often be small. Under these circumstances, the incentive to establish a legal structure protective of property rights and unbiased enforcement of contracts will be weak.

Table 2.5 shows the relationship between geographic variables and institutions using regression analysis. Several institutional measures (columns 1 to 7) are the dependent variables. The independent variables are the three main Sachs variables in their original units. Since these variables are in their original units, distance to major markets and malaria ecology are expected to exert a negative impact on institutional quality, while the share of the population close to an ocean coastline is expected to have a positive sign. Panel A shows the regression results for the year 1985, panel B is for the year 2000, and panel C is for the year 2015.

Columns 1 to 4 of Table 2.5 use the Economic Freedom of the World (EFW) dataset to analyze the impact of geography on economic institutions. The EFW summary rating is the dependent variable in column 1, while the dependent variables for columns 2, 3, and 4 are respectively the EFW area 2 rating for legal structure and protection of property rights, area 3 rating for access to sound money, and area 4 rating for freedom of international exchange.

Distance to major markets was negative and highly significant (generally at the 1 percent level) in each of the first four regressions, and this was true for all three years. In 1985, Malaria ecology was negative in the first four equations but only significant when the legal system is the dependent variable (column 2). However, in 2000 and 2015 (panels B and C), malaria ecology was negative and highly significant for each of the measures of economic institutions. Coastal population was significant for the summary EFW rating and for the area 4 (international exchange) of EFW for all three years.

The explanatory power of the three geography variables was particularly strong for the summary EFW index, the legal system, and international exchange. When these measures were the dependent variable, the r-squared of the regressions was generally between 20 percent and 36 percent. The explanatory power relative to monetary institutions and policy was weaker, ranging from 12 percent to 20 percent.

These results indicate that distance to major markets and malaria ecology have exerted a significant impact on the formation of economic institutions. Moreover, the impact persists to the present. The evidence is weaker for coastal population. This factor, however, significantly impacts the summary rating and the freedom of international exchange. These findings are consistent with the theory that incentives play an important role in the development of institutions.

The geography factors exerted less impact on political democracy. When the polity measure of democracy was the dependent variable (column 5), malaria ecology and coastal population were significant in 1985 and malaria ecology was significant in 2000, but not 2015. Distance to major markets was insignificant in 1985, but significant at the 5 percent level in 2000 and 10 percent level in 2015. The r-squared values for these regressions were low, particularly during 2000 (10 percent) and 2015 (5 percent), indicating that the geographic factors exerted a smaller impact on democracy. Turning to the Freedom House measure of civil liberties and political rights (column 6), all three geographic variables were significant with the expected sign in each of the three years. However, except for 1985, the explanatory power of the geographic variables was substantially lower than was the case when economic institutions were the dependent variable.

Panels B and C (column 7) presents the results when the Kaufman rule of law measure is the dependent variable. These data are unavailable for years prior to the late 1990s. Thus, the rule of law variable can only be examined for 2000 and 2015. In both 2000 and 2015, the distance to major markets and malaria ecology variables were negative and significant at the 1 percent level, while the share of population near an ocean coastline was barely significant (10 percent level) in both years. The explanatory power of the geographic variables on the rule of law variable was 28 percent in 2000 and 27 percent in 2015.

Table 2.5 shows that, across time and institutional measures, at least one of the geographic factors always exerted an adverse impact on the quality of institutions. Moreover, the impact was generally stronger for economic and legal institutions than for political democracy. This pattern is consistent with the view that geography has continuously impacted institutional quality in one way or another and, as a result, geographically disadvantaged countries generally have economic and legal institutions that are less supportive of economic growth and development.

2.4.2 Geography and Per Capita GDP

Rodrik et al. (2004) and Acemoglu et al. (2001, 2002) argue that once institutions are accounted for, geographic conditions do not exert any direct impact on current economic development. This idea, however, fails to recognize the potential indirect effect that geography may have on economic development through its impact on institutions. If unfavorable geographic conditions have reduced the quality of economic institutions, then the usual cross-country regression analyses where the dependent variable is the level of per capita GDP, and the independent variables include both geographic and institutional variables will undermine the importance of geography. This is because a large portion of the effect of geography on levels of per capita GDP operates through its deteriorating effect on economic institutions. The goal of this section is, therefore, to measure both the direct impact of geographic variables and the total impact, including the indirect effects through institutions, on cross-country variations in per capita GDP.

Table 2.6 examines the impact of geographic factors on real per capita GDP in 1985, 2000, and 2015. The dependent variable of the regression model is the natural logarithm of the real per capita GDP. In addition to the three Sachs geographic variables, the regression model also includes (1) the share of the population in the prime working-age 25-59 category, (2) the summary economic freedom rating, and (3) a dummy variable for major Middle Eastern oil-exporting countries. Columns 1, 2, and 3 show the results for 1985, 2000, and 2015, respectively. All the control variables have the expected sign and are significant at the 5 percent level or higher. Because economic freedom is included as a control variable in these equations, the geographic variables will reflect only their direct impact on per capita GDP. In all three years, distance to major markets and malaria ecology were significant, but the share of population near an ocean coast was not. The explanatory power of the model was high, ranging from 72 percent in 1985 to 85 percent in 2000.

To capture the total (direct plus indirect) impact of geography on levels of per capita GDP, a two-stage analysis is performed. In the first stage, economic freedom is regressed against the three key geographic variables (Table 2.5, column 1, panels A, B, and C) and the residuals are saved. In the second stage, the residuals from the first stage are used in place of economic freedom in regressions parallel to those in columns 1, 2, and 3. Since the residuals capture the variation in economic freedom that is unexplained by the geographic variables, adding the residuals in lieu of economic freedom will allow the geographic variables to reflect both their direct impact and indirect impact through economic freedom. Therefore, the regression equations of columns 4 through 6 will reflect the total impact of the geographic variables. When the impact of the geographic variables through institutions is registered, the coefficient of each of the geographic variables is larger and more significant than when only their direct effects are reflected. When the total effects are measured, distance to major markets and malaria are highly significant in all three years and the share of population near an ocean coastline is significant in 1985 and 2000, but not 2015. This implies that when both the direct and the indirect impact through economic institutions are considered, geographic factors, particularly distance to major markets and malaria ecology, exert a strong adverse impact on per capita GDP.

Table 2.6 indicates that location (distance to major markets and access to an ocean coastline) and climate (malaria ecology) exert both a direct and an indirect impact on per capita GDP. When both the direct and indirect impact through economic institutions are accounted for, the adverse effects of geography are both large and highly significant. These findings are not surprising because the per capita GDP figures reflect not only the current situation but also history. Put another way, if location/climate adversely impacted growth rates and income levels historically prior to 1985, then the per capita GDP figures after 1985 will continue to reflect the historical lag.

2.4.3 Geography and Economic Growth

Even though geography has exerted a historical impact on institutions and on levels of per capita GDP, this does not mean that it is continuing to impact economic growth. This section seeks to determine if this is the case.[7]

Table 2.7 provides insight into the impact of the geographic variables on the growth rate of per capita GDP after adjusting for initial per capita GDP, economic institutions, and population. The dependent variable is the annual growth rate of per capita GDP during the 15-year periods 1985-2000, and 2000-2015. In columns 1 to 4, the main control variables are the log of per capita GDP and the EFW summary rating, both five years prior to the beginning of the period, and the change in the EFW summary rating during the subsequent 20 years. The main independent variables are the geographic variables. In odd-numbered equations (1 and 3) the three Sachs variables enter the equations in their original units. In even-numbered equations, the standardized geographic disadvantage index is utilized instead. Columns 1 and 2 are for 1985-2000, while columns 3 and 4 are for 2000-2015.

Per capita GDP five years prior to the beginning of the period is always negative and statistically significant, indicating convergence after adjustment for institutional quality and

[7] A two-stage analysis like the one performed in the last section is inappropriate in this case for at least two reasons. First, the historical impact of geographic disadvantages on initial income levels (which in turn have been impacted by still earlier institutional levels) is negative and large in magnitude. This will potentially induce an artificially positive effect of geographic disadvantages on growth by depressing the initial income level and therefore inflating the growth rate during the period. Second, the impact of geography on changes in institutional quality across time is very low (with r-squares of less than 1 percent) suggesting that there is not a significant indirect effect through this channel.

geographic factors. In other words, other things constant, low-income countries grew more rapidly than their higher-income counterparts. The summary EFW rating and the increases in EFW were both positive and significant in the first period (1985-2000), but only the increase was positive and statistically significant in the second period (2000-2015).

Turning to the geographic variables, malaria ecology and coastal population are statistically significant in the first period, but not in the second, while distance to major markets is insignificant in both periods (see columns 1 and 3). As equations 2 and 4 indicate, the standardized geographic disadvantage variable is negative and significant in the first period (1985-2000, column 2), but not during the second period (2000-2015, column 4). The estimated coefficient of this variable during the first period was -1.02 indicating that other things constant, a one unit increase in the standardized geographic disadvantage measure is associated with a lower annual growth rate of 1.02 percent during 1985-2000. The insignificance of the geographic variables during the second period (2000-2015) indicates that after adjusting for initial per capita GDP and economic institutions, the geographic disadvantages did not significantly impact economic growth. The r-squares were 50 percent and 49 percent for the earlier period (columns 1 and 2) and 17 percent and 15 percent for the latter period (columns 3 and 4).

Columns 5 to 8 present a more comprehensive model which incorporates an additional set of control variables: the log of population at the beginning of each period, the change in the share of total population in the prime working-age 25-59 category, the average net fuel exports during the period, the dummy for six Middle Eastern oil-exporting countries, and a dummy for deadly war conflicts taking place on the soil of the country in the last five years of the period. Columns 5 and 6 are for 1985-2000, and columns 7 and 8 are for 2000-2015.

In the more comprehensive model, all of the control variables have their expected signs. Initial income level was negative and significant in both periods, and economic freedom (both level and change) was always positive and significant. The change in the share of population in the prime working-age 25-59 category was also positive and significant in both periods, and the dummy for deadly war conflicts was negative and significant in both periods. In the second period, the initial population was positive and significant, the average net fuel exports variable was positive and significant, and the dummy for Middle Eastern oil-exporting countries was negative and significant. With regard to the geographic variables, none of them are statistically significant during the second period. In the first period, coastal population has a positive sign (as expected) with a coefficient of 1.22 and a t-ratio of 1.93. The standardized geographic disadvantage measure has a negative sign (as expected) and was statistically significant at the 1 percent level with a coefficient of -0.71. Other things constant, this implies that a one unit increase in the standardized geographic disadvantage is associated with a reduction in the annual growth rate of per capita GDP of 0.72 percent during 1985-2000. The r-squares indicate that the explanatory power of this model is 58 percent for the first period (columns 5 and 6) and 47 percent for the second period (columns 7 and 8).

The results of this section are consistent with the view that the adverse impact of unfavorable geographic conditions on growth of per capita GDP has declined in recent years, and it is now relatively small. To further investigate if this is the case and that the results above are not driven by low statistical power in the second period, the next section focuses on the impact of geography on the growth of per capita GDP over time using a panel data analysis.

2.4.4. Impact of Geography on Economic Growth Over Time

Even though geographic conditions are time-invariant, their impact on economic growth and development may change over time in complex ways. This section seeks to determine if this has been the case by interacting the standardized geographic disadvantage measure with period dummies for the seven 15-year overlapping periods that start in 1970-1985 and end in 2000-2015. Employing the 135 countries of the main sample, this analysis uses a balanced sample of 945 observations (135 countries times seven periods).

Table 2.8 presents the results of this analysis. The main effect for the standardized geographic disadvantage index was negative and statistically significant at the 1 percent level, with a coefficient of -0.81. This indicates that a one standard deviation increase in the geographic disadvantage measure is associated with a decline in growth of 0.81 percent per year during the period 1970-1985, which is the first period of this analysis and the omitted category in the regression.

The coefficients for the interactions between the period and the standardized geographic disadvantage measure indicate the additional effect on growth relative to the main effect of -0.81 (or equivalently, relative to the marginal effect for the first period which is the omitted category). In other words, in each period, the marginal effect of unfavorable geographic conditions, as measured by the standardized geographic disadvantage index, is just the sum of the main effect (which equals -0.81) plus the interaction coefficient corresponding to that period. Therefore, the impact of the standardized measure of geographic disadvantage on growth is a function of time in this model.

The interaction coefficients are not statistically different from zero for the first four periods (1975-1990, 1980-1995, 1985-2000 and 1990-2005) indicating that the marginal effect of unfavorable geographic conditions on growth was not statistically different than -0.81, which is the marginal effect in the base period, 1970-1985. However, in the last two periods, the situation is different. The interaction terms corresponding to the last two periods (0.71 for 1995-2010 and 1.19 for 2000-2015) are positive, large, and statistically significant, indicating that the effect of geographic disadvantages on growth in these two periods is significantly smaller in magnitude than was the case in the prior periods.

Has the effect of geographic disadvantages disappeared? To answer this question, panel B estimates the standard errors of the marginal effects of geographic disadvantages on growth over time using the delta method. For convenience, the 95 percent confidence intervals are presented, and panel C graphically illustrates the marginal effects over time, along with their 95 percent confidence regions.

As expected, the marginal effects were negative and significantly different than zero during the first four periods spanning 1970-2005. The point estimates ranged from -0.70 in 1975-1990 to -1.03 in 1985-2000. During the second to last period, 1995-2010, the marginal effect was -0.09 with a 95 percent confidence interval ranging from -0.42 to +0.23. This indicates that during this period, for the first time, the effect of geographic disadvantages on growth is insignificant. During 2000-2015, the marginal effect was positive (with a point estimate of 0.38) and statistically significant at the 5 percent level[8]. This indicates that, without controlling for any other factor, countries with larger geographic disadvantages grew more rapidly than countries without them during the last period 2000-2015. Because it was the other way around during the first four periods, this finding is consistent with the view that the geographically disadvantaged countries finally started a process of catch-up growth[9].

Overall, the regression analysis conducted above indicates that the impact of unfavorable geographic conditions on growth of per capita GDP, as measured by the standardized geographic

---

[8] The p-value was similar, 4 percent, when the estimates were derived using Seemingly Unrelated Regressions (SUR).

[9] In similar models that control for the initial income level, the pattern is qualitatively the same, but the impact during the 1970-1985 base period was larger in magnitude (generally around -1 percent). As a result, the marginal effect in the last period was not statistically significant. This last result is also present after controlling for one or several of the following variables: the population at the beginning of the period, change in the share of the population in the prime working age (25-59) category, and a dummy for Middle-Eastern oil-exporting countries. The pattern is also present when controlling for the change in economic institutions during the period but the number of observations decline. All results are similar when Seemingly Unrelated Regressions (SUR) is utilized instead of OLS. See Table B.1 of Appendix B.

disadvantage index, has been generally negative and large in magnitude, but it has declined over time. However, one should be cautious in saying that it is exerting no impact on growth and development.

Further, it is important to recognize that even modest growth rates for high-income countries may translate into much larger dollar gains than higher growth rates for low-income countries. For example, the 2015 per capita GDP of the United States was $52,591 per person, and the corresponding figure for Malawi was $1,042 per person. If the U.S. grows at a modest 1 percent annually over the next 15-year period, its per capita GDP would be 61,057 dollars in 2030 (an increase of 8,466 dollars). The same annual growth rate of 1 percent would increase Malawi's per capita GDP by only 168 dollars over the same 15-year period. Even larger annual growth rates of 3 percent and 5 percent would increase Malawi's per capita GDP by 843 dollars and 1,473 dollars, respectively, over the next 15 years. It would take a much longer time horizon before modestly higher growth rates in low-income countries would pick up their income levels enough so that the catch-up process becomes apparent.

In addition, it is possible that geographic disadvantages may be exerting a differential impact on other variables such as international trade. International trade is a vital contributor to economic growth and the development process. The analysis of how the volume of international trade has changed during the last half-century may provide additional insight into the potential impact of geography on economic development. The next section will explore this topic.

2.5 Changes in Transportation and Communication Cost, International trade, Geography, and the Pattern of Economic Development During 1970-2015

During the past century, the world has witnessed an unprecedented reduction in transportation and communication costs. Glaeser and Kohlhase (2004) estimate that the railroad costs (in real dollars per ton-mile) have steadily fallen from about 19 cents in 1890 to 2 cents in 2000, a reduction of 88 percent over the last century, or about 2 percent per year. They estimate that this annual rate of decline in transportation costs was similar for other modes of transportation, including trucks, pipelines, and air travel.

During the second half of the past century, the reductions in transportation costs may have been even larger, particularly when it comes to ocean shipping across countries. The invention of the shipping container, for example, reduced the costs of hand-loading cargo onto a ship in a U.S. port from 48.46 dollars in 1956 to 18 cents[10] in 2006, a reduction of 99.6 percent (Hammond, 2019). Because these containers are standardized in size and design, thousands of them can be stacked on large ships, and transported at a low cost to ports throughout the world. Upon arrival, machines can lift them on to rail cars and trucks for transport to inland distribution centers and manufacturing facilities. These containers have transformed ocean shipping and movement of goods throughout the world.

These large reductions in transportation costs of goods surely provided a major boost to international trade. Table 2.9 supports this view and Table 2.10 breaks down the figures to see if there is any differential increase in trade volume among the 40 most geographically disadvantaged countries, the 21 high-income economies, and the 74 other developing economies of our primary dataset.

Table 2.9 shows the figures for the volume of international trade of merchandise goods for the world from 1970 to 2015 in 5-year intervals. Columns 1, 2, and 3 show the figures for total merchandise trade (imports plus exports), exports, and imports respectively as a percent of world GDP. Columns 4, 5, and 6 show the parallel figures in dollars per capita.

The total world trade as a share of GDP (column 1 of Table 2.9) was 21.9 percent in 1970, and it increased to 49.0 percent in 2015, more than doubling in this 45-year period which is consistent with the huge reductions in transportation and communication costs of the last half-century. The increase in international exchange as a share of GDP was relatively steady except for 1985 and 2015, two years for which the world price of oil declined sharply relative to the previous five years. In per capita terms (column 4), the volume of international trade was $1,288 per person in 1970, but it rose to $7,156 per person in 2015, an increase of 455.8 percent. The increase was persistent except for the small decline during 1985.

Column 2 presents the figures for exports as a share of world GDP. This number reveals the percentage of goods that are produced in a country different than the one in which they are consumed. The figure was 10.7 percent in 1970 and 24.1 percent in 2015, an increase of 125 percent. This huge increase indicates that the economies of the world were substantially more integrated in 2015 than in 1970. The other side of the integration is provided by imports. As column 3 shows, imports also increased sharply as a share of GDP, rising from 11.2 percent in 1970 to 24.1 percent in 2015 (an increase of 121 percent).

---

[10] Both figures are in 2011 U.S. dollars. See Alexander Hammond (2019) for details. Available at: https://humanprogress.org/article.php?p=1905

These figures show that the increase in international trade during 1970-2015 were substantial. Given the sharp reduction in transportation and communication costs during the last half-century, the sharp increase in the volume of international trade is an expected result. How have the reductions in transportation and communication costs and the accompanying increase in international trade impacted economic development? Has the increased volume of international trade exerted a differential effect on the geographically disadvantaged and other developing economies relative to each other and to the world's high-income countries? Table 2.10 breaks down the volume of international trade according to each of the three country-groups in order to examine these questions.

Panel A of Table 2.10 is for the 40 most geographically disadvantaged countries. Panel B is for the 21 high-income countries, and panel C is for the 74 other developing economies. Column 1 of Table 2.10 presents the total dollar volume of the international exchange of goods (imports plus exports) for each group. These figures are expressed in trillions of 2011 PPP U.S. dollars. Columns 2 to 5 show these figures as a share of different totals. Column 2 is relative to the total GDP of each group. Column 3 is relative to the world's GDP. Column 4 is relative to the world's total international trade, and finally, column 5 is relative to the population of each group, that is, per capita.

Panel A of Table 2.10, column 1, indicates that the total trade for the 40 most geographically disadvantaged countries summed to $0.24 trillion (240 billion) dollars in 1970 and 2.09 trillion dollars in 2015, an increase of 770 percent during the 45-year period. Column 2 shows a much more modest increase of 79 percent when the figures are expressed relative to the GDP of the group: from 15.9 percent in 1970 to 28.4 percent in 2015. Column 3 indicates an even smaller increase when the figures are relative to the world's GDP, from 1.2 percent in 1970 to 2.1 percent in 2015 (an increase of 74 percent). As column 4 shows, the international trade of the disadvantaged group declined as a share of total international trade from 5.6 percent in 1970 to 4.3 percent in 2015 (a decrease of 22 percent). Finally, column 5 shows an increase of 196 percent when the figures are expressed in per capita terms (from 599 dollars in 1970 to 1,773 dollars in 2015). Comparing the 770 percent increase of column 1 to the 196 percent increase of column 5 reveals that most of the trade increase for this group was due to a population increase. The population of this group increased from 400 million in 1970 to 1,177 million in 2015, an increase of 2.4 percent per year.

Panel B of Table 2.10 shows the comparable figures for the 21 high-income economies. Their total trade volume was $3.12 trillion in 1970, and it increased to $22.98 trillion in 2015, an increase of 636 percent (column 1). Relative to their GDP, the trade sector of the high-income countries expanded monotonically from 24.4 percent in 1970 to 56.9 percent in 2015 (an increase of 133 percent, see column 2). Relative to the world's GDP, however, their trade volume only rose from 15.9 percent in 1970 to 23.4 percent in 2015 (see column 3). Most interestingly, the high-income countries' share of world international trade fell from 72.8 percent in 1970 to 47.8 percent in 2015, a decline of 34 percent during 1970-2015 and a 23 percent decline in the last 15 years alone. In per capita terms, the international trade of the high-income countries increased from $4,587 in 1970 to $25,180 in 2015, an increase of 449 percent. To a degree, this increase reflects a declining share of the population of this group relative to the world's population, from about 20.4 percent in 1970 (681 million) to about 13.6 percent in 2015 (913 million).

Panel C of Table 2.10 shows the parallel figures for the 74 other developing economies. From 1970 to 2015, their trade volume increased from $930 billion to $22.99 trillion, nearly a 25-fold increase (see column 1). As a share of their GDP, the figure increased from 17.6 percent in 1970 to 45.6 percent in 2015 (an increase of 159 percent, see column 2), reflecting the fact that the GDP of these economies has also grown rapidly. As a share of the world's GDP, the trade sector of this group expanded from 4.7 percent to 23.4 percent, a 394 percent increase (see column 3). Most importantly, relative to the total volume of international trade, the trade sector of these economies rose from 21.6 percent in 1970 to 47.8 percent in 2015, approximately the same share as that of the 21 high-income countries (see column 4). In per capita terms, the international trade of these 74 economies rose by a whopping 12-fold from $412 in 1970 to $4,970 in 2015. Interestingly, the population of this group as a share of the world's total has remained approximately constant at 69 percent during the entire period.

Taken together, panels A to C of Table 2.10 paint a clear picture of the trade sectors of the three groups over time. The big-time gainers from the reduction in transportation and communication costs are the group of 74 other developing economies, followed by the 21 high-income countries. In contrast, the international trade sector of the 40 most geographically disadvantaged economies was exceedingly small in 1970, and their increases were substantially less than for the other economies. Clearly, their gains from the huge reductions in transportation and communication cost and the increase in the volume of international trade during the past half-century have been far less than those of other countries, including other developing economies. To some degree, the smaller increases in the volume of international trade of the geographically disadvantaged group may reflect their weak institutions, including trade barriers. However, the slower growth of trade for this group is also consistent with the view that geography continues to exert an adverse impact on the economic development of these economies.

Tables 2.9 and 2.10 also provide information about the development process of the past half-century. Table 2.9 shows that there is now more international trade than at any time in history and Table 2.10 suggests that there are more individuals potentially being impacted by this integration into the world market network than ever before (even though the impact in the most geographically disadvantaged countries is smaller). The impact of the reduction in transportation and communication costs on the development process is much broader and deeper than in the past. To put things in perspective, consider the Industrial Revolution. The Industrial Revolution resulted in substantial income gains for between 12 and 15 percent of the World's population, but the effect on the rest of the world was minimal. In contrast, the transportation and communication revolution is exerting a positive impact on more than 80 percent of the world's population. This impact is dramatically changing life in a large portion of the developing world.

2.6 The Impact of Geography on Other Measures of Economic Development

How has geography affected other measures of economic development over time? Table 2.11 uses regression analysis to measure the impact of geographic disadvantages on trade, poverty rates, and under-5 mortality rates, through time. The dependent variables are international trade as a share of GDP (columns 1 and 2), international trade per capita (columns 3 and 4), and poverty rates and under-5 mortality rates (columns 5 and 6, respectively).

Columns 1 and 3 of Table 2.11 essentially replicate the results of Table 2.9 but using regression analysis. The intercepts for these models are the corresponding world trade figures for 1970. The coefficients for the years represent the difference between the trade figure for each year and the trade figure in 1970. For example, in column 1, the intercept indicates that the total trade as a share of GDP was 21.94 percent in 1970, and the coefficient of 27.02 percent for 2015 indicates that the world trade as a share of GDP in 2015 was 27.02 percentage points larger than in 1970 (that is 48.96 = 21.94 + 27.02), as indicated in Table 2.9. The increase was statistically significant at the 1 percent level. Similarly, in column 3, the intercept indicates that the total world trade volume in 1970 summed to $1,288 per person and the coefficient of 5,868.65 for 2015 (significant at the 1 percent level) indicates that the total world trade volume increased by $5,868 by 2015. That is, the world trade per capita figure for 2015 was $7,156 ($5,868 + $1,288). In order to make the figures for the world identical to those of Table 2.9, the regressions for trade as a share of GDP are weighted by GDP, and the regressions for trade per capita are weighted by population.

Columns 2 and 4 add the standardized measure of geographic disadvantage. The main effects for the years are interpreted as before, except they would correspond to a value of zero for the index of geographic disadvantage (GeoDis = 0). Recall that this index has mean zero and a standard deviation of 1. In this model, the marginal effect for geographic disadvantage is a function of time and is calculated by adding the base-year effect (corresponding to the value in 1970) plus the interaction term in each year. Column 2 shows that both the main effect and all interaction terms are negative, but none of them are statistically significant. Column 4 shows that both the base-year effect and the interaction terms are negative and significant, and the magnitude of the interaction terms increase over time. This is consistent with the findings of Table 2.10 showing that the impact of the geographic disadvantages on the dollar value of trade per person is not only negative and large, but it has increased in magnitude over time.[11]

Columns 5 and 6 indicate that the pattern is slightly different when the dependent variables are poverty rates and under-5 mortality rates. The year effects are negative, increasing in magnitude over time, and statistically significant. This is consistent with the view that both the poverty rates and the under-5 mortality rates have been declining over time regardless of geography. The base-year effect for geographic disadvantage, however, is positive and statistically significant. This indicates that in 1970, a one standard deviation increase in the geographic disadvantage index was associated with 22.65 percentage points higher poverty rates (column 5) and 62.56 higher deaths per thousand children under the age of five (column 6). The interaction terms are negative and increasing in magnitude over time, suggesting that the effect of geography on both poverty rates and under-5 mortality rates has been declining over time. The interaction terms, however, are not statistically significant until after 2000 for the poverty rates and after 1990 for the under-5 mortality rates. The interaction terms partially compensate for the base-year effect, but they do not fully offset it, indicating that geography still matters for poverty rates and for under-5 mortality rates, but to a lesser extent than during the earlier years.

Taken together, these results lead to a new question. How can the effect of unfavorable geographic conditions over time be increasing in magnitude for the dollar value of trade but decreasing in magnitude for both the poverty rates and the under-5 mortality rates? A plausible answer lies in the emergence of local entrepreneurship which helps alleviate social conditions, including poverty and under-5 mortality rates. This idea is consistent with the reductions in both

---

[11] The results are robust to alternative econometric techniques and control variables. See Table B.2 of Appendix B for the results after controlling for the log of initial population using Seemingly Unrelated Regressions (SUR).

transportation and communication costs, but the particularly large reduction in communication costs over the last 20-years. First, even if people in geographically disadvantaged countries are not trading more relative to other countries, they are still trading much more than they were doing before. The dollar value of the trade per capita for the group of 40 most geographically disadvantaged countries increased by almost 200 percent during 1970-2015, from 599 dollars in 1970 to 1,773 dollars in 2015. This increase in trade per person may have fostered local entrepreneurship and the adoption of improved technologies as important sources of economic progress.

Second, and perhaps even more important, the reduction in communication costs of the past quarter of a century has facilitated a new type of integration through virtual channels, like the Internet. This virtual integration has allowed the communication of ideas to be much faster, much more reliable, and far less costly, than ever before. Because this virtual integration makes no distinction among geographic characteristics and physical barriers, all countries have relatively equal access to it at a minuscule cost. In this case, the most geographically disadvantaged countries receive the most benefit by using new technologies that were developed abroad, by acquiring the necessary knowledge to operate these new technologies, and by having access to ideas they would not have had without the virtual integration with the rest of the world. Some of these ideas can be adapted locally, and some others can lead to even new entrepreneurial ideas. Interestingly, this new type of integration boost development, as suggested by the declining differential impact on poverty rates, but it does not impact the trade figures, which merely reflect the international exchange of physical goods. A further examination of these issues is an important topic for future research.

2.7 Summary and Conclusions

This chapter examined the impact of geography on economic development and how the impact has changed through time. The major findings of this study are:

The 40 countries with the largest geographic disadvantages were identified using the standardized values of the distance to major markets, malaria ecology, and the share of the population residing within 100 kilometers of an ocean coastline. Thirty-six of these countries were in Sub-Saharan Africa, and the other four were South American. See Table 2.1.

The per capita GDP and various measures of institutional quality were derived for 21 high-income, 40 geographically disadvantaged, and 74 other developing countries. In 1970 and 1985, the per capita GDP of the 40 most geographically disadvantaged countries was higher than the parallel figure for the 74 other developing countries, but the reverse was the case for 2000 and 2015. This reversal reflects the more rapid growth of per capita GDP of the less disadvantaged developing countries relative to the 40 most geographically disadvantaged group. See Table 2.2.

The average Economic Freedom of the World (EFW) rating of the 21 high-income countries was higher than for the developing countries. In turn, the average EFW summary rating of the 74 other developing countries was higher than for the 40 most geographically disadvantaged group. This suggests that geographic disadvantages exert a negative impact on the quality of economic institutions. See Table 2.3.

Using the World Bank's irregular data for extreme poverty rate ($1.90 per day), a non-linear iterative algorithm was used to derive a poverty rate dataset for 176 countries from 1970 to 2015. See Appendix A. In 1970, on average, the poverty rates were low (less than two percent) for the high-income countries but about 60 percent for each group of the developing economies. However, between 1970 and 2015, the group of 40 most geographically disadvantaged countries experienced a much slower reduction of poverty (from 59 percent to 32 percent) than the group of 74 other developing economies (from 62 percent to 7 percent). This suggests that geography still matters for poverty rates. See Table 2.4.

Because of the weak economic institutions of the geographically disadvantaged countries, it is not easy to disentangle the impact of geography from that of institutional quality. Regression analysis was used to address this issue. The impact of geography on both economic institutions and per capita GDP was estimated for 1985, 2000, and 2015. After adjusting for cross-country differences in economic freedom, the geographic variables exerted a negative impact on per capita GDP during all three years. The negative impact on per capita GDP was even larger once the indirect impact of geography operating through institutions was also considered. See Tables 2.5 and 2.6. This is strong evidence that, historically, geography has exerted a negative impact on the per capita GDP of the countries with the largest geographic disadvantage.

Regression analysis was also used to examine the impact of geography and institutions on the growth of per capita GDP during 1985-2000 and 2000-2015. After adjusting for initial per capita GDP and economic freedom, the geographic disadvantage variables exerted a negative impact on the growth of per capita GDP during 1985-2000, but their impact was insignificant during 2000-2015. Economic freedom, both level and change, consistently exerted a positive impact on economic growth. Similar results were obtained when control variables for population, fuel exports, and demographic changes were added to the model. See Table 2.7. This is consistent with the view that the adverse impact of geographic factors on the growth of per capita GDP has declined in recent years, and it is now relatively small. Regression analysis of overlapping 15-year periods since 1970 provides additional support for this view. See Table 2.8.

During the past half-century, there has been a huge reduction in transportation and communication cost. This cost reduction has increased international trade and the gains from specialization and adoption of mass production processes. As a share of world GDP, international trade rose from 21.9 percent in 1970 to 49 percent in 2015. See Table 2.9.

The gains from reductions in transportation and communication costs have exerted a differential impact on developing economies. The volume of international trade is much smaller, and it has increased less, in the geographically disadvantaged countries than in the other developing and high-income countries. International trade is a vital ingredient in the growth process. The relatively slow growth of international trade in countries with the largest geographic disadvantages indicates that geography is continuing to impact the economic growth of these countries adversely.

Regression analysis indicates that adverse geographic conditions have also impacted the poverty and under-five mortality rates, but the magnitude of the adverse impact has declined over time. The reductions in the poverty rate were substantially larger for the 74 developing countries than for the 40 most geographically disadvantaged group. As of 2015, geography continues to exert an impact on poverty rates. However, the magnitude of this impact in 2015 was about half what it was in 1970. See Table 2.11. A new emergence of local entrepreneurship influenced by the reduction in transportation and communication costs provides a plausible explanation for the reduction in the impact of geographic disadvantages on poverty.

Table 2.1: Forty most geographically disadvantaged countries

Rank	Country	Malaria Ecology	Distance to Major Markets	Coastal Population	Standardized Geographic Disadvantage
1	Burkina Faso	31.5	4.5	0	2.79
2	Mali	30.1	4.5	0	2.68
3	Niger	21.9	4.5	0	2.06
4	Chad	21.5	4.6	0	2.04
5	Central African Republic	18.0	5.5	0	1.96
6	Nigeria	21.6	4.8	0.23	1.79
7	Ghana	23.3	5.2	0.45	1.77
8	Botswana	5.8	8.8	0	1.70
9	D.R. of the Congo	12.1	6.4	0.01	1.69
10	Mozambique	10.5	9.1	0.45	1.62
11	Togo	21.1	5.1	0.42	1.61
12	Côte d'Ivoire	19.7	5.3	0.37	1.58
13	Guinea	18.7	4.9	0.24	1.57
14	Malawi	6.2	7.9	0	1.56
15	Congo	12.9	6.3	0.16	1.52
16	Zambia	5.7	7.8	0	1.51
17	Zimbabwe	4.1	8.2	0	1.46
18	Namibia	3.7	8.4	0.04	1.42
19	Cameroon	13.2	5.5	0.13	1.41
20	Lesotho	0.0	9.3	0	1.38
21	U.R. of Tanzania: Mainland	7.6	7.3	0.16	1.35
22	Uganda	7.5	6.2	0	1.32
23	Benin	17.5	5.0	0.51	1.22
24	Paraguay	2.3	7.6	0	1.21
25	Kenya	4.8	6.7	0.07	1.13
26	Eswatini	3.1	9.1	0.36	1.12
27	Liberia	17.3	5.3	0.57	1.10
28	Madagascar	5.0	8.9	0.49	1.09
29	Sierra Leone	16.7	5.1	0.49	1.08
30	Gabon	13.0	5.8	0.28	1.06
31	Argentina	0.1	8.6	0.2	1.00
32	Burundi	1.6	6.6	0	0.95
33	South Africa	1.0	8.9	0.38	0.91
34	Bolivia	1.2	6.5	0	0.90
35	Angola	4.4	6.8	0.22	0.87
36	Senegal	15.3	4.8	0.51	0.85
37	Rwanda	0.5	6.5	0	0.84
38	Gambia	15.6	4.7	0.58	0.83
39	Ethiopia	2.0	5.7	0.02	0.79
40	Brazil	1.9	7.7	0.34	0.77
	Simple Averages:				
	40 Most Disadvantaged Countries	**11.0**	**6.5**	**0.2**	**1.39**
	21 High Income Countries	**0.0**	**1.5**	**0.6**	**-0.95**
	74 Other Economies	**1.4**	**3.9**	**0.6**	**-0.44**

Notes: Malaria Ecology is a purely climatological variable indicating the ecological conditions for the prevalence of malaria. Higher numbers indicate a higher disadvantage. Distance to major markets indicates the minimum distance, in thousands of kilometers, to Tokyo, New York, or Rotterdam. Higher values indicate a higher disadvantage. Coastal population measures the fraction of the population living within 100 kilometers from the ocean coast. Lower values of this variable indicate a higher disadvantage. These variables come from Gallup, Sachs, and Mellinger (1999) and later revised by Sachs (2003). The standardized geographic disadvantage measure was computed by first standardizing, and then adding these three variables in such a way that higher numbers indicate a higher geographic disadvantage. The final sum was then standardized to have zero mean and a standard deviation of one.

Table 2.2: Per capita GDP (in 2011 PPP dollars) and economic growth for the forty most geographically disadvantaged countries

		Per Capita GDP (2011 PPP dollars)				Growth of Per Capita GDP (percent)		
Country	**GeoDis**	**1970**	**1985**	**2000**	**2015**	**1970-1985**	**1985-2000**	**2000-2015**
Burkina Faso	2.79	781	818	1,024	1,450	0.3	1.5	2.3
Mali	2.68	778	907	1,048	1,553	1.0	1.0	2.6
Niger	2.06	1,298	923	683	913	-2.3	-2.0	1.9
Chad	2.04	1,076	786	796	2,384	-2.1	0.1	7.3
Central African Rep.	1.96	1,497	1,139	960	576	-1.8	-1.1	-3.4
Nigeria	1.79	2,850	2,649	2,774	5,578	-0.5	0.3	4.7
Ghana	1.77	2,236	1,537	2,084	3,809	-2.5	2.0	4.0
Botswana	1.70	1,446	5,259	10,266	14,805	8.6	4.5	2.4
D.R. of the Congo	1.69	2,119	1,572	552	836	-2.0	-7.0	2.8
Mozambique	1.62	530	280	502	1,103	-4.3	3.9	5.2
Togo	1.61	2,006	1,526	1,282	1,370	-1.8	-1.2	0.4
Côte d'Ivoire	1.58	4,328	4,109	2,912	3,218	-0.3	-2.3	0.7
Guinea	1.57	1,052	1,084	1,211	1,364	0.2	0.7	0.8
Malawi	1.56	653	885	923	1,124	2.0	0.3	1.3
Rep. of Congo	1.52	3,888	7,276	5,360	6,272	4.2	-2.0	1.0
Zambia	1.51	3,224	2,354	1,990	3,478	-2.1	-1.1	3.7
Zimbabwe	1.46	2,112	2,198	2,249	1,560	0.3	0.2	-2.4
Namibia	1.42	6,354	5,561	6,067	9,462	-0.9	0.6	3.0
Cameroon	1.41	2,188	3,613	2,337	2,778	3.3	-2.9	1.2
Lesotho	1.38	661	985	1,526	2,710	2.7	2.9	3.8
Tanzania	1.35	1,573	1,465	1,534	2,566	-0.5	0.3	3.4
Uganda	1.32	1,346	863	1,176	1,954	-3.0	2.1	3.4
Benin	1.22	1,262	1,542	1,718	2,055	1.3	0.7	1.2
Paraguay	1.21	3,021	5,343	5,072	8,539	3.8	-0.3	3.5
Kenya	1.13	2,104	2,313	2,320	3,046	0.6	0.0	1.8
Eswatini	1.12	2,600	4,290	6,107	7,969	3.3	2.4	1.8
Liberia	1.10	1,422	1,043	534	865	-2.1	-4.5	3.2
Madagascar	1.09	2,477	1,643	1,403	1,360	-2.7	-1.1	-0.2
Sierra Leone	1.08	1,573	1,631	834	1,563	0.2	-4.5	4.2
Gabon	1.06	14,612	21,268	17,603	18,389	2.5	-1.3	0.3
Argentina	1.00	12,826	12,006	15,119	19,502	-0.4	1.5	1.7
Burundi	0.95	803	951	700	694	1.1	-2.0	-0.1
South Africa	0.91	9,598	9,506	9,340	12,246	-0.1	-0.1	1.8
Bolivia	0.90	3,661	3,668	4,293	6,200	0.0	1.0	2.5
Angola	0.87	4,727	3,882	3,659	8,689	-1.3	-0.4	5.8
Senegal	0.85	2,027	1,773	1,862	2,311	-0.9	0.3	1.4
Rwanda	0.84	786	953	775	1,693	1.3	-1.4	5.2
Gambia	0.83	1,662	1,696	1,564	1,786	0.1	0.5	0.9
Ethiopia	0.79	793	735	703	1,553	-0.5	-0.3	5.3
Brazil	0.77	6,005	10,185	11,263	15,826	3.5	0.7	2.3
Population Weighted Averages:								
40 Most Disadvantaged	**1.39**	**4,052**	**4,816**	**4,782**	**6,286**	**1.15**	**-0.05**	**1.82**
21 High Income	**-0.95**	**19,944**	**28,112**	**38,831**	**44,060**	**2.29**	**2.15**	**0.84**
74 Other	**-0.44**	**2,581**	**3,883**	**5,801**	**11,005**	**2.72**	**2.67**	**4.27**

Note: This table makes use of the RGDPNApc series (expressed in 2011 PPP $US, single benchmark) which is the most suitable measure of per capita GDP for growth calculations and comparisons over time (but not necessarily across countries). Source: Maddison Project Database (2018) and own calculations.

Table 2.3: Economic Freedom of the World (EFW) summary rating and ranking for the 40 most geographically disadvantaged countries.

Country	1985	2000	2015
Burkina Faso			6 (127)
Mali	4.6 (78)	5.9 (89)	5.8 (134)
Niger	5 (60)	5.1 (113)	5.7 (143)
Chad	4.5 (83)	4.9 (116)	5.2 (152)
Central African Rep.	4.3 (89)	5.3 (111)	4.6 (158)
Nigeria	3.7 (94)	5.4 (110)	6.4 (113)
Ghana	3.3 (104)	5.9 (88)	6.5 (106)
Botswana	5.4 (47)	7.2 (35)	7.4 (51)
D.R. of the Congo	3.7 (96)	3.8 (123)	5.8 (136)
Mozambique			5.6 (145)
Togo	4.9 (70)	5.5 (103)	5.7 (144)
Côte d'Ivoire	5.7 (38)	5.7 (100)	5.9 (129)
Guinea			5.7 (141)
Malawi	5.2 (53)	5.2 (112)	5.8 (138)
Congo	4.2 (90)	4.2 (122)	4.8 (157)
Zambia	3.3 (103)	6.4 (76)	6.7 (91)
Zimbabwe	4.3 (88)	4.4 (120)	6 (128)
Namibia		6.5 (73)	6.6 (98)
Cameroon	5.1 (55)	5.5 (104)	5.8 (132)
Lesotho			6.5 (109)
Tanzania	3.5 (99)	6.2 (80)	6.9 (77)
Uganda	2.7 (107)	6.8 (56)	7.3 (55)
Benin	4.7 (76)	5.4 (108)	5.8 (135)
Paraguay	4.6 (81)	6.5 (71)	6.9 (78)
Kenya	5.3 (50)	6.7 (60)	7.1 (71)
Eswatini			6.4 (111)
Liberia			6.9 (80)
Madagascar	4.3 (87)	5.8 (97)	6.3 (119)
Sierra Leone	3.6 (98)	5 (114)	5.8 (137)
Gabon	5.1 (59)	5.9 (94)	5.8 (133)
Argentina	3.1 (105)	7.2 (37)	5 (153)
Burundi	4.4 (86)	4.9 (117)	5.9 (131)
South Africa	4.9 (67)	7 (47)	6.8 (82)
Bolivia	3.4 (100)	6.9 (49)	6.1 (126)
Angola			5.4 (148)
Senegal	5 (62)	5.8 (96)	6.1 (123)
Rwanda		6 (83)	7.6 (30)
The Gambia			7.2 (63)
Ethiopia			5.6 (146)
Brazil	3 (106)	5.9 (91)	5.8 (140)
Simple Averages:			
40 Most Geog. Disadvantaged	**4.30 (80)**	**5.77 (90)**	**6.14 (117)**
21 High Income	**6.68 (19)**	**7.90 (14)**	**7.74 (25)**
74 Other	**5.23 (56)**	**6.58 (63)**	**6.89 (75)**

Note: The EFW ranking is in parenthesis. The rankings are out of 109 countries in 1985, 123 countries in 2000, and 159 countries in 2015 — source: Gwartney, Lawson, Hall, and Murphy (2018).

Table 2.4: Extreme poverty rate (percentage of the total population living under $1.90 per day) and under-five mortality rate (per 1,000 living birth) for the forty most geographically disadvantaged countries

	Extreme Poverty Rate (percent)				Under 5 Mortality Rate (per 1,000 people)			
Country	**1970**	**1985**	**2000**	**2015**	**1970**	**1985**	**2000**	**2015**
Burkina Faso	91.7	87.3	73.3	41.8	235.6	225.5	206.3	88.9
Mali	91.5	88.4	63.3	42.5	72.3	31.1	19.8	11.4
Niger	86.6	81.5	78.0	42.7	248	176.3	156.7	67.1
Chad	84.9	77.2	65.7	35.6	265.4	197.5	143.2	103.7
Central African Rep.	92.6	87.6	71.1	58.7	314.7	215.5	180.4	88.4
Nigeria	66.2	53.3	57.9	45.1	229.1	147.7	79.6	37.5
Ghana	60.1	44.8	32.3	13.0	132.7	77.1	34.7	15.7
Botswana	60.8	42.6	30.9	16.1	120.5	55	87	40.6
D.R. of the Congo	98.2	97.1	94.9	71.2	222.3	177.4	175.2	130.2
Mozambique	91.9	87.6	81.7	60.0	243.4	152.9	146.8	94.9
Togo	85.3	76.3	62.2	49.2	211.3	151.2	150.3	90.1
Côte d'Ivoire	12.2	6.8	24.5	28.2	246.3	197.3	161.3	97.6
Guinea	95.3	93.0	59.1	31.2	141.4	93.6	114.3	51.3
Malawi	80.7	72.8	67.8	70.5	242.6	221.8	142.6	64.2
Congo	85.9	75.0	59.0	28.6	125.6	100	83.1	52.5
Zambia	74.2	60.2	45.7	57.5	201.9	154	99.2	54.7
Zimbabwe	65.2	50.2	32.0	16.9	322.5	258.7	165.4	91.7
Namibia	70.9	53.7	34.7	13.4	300.4	203.8	118.4	67.9
Cameroon	73.5	60.2	27.3	22.8	150	97.4	104.5	48.7
Lesotho	66.5	50.5	58.6	50.0	284.9	237.7	186.1	80.1
Tanzania	85.6	76.7	86.0	39.3	177.2	99.2	116.9	93.8
Uganda	74.2	61.6	66.3	40.2	150.6	181.6	107.1	47.8
Benin	77.7	67.1	52.1	49.5	399.3	284.9	219.5	113.7
Paraguay	3.6	1.6	9.5	1.9	273.3	254.1	170.4	78.6
Kenya	56.6	39.1	36.1	36.8	339.7	245.7	171.9	61.7
Eswatini	93.0	87.2	48.4	30.6	97.9	86.5	76.2	47.2
Liberia	88.8	83.0	74.5	39.7	324	331.2	223.7	93.5
Madagascar	56.9	55.9	66.5	69.6	283.7	208.8	186.2	107.5
Sierra Leone	78.1	69.8	61.9	47.9	77.7	54.8	33.9	22.4
Gabon	33.5	19.7	10.2	3.9	221.2	159.3	181.4	42
Argentina	0.7	0.6	5.7	0.6	287.1	171.4	131.7	49.8
Burundi	90.5	85.0	82.7	66.8	332.1	270.2	233.1	122.2
South Africa	59.1	41.1	35.0	17.5	177.6	85.7	126.1	57.8
Bolivia	15.5	8.9	28.6	6.4	250	226.8	186.5	130.8
Angola	59.2	46.0	32.3	23.8	223.1	158.8	120.6	77.7
Senegal	82.2	73.1	49.5	29.4	212.6	175.6	130.4	58.3
Rwanda	74.0	64.0	77.2	55.9	188.5	192.3	146	55.3
Gambia	86.9	80.3	61.0	10.1	129.5	73.5	78.4	40.3
Ethiopia	85.8	78.3	56.5	27.3	181.1	169.2	165.1	64.9
Brazil	31.6	23.1	12.5	3.4	113.3	81.2	101.8	57
Population Weighted Average:								
40 Most Geog. Disadv.	**58.65**	**50.13**	**46.01**	**32.44**	**200.7**	**150.7**	**119.4**	**64.1**
21 High Income	**1.85**	**0.81**	**0.49**	**0.67**	**22.5**	**10.9**	**6.4**	**4.8**
74 Other	**62.34**	**49.03**	**30.13**	**6.57**	**147.2**	**90.1**	**55.7**	**27.1**

Source: World Bank (2019) and own calculations. See Appendix A.

Table 2.5: Geography and institutions, 1985, 2000, and 2015

Panel A: 1985	(1) Summary EFW Index	(2) Legal Sys. & Prop. Rights (Area 2)	(3) Access to Sound Money (Area 3)	(4) Trade Freedom (Area 4)	(5) Demo-cracy (Polity IV)	(6) Demo-cracy (Freedom House)	(7) Rule of Law (WGI)
Distance to Major	-0.14***	-0.27***	-0.27***	-0.28***	-0.51*	-0.18**	
Markets	(-2.87)	(-3.64)	(-3.39)	(-2.91)	(-1.69)	(-2.45)	
Malaria Ecology	-0.02	-0.07***	-0.04	-0.03	-0.29***	-0.10***	
	(-1.12)	(-3.36)	(-1.16)	(-0.55)	(-4.52)	(-6.01)	
Coastal	0.89**	0.04	0.28	1.36**	4.41**	1.39***	
Population	(2.45)	(0.07)	(0.48)	(2.01)	(2.26)	(2.97)	
Intercept	5.44***	5.71***	7.39***	5.44***	0.44	4.32***	
	(14.42)	(11.51)	(15.25)	(7.66)	(0.22)	(8.25)	
Observations	108	105	112	98	124	133	
Adj. R-squared	0.21	0.24	0.12	0.17	0.21	0.33	

Panel B: 2000	(1)	(2)	(3)	(4)	(5)	(6)	(7)
Distance to Major	-0.07*	-0.22***	-0.12*	-0.13***	-0.48**	-0.17**	-0.12***
Markets	(-1.88)	(-3.11)	(-1.68)	(-2.80)	(-2.16)	(-2.48)	(-3.17)
Malaria Ecology	-0.06***	-0.11***	-0.05**	-0.07***	-0.13*	-0.04*	-0.04***
	(-4.37)	(-5.11)	(-2.02)	(-4.17)	(-1.88)	(-1.94)	(-3.94)
Coastal	0.74***	0.30	0.87*	0.83**	2.16	0.92**	0.55**
Population	(2.78)	(0.66)	(1.76)	(2.61)	(1.35)	(2.05)	(2.52)
Intercept	6.72***	6.41***	7.90***	7.59***	5.27***	5.01***	0.44*
	(24.19)	(14.03)	(15.55)	(24.83)	(3.63)	(11.17)	(1.81)
Observations	112	112	112	112	126	135	135
Adj. R-squared	0.34	0.34	0.15	0.35	0.11	0.16	0.31

Panel C: 2015	(1)	(2)	(3)	(4)	(5)	(6)	(7)
Distance to Major	-0.07**	-0.17***	-0.13***	-0.10***	-0.39*	-0.17**	-0.12***
Markets	(-2.29)	(-2.91)	(-3.17)	(-2.73)	(-1.90)	(-2.60)	(-3.15)
Malaria Ecology	-0.04***	-0.08***	-0.06***	-0.04***	-0.06	-0.05**	-0.04***
	(-4.24)	(-5.10)	(-4.30)	(-3.23)	(-0.91)	(-2.10)	(-4.23)
Coastal	0.56***	0.55	0.38	0.87***	1.36	1.02**	0.48**
Population	(2.81)	(1.46)	(1.28)	(3.71)	(0.88)	(2.37)	(2.14)
Intercept	6.97***	6.08***	8.85***	7.17***	5.95***	5.12***	0.47*
	(33.87)	(15.80)	(32.23)	(29.46)	(4.31)	(11.58)	(1.88)
Observations	135	135	134	135	127	135	135
Adj. R-squared	0.25	0.27	0.20	0.29	0.06	0.19	0.28

Notes: Robust t-Statistics are in parenthesis. The symbols ***, **, and * denote statistical significance at the 1%, 5%, and 10% level respectively.

Table 2.6: The direct and the total impact of geography on real per capita GDP: 1985, 2000, and 2015

The dependent variable is the log of real per capita GDP

	Direct Effect (Columns 1 -3)			Total (direct + indirect) effect Columns (4 – 6)		
	(1)	(2)	(3)	(4)	(5)	(6)
Independent variables:	1985	2000	2015	1985	2000	2015
Prime age 25-59 share of pop	0.08***	0.09***	0.10***	0.08***	0.09***	0.10***
	(7.22)	(8.11)	(8.13)	(7.22)	(8.11)	(8.13)
EFW	0.12**	0.35***	0.23***			
	(2.40)	(4.53)	(2.66)			
EFW Residuals				0.12**	0.35***	0.23***
				(2.40)	(4.53)	(2.66)
Distance to Major Markets	-0.05**	-0.05**	-0.06**	-0.07***	-0.07***	-0.07***
	(-2.04)	(-2.60)	(-2.45)	(-2.66)	(-3.82)	(-3.07)
Malaria Ecology	-0.04***	-0.02**	-0.02*	-0.04***	-0.04***	-0.03***
	(-4.21)	(-2.53)	(-1.90)	(-4.36)	(-4.62)	(-2.73)
Coastal Population	0.21	0.07	0.08	0.31**	0.33**	0.21
	(1.28)	(0.54)	(0.53)	(2.00)	(2.24)	(1.37)
Middle East oil exporter	1.10***	0.95***	(0.34)	1.10***	0.95***	(0.34)
	(3.98)	(3.91)	(-0.99)	(3.98)	(3.91)	(-0.99)
Intercept	5.59***	3.38***	3.66***	6.22***	5.74***	5.25***
	(12.71)	(7.35)	(5.33)	(12.50)	(12.42)	(9.13)
No. of obs.	108	112	135	108	112	135
Adjusted r-squared	0.73	0.84	0.77	0.73	0.84	0.77
F-value	70.3	108.14	74.62	70.3	108.14	74.62
P-value	0	0	0	0	0	0

Notes: Robust t-statistics are in parenthesis. The symbols ***, **, and * denote statistical significance at the 1%, 5%, and 10% level respectively.

Table 2.7: The impact of geography on the growth of per capita GDP

	The dependent variable is the annual growth rate of real per capita GDP during the period						
	(1) 1985-2000	(2) 1985-2000	(3) 2000-2015	(4) 2000-2015	(5) 1985-2000	(6) 1985-2000	(7) 2000-2015
Income per capita (log, 5 years prior)	-0.78***	-0.78***	-0.71**	-0.62**	-0.47*	-0.50*	-0.88***
	(-3.32)	(-3.33)	(-2.38)	(-2.14)	(-1.72)	(-1.97)	(-3.09)
EFW (5 years prior)	1.27***	1.28***	0.29	0.28	0.83***	0.83***	0.75**
	(5.90)	(5.72)	(1.05)	(1.04)	(3.60)	(3.85)	(2.31)
Change in EFW (20 years)	1.01***	1.07***	0.41*	0.51**	0.63***	0.65***	0.61***
	(4.54)	(4.76)	(1.68)	(2.29)	(2.74)	(2.91)	(2.83)
Distance to major markets	-0.11		-0.01		-0.11		-0.02
	(-1.43)		(-0.03)		(-1.46)		(-0.28)
Malaria Ecology	-0.10**		-0.06		-0.06		-0.04
	(-2.58)		(-1.50)		(-1.32)		(-1.13)
Population within 100km of coast	1.50***		-0.57		1.22*		-0.02
	(2.71)		(-1.13)		(1.93)		(-0.05)
Geographic disadvantage		-1.02***		-0.1		-0.71***	
		(-3.94)		(-0.41)		(-2.86)	
Log of population, initial					0.07	0.05	0.32***
					(0.59)	(0.50)	(3.41)
Change in prime age share					0.12**	0.13***	0.11**
					(2.49)	(3.02)	(2.37)
Net fuel exports, period average					-0.03	-0.03	0.04**
					(-1.44)	(-1.60)	(2.50)
Middle East oil exporter					-0.66	-0.55	-3.22**
					(-0.63)	(-0.53)	(-2.50)
War on Soil					-1.61**	-1.62***	-5.15***
					(-2.34)	(-3.13)	(-7.50)
Intercept	0.27	0.03	6.95**	5.67**	-0.15	-0.07	3.96
	(0.13)	(0.01)	(2.21)	(2.06)	(-0.07)	(-0.04)	(1.22)
Number of Observations	102	102	123	123	95	95	117
Adjusted r-squared	0.50	0.49	0.17	0.15	0.58	0.57	0.47

Table 2.8: The impact of geographic disadvantages (GeoDis) over time

Panel A: Regression Analysis

Dependent variable is growth rates of real per capita GDP over 15 year (overlapping) periods

	Coef.	Robust t	p-value	[95% C.I.]
Period Effect				
1975-1990	-0.57*	-1.93	0.053	[-1.15, 0.01]
1980-1995	-0.95***	-3.06	0.002	[-1.56, -0.34]
1985-2000	-0.19	-0.71	0.477	[-0.71, 0.33]
1990-2005	0.43*	1.79	0.073	[-0.04, 0.9]
1995-2010	1.09***	4.31	0.000	[0.59, 1.59]
2000-2015	0.99***	3.92	0.000	[0.5, 1.5]
GeoDis Effect	-0.81***	-4.46	0.000	[-1.16, -0.45]
Interaction: Period × GeoDis				
1975-1990	0.10	0.38	0.703	[-0.43, 0.63]
1980-1995	0.03	0.11	0.913	[-0.53, 0.59]
1985-2000	-0.22	-0.85	0.396	[-0.73, 0.29]
1990-2005	0.08	0.35	0.728	[-0.39, 0.56]
1995-2010	0.71***	2.90	0.004	[0.23, 1.19]
2000-2015	1.19***	4.85	0.000	[0.71, 1.67]
Intercept	1.52***	8.52	0.000	[1.17, 1.87]

Number of countries = 135, number of periods = 7

Total number of observations = 945, R-squared = 0.1674

Note: GeoDis is the aggregate measure of geographic disadvantage which is standardized to have a mean of zero and standard deviation of one

Panel B: Marginal effect of GeoDis over time

Period	dy/dx	Delta Method Robust SE	t-stat	p-value	[95% Conf. Interval]
1970-1985	-0.806	0.181	-4.46	0.000	[-1.16, -0.45]
1975-1990	-0.703	0.202	-3.49	0.001	[-1.1, -0.31]
1980-1995	-0.775	0.221	-3.5	0.000	[-1.21, -0.34]
1985-2000	-1.027	0.187	-5.49	0.000	[-1.39, -0.66]
1990-2005	-0.722	0.159	-4.54	0.000	[-1.03, -0.41]
1995-2010	-0.093	0.166	-0.56	0.574	[-0.42, 0.23]
2000-2015	0.384	0.166	2.32	0.021	[0.06, 0.71]

Panel C: Line graph of the marginal effects of GeoDis over time

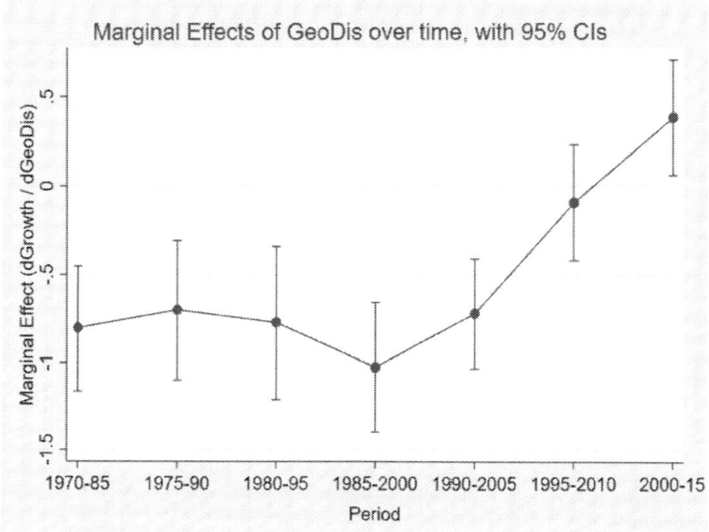

Table 2.9: World total trade as a share of the World's GDP and per capita

	(1)	(2)	(3)	(4)	(5)	(6)
	As a share of GDP (percent)			**Per capita (2011 PPP $)**		
Year	**Trade**	**Exports**	**Imports**	**Trade**	**Exports**	**Imports**
1970	21.9	10.7	11.2	1,288	628	660
1975	29.1	14.4	14.7	1,913	948	965
1980	33.3	15.9	17.3	2,449	1,173	1,276
1985	30.8	14.8	16.0	2,322	1,117	1,205
1990	32.3	15.9	16.4	2,653	1,304	1,349
1995	37.1	18.3	18.8	3,346	1,649	1,697
2000	43.7	22.2	21.5	4,422	2,242	2,180
2005	49.5	24.9	24.6	5,687	2,861	2,826
2010	50.0	24.8	25.2	6,557	3,254	3,303
2015	49.0	24.1	24.9	7,156	3,518	3,638
%Increase 1970-2015	123.15%	125.06%	121.33%	455.82%	460.58%	451.29%
%Increase 2000-2015	12.07%	8.68%	15.56%	61.83%	56.93%	66.88%

Table 2.10: Trade shares of different groups of countries

Year	Total trade ($ 10^12)	As a share of the group's GDP	As a share of the World's GDP	As a share of the World's trade	Per capita
Panel A: 40 Most Geographically Disadvantaged Countries					
1970	0.24	15.9%	1.2%	5.6%	$599
1985	0.46	17.8%	1.4%	4.5%	$775
2000	0.95	25.7%	1.7%	3.8%	$1,125
2015	2.09	28.4%	2.1%	4.3%	$1,773
%Increase 1970-2015	770%	79%	74%	-22%	196%
%Increase 2000-2015	119%	11%	27%	13%	58%
Panel B: 21 High-Income Countries					
1970	3.12	24.4%	15.9%	72.8%	$4,587
1985	7.12	36.0%	21.4%	69.6%	$9,426
2000	15.42	48.2%	27.2%	62.3%	$18,501
2015	22.98	56.9%	23.4%	47.8%	$25,180
%Increase 1970-2015	636%	133%	47%	-34%	449%
%Increase 2000-2015	49%	18%	-14%	-23%	36%
Panel C: 74 Other Developing Economies					
1970	0.93	17.6%	4.7%	21.6%	$412
1985	2.65	24.3%	8.0%	25.9%	$865
2000	8.37	39.9%	14.8%	33.8%	$2,137
2015	22.99	45.6%	23.4%	47.8%	$4,970
%Increase 1970-2015	2375%	159%	394%	121%	1107%
%Increase 2000-2015	175%	14%	58%	41%	133%

Table 2.11: Geographic disadvantages, trade, poverty, and under-5 mortality rates

	(1)	(2)	(3)	(4)	(5)	(6)
	International Trade (% of GDP)		International Trade (dollars per capita)		Extreme Poverty	Under 5 Mortality
Year Effect						
1975	7.13	7.47	625.80	585.70	-2.44	-14.24*
	(1.20)	(1.21)	(0.81)	(0.80)	(-0.85)	(-1.77)
1980	11.33*	11.72**	1,161.63	1,102.29	-4.99*	-30.95***
	(1.92)	(1.97)	(1.27)	(1.28)	(-1.77)	(-4.04)
1985	8.88	6.51	1,034.02	1,007.39	-7.37***	-44.94***
	(1.50)	(1.18)	(1.18)	(1.22)	(-2.69)	(-6.07)
1990	10.36	7.74	1,365.50	1,363.94	-9.13***	-54.77***
	(1.60)	(1.27)	(1.40)	(1.44)	(-3.41)	(-7.57)
1995	15.13**	12.43*	2,058.32*	2,094.19*	-11.38***	-61.61***
	(2.21)	(1.89)	(1.82)	(1.89)	(-4.40)	(-8.77)
2000	21.75***	17.98***	3,134.46**	3,223.29**	-13.26***	-70.50***
	(3.19)	(2.72)	(2.24)	(2.36)	(-5.28)	(-10.51)
2005	27.59***	23.13***	4,399.27***	4,596.83***	-16.50***	-81.55***
	(3.63)	(3.30)	(2.71)	(2.91)	(-6.72)	(-12.64)
2010	28.04***	23.72***	5,269.72***	5,601.74***	-19.66***	-90.38***
	(3.71)	(3.52)	(3.17)	(3.52)	(-8.10)	(-13.99)
2015	27.02***	23.02***	5,868.65***	6,357.64***	-22.43***	-98.68***
	(3.86)	(3.69)	(3.47)	(4.09)	(-9.49)	(-15.99)
GeoDis Effect		-4.67		-1,310.23***	22.65***	62.56***
		(-1.52)		(-4.94)	(14.49)	(12.00)
Interactions:						
1975×GeoDis		0.38		-516.93	-0.40	-1.91
		(0.07)		(-1.11)	(-0.18)	(-0.27)
1980×GeoDis		0.52		-1,075.20**	-1.05	-6.08
		(0.10)		(-1.96)	(-0.48)	(-0.89)
1985×GeoDis		-3.96		-1,323.64**	-1.77	-8.92
		(-0.80)		(-2.36)	(-0.82)	(-1.32)
1990×GeoDis		-4.06		-1,852.73***	-2.11	-10.65
		(-0.68)		(-2.62)	(-1.00)	(-1.59)
1995×GeoDis		-4.40		-2,572.47***	-2.94	-11.41*
		(-0.67)		(-3.23)	(-1.44)	(-1.81)
2000×GeoDis		-6.12		-3,874.77***	-4.05**	-15.43***
		(-0.89)		(-3.69)	(-1.99)	(-2.60)
2005×GeoDis		-8.17		-5,088.53***	-5.70***	-23.92***
		(-1.06)		(-4.12)	(-2.79)	(-4.20)
2010×GeoDis		-10.04		-5,505.12***	-7.54***	-33.30***
		(-1.30)		(-4.23)	(-3.76)	(-5.73)
2015×GeoDis		-10.62		-5,857.92***	-9.80***	-38.57***
		(-1.36)		(-4.33)	(-5.04)	(-7.00)
Intercept	21.94***	18.97***	1,287.50	1,109.48***	34.69***	130.63***
	(6.03)	(5.51)	(1.24)	(2.78)	(16.80)	(22.12)
Observations	1,346	1,346		1,346	1,330	1,330
R-squared	0.05	0.10		0.20	0.57	0.62

Robust t-statistics in parentheses. *** $p<0.01$, ** $p<0.05$, * $p<0.1$

CHAPTER 3

INSTITUTIONS AND ECONOMIC DEVELOPMENT

"If it matters, measure it."
Michael Walker.

3.1. Introduction

Following a session on *1984,* the classic novel of George Orwell at the 1984 Mont Pelerin Society meeting, a series of Liberty Fund conferences inspired by Michael Walker was held with the purpose of differentiating between economic freedom and political freedom. Led by Milton and Rose Friedman, these conferences facilitated a close interaction among academics of the caliber of Gary Becker, Douglas North, and Gordon Tullock, in addition to the Friedmans. The Economic Freedom of the World index was an outgrowth of this series of conferences. See Gwartney (2008) for additional details.

At the time, the neoclassical model of Robert Solow dominated the theory of economic growth. In this model, the main drivers of growth were improvements in technology and increases in physical and human capital. However, Douglass North argued that these so-called "drivers" of growth were mere reflections of growth itself and not the fundamental cause of growth and development. Besides, the predictions from the neoclassical growth theory alone were unable to explain basic cross-country differences in rates of return, productivity, and investment. With this background, and following the eminent work of North, a group of economists often referred to as "new institutional economists" arose during the 1990s. These economists argued that institutions not only supplement the neoclassical analysis, but they are the fundamental cause of long-run economic performance.

With the increasing recognition of the role of institutions in facilitating economic development, there is also a growing controversy over which institutions are the most influential. At the heart of this controversy is the question of whether it is political or economic institutions that really matter for sustained economic development. The distinction between the two is subtle, and this distinction was at the heart of the debate about whether George Orwell was right held at the 1984 meeting of the Mont Pelerin Society.

Economic institutions reduce transactions costs that impede mutually beneficial exchanges, and as such reflect the degree to which individuals can voluntarily engage in trade, have access to sound money, and can depend on the legal system to protect their property and enforce contracts in an unbiased manner. Thus, economic institutions refer to legal structures and political actions that determine the structure of the economy, particularly the extent to which it is directed by markets rather than political allocation. In contrast, political institutions refer to the structural organization of the political process, including how officials are chosen, constraints on their actions, and the openness of the process.

The effects of economic and political institutions have been widely analyzed separately, but not together. On one hand, Daron Acemoglu and his collaborators have largely argued that inclusive political institutions that constrain the power of government are necessary to facilitate sustained economic development (Acemoglu, Johnson, and Robinson, 2001 and 2005; Acemoglu and Johnson 2005; Acemoglu and Robinson, 2012; Acemoglu, Naidu, Restrepo, and Robinson, 2019; Rodrik 2000). On the other hand, a large and growing number of scholars find that economic institutions that protect private property and enforce contracts evenhandedly are the central institutional factors underlying the growth process (Knack and Keefer, 1995; Dawson, 1998; Heckelman, and Stroup, 2000; Rodrik, Subramanian, and Trebbi, 2004; Gwartney, Holcombe, and Lawson, 2006; Bjørnskov and Foss, 2008; Faria and Montesinos, 2009; Hall, Sobel, and Crowley, 2010; Faria, Montesinos, Morales, and Navarro, 2016; Bennett, Faria, Gwartney, and Morales, 2016).

Disentangling the effects of economic and political institutions is not easy. According to the Grand Transition view advanced by Paldam and Gundlach (2008), the process of development is a unified phenomenon in which both institutions and economic development occur simultaneously. Two figures have emerged from the efforts to mitigate the endogeneity problem and better identify the causal impact of economic and political institutions: Daron Acemoglu on the side of political institutions and Hugo Faria on the side of economic institutions. Acemoglu et al. (2001, 2002, 2005), used settler mortality rates and population density in 1500 as instruments for political institutions. Faria et al. (2009, 2012, 2013, 2016) have used a variety of identification strategies to isolate an exogenous source of variation in economic institutions and policies. The objective of this research is to identify what Douglas North called the fundamental cause of economic development.

This chapter builds on a working paper by Bennett, Faria, Montesinos, Morales, and Navarro (2017). In this working paper, the authors examined and sought to disentangle the relative merits of economic freedom and executive constraints, the preferred political measure of Acemoglu and his collaborators. This chapter differentiates from Bennett et al. (2017) in multiple ways. First, the working paper focused solely on the constraints on the executive as the measure of institutional quality, while this chapter examines a wider set of institutional measures. Second, while Bennett et al. (2017) focus only on an instrumental variable approach to isolate a causal link between institutions and economic development, this research will also consider the importance of lagged changes in institutions and their subsequent effect on development. Bennett et al. (2017) ran only cross-country regressions, this chapter will analyze and exploit variations across both countries and time. Third, Bennett et al. (2019) focus only on per capita GDP in 2010 as the dependent variable, while this research will examine a broader set of performance measures, including the growth of per capita GDP, poverty rates, and changes in poverty rates. Fourth, the latest available data will be utilized and as a result, the sample sizes will be larger.

Regarding the relationship between political and economic institutions, this chapter is also related to Rode and Gwartney (2012). The two approaches, however, are methodologically different and use different data sources. While Rode and Gwartney used data from Cheibub et al. (2010) to study the effect of democratization on economic liberalization, this chapter will verify their results using a different dataset and perform Granger causality tests in both directions: from democratization to economic liberalization and vice versa. The Granger causality tests will be conducted both for the levels and for the changes in the measures of economic and political institutions.

This chapter is organized as follows: The following section 2 describes the data, provides their sources, and discusses summary statistics of the variables. Section 3 presents results using levels of economic and political institutions and levels of per capita GDP and extreme poverty rates. Section 4 examines changes in economic and political institutions and their impact on growth rates of per capita GDP and changes in poverty rates. Section 5 presents an instrumental variable analysis. Section 6 discusses the relationship between economic and political institutions, and section 7 concludes.

3.2. Data

As in Chapter 2, the primary database for this chapter consists of the 135 countries for which per capita GDP data are continuously available since 1970 and the Economic Freedom of the World data are available in 2015. These 135 countries constituted approximately 93 percent of the World's population in 2015. The primary variables utilized in this chapter are presented and defined in Table 3.1.

3.2.1 Economic Institutions

The variables EFW, Area 2 of EFW, and Rule of Law (WGI), are the three main measures of economic institutions. The first variable stands for the Economic Freedom of the World (EFW) index which is a comprehensive measure of the degree to which the policies and institutions of a country are supportive of personal choice, voluntary exchange, market allocation of goods and services, free trade, and protection of individuals and their property from aggression by others. The summary index is based on ratings ranging from zero to ten for 42 different components which are classified in 5 separate areas and then averaged. Higher ratings are indicative of more economic freedom. This variable is from Gwartney et al. (2018).

Economic theory indicates that high and sustained levels of economic freedom and increases in economic freedom are important sources of economic growth and development. This is because economic freedom facilitates and encourages gains from trade, entrepreneurship, innovation, and capital formation. To capture high and sustained levels of economic freedom, the average of summary EFW rating was calculated over an extended period of 30 years. The nomenclature or abbreviated name for this variable is "efm30" and this name stands for "economic freedom, mean, 30-years". For example, in 2015, the variable efm30 is the average EFW rating for the period 1985-2015. Similarly, in 2010, the variable efm30 is the average EFW rating for the period 1980-2010. A minimum of five (out of the seven possible) observations is required for the calculation of the mean for this variable. The next two variables are area 2 of EFW and rule of law (WGI). These two variables measure an important aspect of economic institutions: the quality of the legal system and the presence of rule of law. These two variables are from different sources. Nevertheless, it is expected that they will be highly correlated since they are measuring roughly the same institutional characteristics.

Specifically, area 2 of EFW measures the integrity of the legal system and the protection of property rights. This variable is the average of nine different components: Judicial independence, impartial courts, protection of property rights, military interference in rule of law and politics, the integrity of the legal system, legal enforcement of contracts, regulatory costs of the sale of real property, reliability of police, and business costs of crime. These components are scaled to range from zero to ten and then averaged to obtain the area 2 rating of EFW. Higher ratings are indicative of a legal system consistent with the principles of economic freedom. This variable is from Gwartney et al. (2018). As in the case of the summary EFW rating, the average of area 2 of EFW was also calculated for an extended period of 30 years, and the corresponding variable name is "a2m30" which stands for "area 2, mean, 30-years". In 2015, for example, this variable is the average of area 2 of EFW for the period 1985-2015. A minimum of five (out of the seven possible) observations is required to calculate this average.

The rule of law variable (WGI) is from Kauffman and Kraay (2019) World Governance Indicators from the World Bank group. They define this variable as "capturing perceptions of the extent to which agents have confidence in and abide by the rules of society, and in particular the quality of contract enforcement, property rights, the police, and the courts, as well as the likelihood of crime and violence." The variable is standardized and ranges from minus 2.5 to plus 2.5. Higher numbers reflect closer adherence to the rule of law. The average rule of law (WGI) was also calculated over an extended period of time. Since the original rule of law variable starts in 1996, this variable is the average for the years 1996, 2000, 2005, 2010, and 2015. A minimum of three (out of the five possible) observations was required to calculate this average.

3.2.2 Political Institutions

Several measures of political institutions have been used in the literature. Some of the most important measures are the combined democracy score and executive constraints provided by Polity IV, the political rights and civil liberties variables provided by Freedom House, and the newly develop binary-indicator for democracy from Acemoglu et al. (2019). These variables are listed in Table 1 and a brief explanation is provided below.

The Polity IV democracy score is calculated by combining two separate series: DEMOC and AUTOC. DEMOC intends to measure the degree of institutionalized democracy in a country on a scale from 0 (least democratic) to 10 (most democratic). Similarly, the AUTOC variable is designed to measure the degree of institutionalized autocracy or the degree "Authoritarian regime" in a country on a scale from 0 (least autocratic) to 10 (most autocratic). Both variables measure the competitiveness of political participation, the openness and competitiveness of executive recruitment, and constraints on the chief executive, but using different internal sub-variables and different weights. Therefore, one is not the opposite of the other. The combined democracy variable is obtained by subtracting the AUTOC score from the DEMOC score and has been widely used in the literature. The resulting "unified" or "combined" polity score ranges from +10 (strongly democratic) to -10 (strongly autocratic).

The advantages of using the combined score are obvious as it combines autocratic and democratic elements into a unified democracy/autocracy spectrum and this is reflected by the usage of this variable in the literature. However, as the theory of Eckstein and Gurr (1975) suggests, autocratic and democratic authority are different patterns of authority, elements of which may co-exist simultaneously. Therefore, caution is recommended when utilizing this variable.

One of the Polity IV components, the constraints on the executive, has been widely used by Daron Acemoglu and other researchers. This variable measures the institutionalized constraints on the decision-making powers of chief executives. This variable ranges from 1 (Unlimited Authority) to 7 (Executive Party or Subordination). When the executive constraints measure is equal to seven, accountability groups such as the legislature have effective authority equal to or greater than the executive in most areas of activity. When this variable is equal to one, there are no regular limitations on the executive's actions and the constitutional restrictions, if any, are often ignored.

Two other political variables — political rights and civil liberties — are from Freedom House (FH). The political rights variable is the average of 10 political rights indicators grouped into three subcategories: Electoral Process, Political Pluralism and Participation, and Functioning of Government. This variable ranges from 1 (most free) to 7 (least free). The civil liberties variable is the average of 15 civil liberties indicators grouped into four subcategories: Freedom of Expression and Belief, Associational and Organizational Rights, Rule of Law, and Personal Autonomy and Individual Rights. This variable ranges from 1 (most free) to 7 (least free). Because these two variables are typically highly correlated, and their scales are such that higher numerical values indicate less freedom, a third variable "political freedom" was constructed. This variable is the average of political rights and civil liberties from Freedom House. The scale of this variable was inverted so that the new variable ranges from 1 (least free) to 7 (most free).

A dichotomous measure of democracy developed by Acemoglu, Naidu, Restrepo, and Robinson (2019) is also examined as a measure of political institutions. This variable classifies a country as democratic if both Freedom House assigns a "free" or "partially free" and Polity IV assigns it a positive score. Acemoglu et al. (2019) used the binary classifications provided by Cheibub, Gandhi, and Vreeland (2010) or Boix, Miller, and Rosato (2012) to complete missing values.

Inspired by Acemoglu et al. (2019) and Persson and Tabellini (2006), the author also constructed three additional variables designed to provide a more accurate measure of political democracy. The variable Strong Democracy is a dummy variable that is equal to one if both Freedom House measures assign a "free" or "partially free" and the combined democracy score from Polity IV assigns it a score of 8, 9, or 10. Similarly, the variable Strong Autocracy is a dummy that is equal to one if the country has a combined Polity score of -8, -9, or -10, and both measures of civil liberties and political rights from Freedom House are 6 or 7. Finally, the variable Vulnerable Democracy contains all other cases. Persson and Tabellini (2006) argue that democracy is a blunt concept and that huge heterogeneity across democracies and across political reforms can blur the relevance of democratic political institutions in empirical practice. The rationale behind Strong Democracy, Strong Autocracy, and Vulnerable Democracy is that the potential heterogeneous mix will be captured in the Vulnerable Democracy variable and that this way the Strong Democracy variable will be "cleaner" from noise. The Strong Democracy measure should better capture the idea of democratic political institutions that are unequivocally free. This variable is also related to the measure constructed by Cheibub et al. (2010) and the stable democracy measure constructed by Rode and Gwartney (2012).

Like the economic variables, the political variables were averaged over a 30 year time frame in order to capture high and sustained levels of political-institutional quality. The corresponding variables and their 30-year moving averages are Democracy from Polity IV (polm30), Executive Constraints (xcm30), Political Rights (prm30), Civil Liberties (clm30), Political Freedom (pfm30), Democracy from Acemoglu et al. (dem30), Strong Democracy (sdm30), Strong Autocracy (sam30), and Vulnerable Democracy (vdm30).

3.2.3. Descriptive Statistics

Table 3.2 shows the pairwise Pearson correlation matrix between the economic and political variables organized in three panels. Panel A is for the full period 1980-2015. Panel B is for 2015. Panel C is for the average of the variables over 1985-2015.

The correlation coefficients are higher among the variables that fundamentally measure the same institutional concept. For example, the correlation coefficients between area 2 of EFW and the rule of law from WGI is about 0.91 in all three panels. The correlation coefficient between the summary EFW rating and rule of law was about 0.74 during the full period 1980-2015 (panel A) and 0.76 in 2015 (panel B). Interestingly, the 30-year means between these two correlated much stronger with a value of 0.85 (panel C). This indicates that generally the countries that sustained elevated levels of economic freedom over an extended period also sustained the best legal systems in terms of their protection of property rights.

In contrast, the correlation coefficients between the economic and political variables are lower. For instance, the correlation between the summary EFW rating and the combined democracy score from Polity IV was 0.48 in the full period 1980-2015 (panel A), 0.39 in 2015 (panel B), and 0.54 for the 30-year averages. This indicates that economic institutions and political institutions are generally measuring different aspects of the institutional environment which is a desirable feature for the goal of this research of disentangling the effect of the two. The correlations are, once again, generally higher after averaging the variables over lengthy periods of time. This indicates that the observed correlations are not only a one-time phenomenon but rather a general pattern that gets even stronger as countries sustain high-quality institutions over relatively lengthy periods.

Finally, the correlation coefficients among the political variables are relatively high (typically above 0.8 and in some cases above 0.9) except for the Strong Democracy variable (ranging between 0.57 and 0.83). This indicates that the variable Strong Democracy captures something different than the other political variables. Interestingly, the Strong Democracy variable is the political variable that correlates the least with other political variables and the most with all economic variables. This interesting finding is consistent with the view of Persson and Tabellini (2006) that democracy is a blunt concept. By refining the criteria to Strong Democracies, this concept is sharpened and becomes less blunt.

Table 3.3 presents a summary of descriptive statistics for the main institutional variables for the base sample of 135 countries. The two main outcome variables, per capita GDP and extreme poverty rates, are also included. Panel A is for 1985, panel B is for 2000 and panel C is for 2015 (except for Acemoglu's democracy variable which is for 2010). A companion table showing descriptive statistics for the average institutional variables during 1985-2015, and for some additional time-invariant variables utilized later in this chapter, is presented in Table C-1 of Appendix C.

Table 3.3 shows that both the means and the medians of all the institutional variables under consideration have increased over time. Recall that lower numerical values for the civil liberties and political rights variables indicate more democratic political institutions. The overall increases in the means and medians of these institutional measures indicate a systematic improvement in institutional quality around the world. It is interesting, however, that the increases appear to be substantially larger during 1985-2000, than during 2000-2015. For instance, the world median EFW increased 1.52 points (from 5.13 to 6.72) between 1985 and 2000, but only 0.18 points (from 6.72 to 6.90) between 2000 and 2015. Similarly, the median polity IV combined democracy score increased from 12 points (from -6 to +6) between 1985 and 2000 but only 1 point (from +6 to +7) between 2000 and 2015. The same pattern is true for the other institutional variables. This indicates that, overall, 1985-2000 was a period of larger institutional changes than 2000-2015.

Table 3.3 also indicates that poverty rates have fallen while per capita GDP has increased, as expected. In 1985, the median poverty rate for this group of countries was 13.30 percent. By 2015, the median poverty rate declined to 1.90 percent, indicating that more than half of the countries in the sample virtually eliminated extreme poverty. The median per capita GDP almost doubled between 1985 and 2015, from $6,178 to $11,849.

3.3. Institutions and Levels of Per Capita GDP and Poverty Rates

This section describes the relationship between the levels of economic and political institutions, and the levels of per capita GDP and poverty rates. In this regard, this section captures the historical association between institutions and contemporary economic development. The main dependent variables are the natural logarithm of the 2015 per capita GDP (in 2011 PPP dollars) and the extreme poverty rates as measured by the estimated percentage of the population living on less than $1.90 per day in 2015. The primary independent variables are the averages of various institutional measures over an extended period, mostly 1985-2015. The first subsection describes the univariate results and the next subsection describes the multivariate results.

3.3.1 Univariate Results

This section seeks to determine the magnitude of the association between the different institutional measures and the outcome variables. Table 3.4 presents a simple regression analysis between the long-term 30-year average of each institutional variable and the log of per capita GDP (panel A) and extreme poverty rates (panel B). Both of the dependent variables are for 2015. All variables are standardized so that the magnitude of the coefficients is comparable across regressions.

Columns 1 to 3 present the results for the economic variables: the summary measure of economic freedom (efm30), area 2 of EFW (a2m30), and rule of law from the WGI (rlm30). Columns 4 and 5 present the results using the two measures of Polity IV: the combined democracy score and executive constraints. Columns 7 and 8 present results using Freedom House measures: Political Rights, Civil Liberties, and the average between the two (with the scale inverted). Column 9 presents the results using the dichotomous democracy measure from Acemoglu et al. (2019). And finally, column 10 shows the results using the Strong Democracy measure described above.

Overall, a distinct pattern is highly visible. The association is much stronger between the economic variables and outcome variables than between the political variables and outcome variables. In panel A, where per capita GDP is the dependent variable, the standardized coefficients range between 0.77 and 0.80 for the economic variables while they are between 0.35 and 0.62 for the political variables. The r-squares are also larger for the economic variables (columns 1-3, ranging from 0.59 to 0.64) than for the political variables (columns 4-10, ranging from 0.12 to 0.38). In panel B, where the extreme poverty rate is the dependent variable, the standardized coefficients range between -0.53 and -0.58 for the economic variables and between -0.29 and -0.43 for the political variables. Correspondingly, the R-squares for the poverty regressions are larger for the economic variables (ranging from 0.28 to 0.33) than for the political variables (ranging from 0.09 to 0.19).

Among the political variables, the strong democracy binary variable (column 10) is the one that is most closely associated with both per capita GDP and poverty rates. In panel A, its standardized coefficient of 0.62 is notably larger than the second largest standardized coefficient of 0.56 corresponding to civil liberties in column 7. In a way, this is not surprising and is consistent with the grand transition view of Paldam and Gundlach (2008) and with the view of Persson and Tabellini (2006) that democracy is a blunt concept. Further, it is remarkable that the less precise measures of democratic political institutions (the independent variables of columns 4 through 9) have dominated the empirical analysis of comparative development, while more refined measures of democracy, like that of column 10 have seldom been examined.

3.3.2. Multivariate Results

Table 3.5 adds to the equations the three main Sachs' geographic variables: Malaria ecology, distance to major markets, and coastal population. If institutions are a channel through which geography affects comparative economic development, then after controlling for geographic characteristics the coefficients of institutional measures should decline in magnitude. The empirical evidence suggests that this is indeed the case.

When per capita GDP is the dependent variable (panel A), the coefficients associated with the economic variables now range from 0.56 to 0.61 (Table 3.5, columns 1 to 3) but remain highly statistically significant with t-ratios ranging between 8.36 and 11.33. In contrast, three of the political variables are statistically insignificant: the combined democracy score, executive constraints, and the binary democracy classification by Acemoglu et al. (2019). The Freedom House variables remain significant, but their standardized coefficients fell substantially to 0.22 for political rights, 0.29 for civil liberties, and 0.25 for the average. This is about half what they were in the univariate results of Table 3.4. Finally, the strong democracy variable (column 10) remained significant with a coefficient of 0.36 and a t-ratio of 6.17, the largest among the political variables.

Panel B of Table 3.5 shows the corresponding results when the extreme poverty rate is the dependent variable. For these equations, the three economic variables are significant with coefficients ranging between -0.19 and -0.25 and t-ratios ranging between -2.87 and -3.17. However, all the political variables of columns 4 through 9 were insignificant. Only the strong democracy variable (column 10) remained significant at the 5 percent level with a standardized coefficient of -0.11.

Each of the three Sachs geographic variables was statistically significant at the 1 percent level in most of the 20 regressions of Table 3.5, panels A and B. Their magnitudes were larger in equations 4 to 10 (when the political variables were the institutional measures) than in equations 1 to 3 (when the economic variables were the institutional measures). This indicates that geographic factors explain a significant amount of the cross-country variation in the levels of per capita GDP and poverty rates, even after holding constant the average institutional quality during the 30-year period 1985-2015.

Taken together, Tables 3.4 and 3.5 indicate that both levels of per capita GDP and poverty rates are more strongly associated with economic institutions than political institutions. After controlling for geographic characteristics, the relative decline in the magnitude of the coefficients was much larger for the political variables than for the economic variables. The latter remained strong and highly significant with the expected signs (positive for income and negative for the poverty rate), while the former weaken and became insignificant for three of the measures. In addition, the political variable with the strongest historical association with contemporary levels of per capita GDP and poverty rates was strong democracy defined as a solid record of high-quality democratic institutions: scores of 8, 9, or 10 in the combined democracy measure, and scores of 1 or 2 in both civil liberties and political rights.

Table 3.6 presents horse races between economic and political institutions. Like before, the dependent variable is the 2015 level of per capita GDP in panel A and the 2015 extreme poverty rate in panel B. In columns 1 to 5 the main measure of economic institutions is the summary rating of the economic freedom of the world index averaged over the period 1985-2015 (efm30). In columns 6 to 10, the main measure of economic institutions is the rule of law variable from the World Governance

Indicators (WGI) averaged over the years 1996, 2000, 2005, 2010, and 2015. The main political institutions are the combined democracy score (polm30, columns 1 and 6), executive constraints (columns 2 and 7), political freedom (columns 3 and 8), democracy from Acemoglu et al. (2019) (columns 4 and 9), and finally the strong democracy variable (columns 5 and 10).[12] The three Sachs' geographic variables are added as additional controls.

Even though these competitions between economic and political institutions are performed using ordinary least squares and there is potential endogeneity, the results are informative. In both panels A and B of Table 3.6, the economic variables are statistically significant, mostly at the 1 percent level, in each of the 20 equations. The economic variables also have the expected signs (positive in panel A and negative in panel B). The political variables, in contrast, are largely insignificant except for strong democracy in column 5 of panel A which enters with the expected positive sign. The other 4 political variables in columns 6 to 9 of panel A, enter with the wrong sign. It is interesting that after controlling for rule of law and geography, the political variables (except strong democracy) are negatively associated with per capita GDP. This unexpected result suggests that on average, two countries with similar geographic conditions and the same perception of rule of law among their citizens, the least democratic country tends to have the largest per capita GDP. But one unequivocal result is much more sensible. When comparing two countries with the same geographic characteristics and the same political institutions (either democratic or autocratic), the most economically free country has, on average, the largest per capita GDP and the lowest poverty rates.

Tables 3.4, 3.5, and 3.6, show a stronger association of levels of economic development (as measured by per capita GDP and extreme poverty rates) with economic institutions than with political institutions. But this association in levels reflects history. Consistent with the grand transition view of Paldam and Gundlach (2008), these findings merely reflect that those countries that historically developed institutions supportive of the rule of law, protective of property rights, and generally consistent with economic freedom, have higher levels of income per capita and lower poverty rates. However, a more interesting question would be if given their history, this is continuing to be the case. Do changes in institutions lead to growth and to reductions in poverty rates, and if so, which institutional changes lead to more rapid economic development? The next section will address these questions.

[12] The correlation coefficient between the 30-year average of civil liberties and political rights and the average of the two is 0.99. Because of this high correlation, only the average of the two (political freedom) is used in the empirical analysis.

3.4. Changes in Institutions, Growth Rates, and Reductions in Poverty Rates

This section will assess if changes in institutions lead to subsequent increases in per capita GDP and reductions in poverty rates. As this issue is addressed, changes in income and poverty over 15 year periods will be considered, along with changes in institutions during a 15 year period lagged by 5 years. For example, for the period 2000-2015, the changes in institutions during 1995-2010 will be examined. Because the changes in institutions during 1995-2010 may have a different impact depending on when they took place, this period will be broken down into three 5-year subperiods: the 5 years prior to the beginning of the period (1995-2000 in the example), the first 5-years of the period (2000-2005), and the second 5-years of the period (2005-2010). Table 3.7 will focus on the impact of economic institutions, Table 3.8 on political institutions, and Table 3.9 will simultaneously include both the economic and political variables. To control and test for convergence, all of the growth equations will include the log of per capita GDP at the beginning of the period. Similarly, all of the equations concerning the reductions in poverty rates will control for the initial poverty rate.

Columns 1 and 2 of Table 3.7 focus on the 1985-2000 period. In this period of rapid increases in economic freedom and trade liberalization around the world, both the level of economic freedom in 1980 and all increases in economic freedom in 5-year intervals from 1980 to 1995 were positive for growth and highly statistically significant. Of these increases, the largest in magnitude in terms of its effect on growth was the change in the summary EFW rating from 1980 to 1985. This was true for both columns 1 and 2.

Column 2 adds a set of control variables. These controls are the same as those employed in the growth analysis of Chapter 2 (see section 2.3.4, Table 7). Of these controls, the following were statistically significant: the standardized geographic disadvantage index with a coefficient of -0.39, the change in the percentage of the population in the prime working-age 25-59 category with a coefficient of 0.12, the dummy for the Middle Eastern oil-exporting countries with a coefficient of -0.93, and the dummy for having a war on soil with a fatality rate of 0.1 percent of the population with a coefficient of -1.30. After controlling for these factors, the coefficient for EFW in 1980 was 0.71, and for the change in EFW during 1980-1985 was 1.34. This last coefficient indicates that on average, and holding all else constant, a unitary increase in EFW during the 5-year period 1980-1985 was associated with an additional 1.34 percent annual growth rate during the following 15-year period 1985-2000. The other two increases were also positive and significant but of smaller magnitude. The coefficient for the change in EFW during 1985-1990 was 0.69, and for the change in EFW during 1990-1995 was 0.79.

Columns 3 and 4 of Table 3.7 are for the period 2000-2015. The impact of economic freedom on the growth of per capita GDP was smaller during this period. The level of EFW in 1995 and the change during the first five years of the period were positive and statistically significant. This was true in both columns 3 and 4. In column 4, the following controls were statistically significant. The log of the initial population with a coefficient of 0.28, the change in the percentage of the population in the prime working-age 25-59 category with a coefficient of 0.10, the dummy for the Middle Eastern oil-exporting countries with a coefficient of -3.88, and the dummy for having a war on soil with a fatality rate of 0.1 percent of the population with a coefficient of -5.85. Even though only two of the EFW variables are significant in this period, their magnitude increased. In column 4, the coefficient for EFW in 1995 was 0.86 and the coefficient for the change in EFW during the 5-year period 2000-2005 was 1.45.

Columns 5 and 6 of Table 3.7 present a panel analysis. In column 5, only two periods are considered: 1985-2000 and 2000-2015, and a dummy for the second period is added. In column 6, the periods are allowed to overlap. Therefore, the following four overlapping periods are included in the equation: 1985-2000, 1990-2005, 1995-2010, and 2000-2015. Both equations are estimated using seemingly unrelated regressions (SUR) to gain efficiency in the estimation, but the results using regular OLS are similar. These equations show that the coefficient for EFW 5-years prior to the beginning of the period was 0.80 in column 5 and 0.77 in column 6, both highly statistically significant. Similarly, all increases were positive, large in magnitude, and statistically significant at the 1 percent level. The largest increases were the 5-years prior and the first 5-years of the period with coefficients ranging from 0.86 to 1.14 in both columns (with and without overlap). This indicates that a one-unit increase in EFW for these variables was associated with, on average, a 1 percent increase in the annual growth of per capita GDP during the 15-year periods.

As expected, the log of the initial population and the change in the demographic composition of the population were positive and significant, and the geographic disadvantage index and the dummies for Middle Eastern oil-exporting countries and for deadly wars in the country were negative and statistically significant. In all equations 1 to 6, it is reassuring that the log of initial per capita GDP was negative and significant, indicating that there is evidence of conditional convergence after controlling for institutions, as indicated by Knack and Keefer (1995).

Turning to poverty rates, equations 7 and 8 of Table 3.7 provide a parallel analysis to that of equations 5 and 6, except that the dependent variable is the change in extreme poverty rate during a period of 15 years and that instead of controlling for the initial income level, the initial poverty level is employed. In these equations, only the level of EFW five years prior to the beginning of the period is associated with further reductions in poverty rates. The coefficient for the level of EFW was -1.94 in column 7 (using two non-overlapping periods) and -1.50 in column 8 (using four overlapping periods). In corresponding regressions for only developing economies (i.e. excluding the 21 high-income economies) the corresponding coefficients are larger: -3.16 in column 7 and -2.72 in column 8, respectively; and the change during the five years prior to the beginning of the period is significant with a coefficient of -1.99, suggesting that not only the levels but the increases toward economic freedom contributed to the reduction in poverty among developing economies. See Tables C.2 to C.6 of Appendix C.

The structure of Table 3.8 is identical to Table 3.7, except the combined democracy score from Polity IV is the primary institutional variable. Informatively, most of the coefficients for both the level of democracy 5 years prior to the beginning of the period and the 5-year changes in the democracy measure are statistically insignificant. The control variables entered with their predicted sign although not all of them were significant. The two control variables that were generally significant were the change in the percentage of the population in the prime working-age 25-59 category (positive and highly significant) and the dummy for having a war on soil with a fatality rate of 0.1 percent of the population (negative and significant). The standardized geographic disadvantage index was negative and significant in both panel equations (columns 5 and 6) but only marginally significant in equation 4 corresponding to the period 2000-2015.

Turning to columns 7 and 8 of Table 3.8 corresponding to the change in poverty rates, puzzling results start to emerge. The coefficient for democracy 5 years prior to the beginning of the period is positive and statistically significant as a determinant of poverty in both equations 7 and 8. In equation 8, all 5-year changes in the democracy measure are associated with increases, not reductions, in poverty rates. The geographic disadvantage index enters positive (as expected) and significant in both equations 7 and 8, and the change in the percentage of the population in the prime working-age 25-59 category enters negative (as expected) and significant in both equations.

Table 3.9 combines the regressors of Tables 8 and 9 simultaneously. The results are similar to the separate analyses of Tables 3.8 and 3.9, except that in general, the coefficients are less significant. Economic freedom, both levels 5-year prior to the period and changes during the period are positive and significant in the equations for growth, but only the level of the summary EFW index matters for the reduction of poverty. However, when only the developing countries are included, the change in EFW is negative and significant (indicating countries with larger increases in economic freedom achieve larger reductions in poverty rates). See Tables C.2 to C.6 of Appendix C for these results.

The combined democratic score from Polity IV is generally statistically insignificant for growth (both levels and changes). However, once again, the political measures are marginally significant (both levels and changes) and with the unexpected sign for the changes in poverty rates.[13] These puzzling results are also present when the regressions are run for the subset of developing economies and for the other standard political variables: political rights and civil liberties (and their average) from Freedom House, executive constraints from Polity IV, and democracy from Acemoglu et al. (2019). The only exception was the newly constructed measure of strong democracy for which levels and changes of democracy were positive, large in magnitude, and highly significantly associated with the growth of per capita GDP, but neither the level nor changes were significantly associated with reductions in poverty rates. The results of these alternative versions of Tables 3.8 and 3.9 are presented in Tables C.7 to C.14 of Appendix C.

Overall, one message is clear about the relative magnitude of the association between levels and changes of different types of institutions and economic development. The evidence strongly indicates that levels and changes in economic institutions are more directly associated with economic development than levels and changes of political institutions. Moreover, democratic political institutions, unless they are strongly democratic, are generally associated with higher and increasing poverty rates. This puzzling result may provide some insight into why there is a rise of democratic and authoritarian populism around the world. This preliminary finding would not be possible without a complete and balanced poverty rate dataset which is one of the contributions of this dissertation, but further investigating these results using this poverty dataset is subject to future research.

3.5. Instrumental Variable Analysis

The results presented above provide information about the level of association between the institutional variables and economic development. However, they cannot be fully interpreted as causal.

[13] This result is consistent with Glaeser, La Porta, Lopez-de-Silanes, and Shleifer (2004). They argue that rather than (political) institutions cause growth, it is human capital that comes first and then the institutions. Therefore, they argue that poor and undemocratic countries first get out of poverty through good policies pursued by dictators, and then they improve their political institutions.

Potential endogeneity concerns due to either reverse causality, relevant omitted variables correlated with the regressors, or measurement error in the variables, could lead to bias and inconsistent results. To alleviate these concerns, this section will employ instrumental variables designed to unveil an exogenous source of variation in the institutional measures.

It is not an easy task to discover and verify a good instrumental variable (IV). An instrument needs to satisfy several requirements before it is acceptable to the researcher. Econometrically, the instruments need to be sufficiently correlated with the endogenous variable and they need to be orthogonal, i.e. uncorrelated, to the structural error term. The first condition, the strength of the IVs, can be tested empirically. Moreover, under weak IVs, the extent of the bias and the magnitude of the size distortions of the inferences can be quantified. For example, see Stock and Wright (2000) and Stock and Yogo (2005). The second condition cannot be unconditionally tested using state-of-the-art econometric techniques. Only tests that are conditionally valid are available. Therefore, intuition and falsification tests play an important role in the credibility of the second condition, or validity, of the instrument.

This section will examine and utilize, when possible, the best available instrumental variables known in the literature for both economic and political institutions. For economic institutions, the best candidate is the predicted human genetic diversity in both linear and quadratic forms as employed by Faria et.al. (2016). For political institutions, the best candidates are the settler mortality rates as employed by Acemoglu et al. (2001) and the refined measure of early disease environment as proposed by Auer (2013) following the critique of the settler mortality rate dataset by Albouy (2012). A more detailed description of each of these instruments is presented below.

3.5.1 Colonial Instruments

This subsection will describe two potentially useful instrumental variables widely utilized in the literature: settler mortality rates (LSMR) and early disease environment (EDE). The first was proposed by Acemoglu (2001) and the second by Auer (2013).

In a very influential article, Acemoglu et.al (2001) used settler mortality rates as an instrument for institutions. They argued that because Europeans were well informed about the potential mortality rates they would face in different places, the actual mortality rates experienced by soldiers, bishops, and sailors who settled in colonies between the 17th and 19th centuries would be a good instrument for institutions. Essentially, the rationale is that when mortality rates were high, Europeans did not plan to settle and therefore they established extractive institutions. In contrast, when the mortality rates were low, Europeans settled and established inclusive institutions protective of private property rights and the rule of law. In either case, the institutions they established persisted over time.

In a similar argument, Acemoglu et al. (2002) argue that Europeans established extractive institutions in places where the indigenous population was highly and densely concentrated. A large and dense indigenous population provided the Europeans with a good source of labor, making extractive institutions more attractive. In contrast, in sparsely populated areas, it was much easier for the Europeans to settle permanently and to establish more inclusive and protective institutions.[14] Since relatively rich places at the time established extractive institutions whereas the relatively poor places established more inclusive institutions, this accounts for the reversal of fortunes over the past 500 years highlighted by the classic article by Acemoglu et al.

The instrumental variables used by Acemoglu et al. (2001) are not without criticism. Most notably, Albouy (2012), argues that their results were driven by severe measurement problems in the data for the settler mortality rate. The problems include the incorrect matching of the mortality rate data because the mortality rates of campaigning soldiers were sometimes intermingled with harshly treated African laborers. Further, Curtin et. al. (1995) notes that the original data reflects maximum rates, not averages, leading to outliers that were driving the results.

Several solutions have been proposed for these problems. The most notable was proposed by Raphael Auer, a former student of Acemoglu. After taking into consideration Albouy's critique and Acemoglu's response, Auer (2013) used geographic variables, disease conditions including the natural prevalence of germs, and climatological information, to construct a measure of the early disease environment (he called it EDE) that the Europeans faced during colonization. The EDE measures the probability of deaths for European males in the age cohort of soldiers. Because the EDE measures the hypothetical, or anticipated, deaths rates rather than the actual ones, this measure is a better indicator of the decisions made by Europeans to either settle or to deter migration to a colony.

[14] Engerman and Sokoloff (2002, 2005, 2012) also argued that early institutional differences associated with initial factor endowments, or initial conditions, had a persistent and diverging effect on the long-run development paths of North and South America.

3.5.2. Ancestral Instruments

This section will build upon new ideas for instrumental variables that go back to the very dawn of human civilization. These ideas will be examined in order to explore potential instruments for economic institutions.[15]

In a recent and influential article, Ashraf and Galor (2013) advance the idea that human genetic diversity is directly linked to current comparative economic development. They take the geographic ideas of Jared Diamond (1997) a step further and argue that the migratory distance from Africa is intrinsically linked to our genetic composition in terms of the diversity of alleles, and that that genetic diversity has been a significant and persistent factor that affected the course of economic development from the cradle of humankind to the present. More specifically, they argue that during *Homo sapiens* exodus out of Addis Ababa, Ethiopia, which took place between tens and hundreds of thousands of years ago, the migrating sub-populations carried with them only a portion of the genes of their parental colonies. Therefore, they argue that the migratory distance from East Africa is intrinsically and ancestrally correlated to human genetic diversity.

Ashraf and Galor (2013) argue that genetic diversity impacts comparative economic development in a humped-shaped manner. According to their views, the optimal level of genetic diversity is determined by the combination of conflicting effects on productivity of trust and creativity. On the one hand, genetic diversity is associated with an increased likelihood of mistrust and disarray, reducing cooperation and socioeconomic order. On the other hand, genetic diversity may facilitate specialization, innovation, and knowledge creation. The result, a net humped-shaped effect on economic development.

Faria et al. (2016) argue that the observed humped-shaped relationship between genetic diversity and economic development is the result of the establishment of institutions that are persistent over time. The authors of that paper argue that genetic diversity affects development only through clusters of economic institutions and policies. In other words, using pre colonial predicted genetic diversity, the authors explain that rather than a direct link between genetic diversity and development, as Ashraf and Galor claim, it is more likely that there is an indirect link through clusters of economic institutions. Too much diversity may reduce the likelihood of agreement on institutional traits that

---

[15] Other colonial variables have been used as instruments for economic institutions. See Bennett et al. (2017). However, in this setting, these colonial instruments are not ideal to disentangle the causal effects of economic and political institutions.

lead to the evenhanded treatment of the population and that foster voluntary transactions, while too little diversity suppresses the need for complex multidimensional institutional arrangements to tackle the tasks occurring in the economy.

Figure 3.1 shows the relationship between the ancestral instruments and current economic development. Panel A of Figure 3.1 illustrates the hump-shaped relationship between prehistoric migratory distance and the 2015 per capita GDP. This relationship is highly statistically significant and robust to a variety of specifications. The 95 percent confidence bands include over 95 percent of the countries. World Bank three-digit codes are used to label the countries, and different symbols (and colors) are used to identify the continent.

As in Ashraf and Galor (2013), the migratory distance from Addis Ababa, Ethiopia, is calculated using five obligatory intermediate waypoints that capture paleontological and genetic evidence on prehistoric human migration patterns. The five waypoints are Cairo (Egypt), Istanbul (Turkey), Phnom Penh (Cambodia), Anadyr (Russia), and Prince Rupert (Canada).

Panel A of Figure 3.1 shows clusters of countries according to their continent. For example, European countries are all clustered in the upper-left quadrant, showing low migratory distances (less than 10 thousand kilometers) and high levels of per capita GDP (generally above $10,000). This observation indicates a direct link between the hump-shaped relationship and the geographic location, and relative size, of the continents.

Panel B of Figure 3.1 illustrates the hump-shaped relationship between unadjusted (pre-colonial) genetic diversity and current economic freedom. Following Ashraf and Galor (2013), genetic diversity is predicted using migratory distance from East Africa. In turn, economic freedom is measured by the average summary EFW rating over the period 1985-2015. As in panel A, the 95 percent confidence bands include mostly all of the countries, which are labeled by their names, and different symbols (and colors) are used to identify their continent. Panel B of Figure 3.1 also shows a clustering of countries according to their continent, indicating a link to the geographic location of the countries.

Figure 3.2 provides a schematic representation of the channel of influence from ancestral/pre-historic instruments to current economic development. Panel A of Figure 3.2 is a general illustration that applies to both ex-colonies and non-colonies. Panel B of Figure 3.2 is specifically for ex-colonies. The general rationale behind Figure 3.2 is that the ancestral instruments reflect a combination of pre-historical and historical factors that shaped culture through a process of migration that took place throughout tens of thousands of years. Examples of these factors include the interactions among tribes, trade, experiences (including the survival to changing weather conditions and perils), genetic diversity, luck, and positive selection. The cultural legacy of these events persisted over time and influenced our current economic institutions. However, the ancestral instruments do not affect development directly because there is no linkage between the ancestral characteristics of the native population and current economic development other than through their culture and possibly their interactions with the colonizers, in the case of ex-colonies. For those reasons, the ancestral instruments are expected to satisfy the usual econometric assumptions of strength and validity (orthogonality).

The following sub-sections will expand on the argumentation above for the ancestral instruments. Empirical evidence for the strength and validity of the instruments is provided, as well as the second-stage results after using the validated instruments. Besides, a new theory is provided explaining why migratory distance is a better instrument than genetic diversity. The theory relies on a more general process of migration in which interactions are a key element that shaped the culture of early civilizations. Through this cultural channel, the ancestral instruments influenced contemporary economic institutions, which in turn lead to divergent economic outcomes. Empirical evidence consistent with this theory is provided.

3.5.3. The Exodus Process, and Migratory Distance as an Instrumental Variable

In contrast to Ashraf and Galor (2013) and Faria et al. (2016), this research also uses migratory distance from East Africa, in addition to predicted genetic diversity, as an instrumental variable for economic institutions. Because genetic diversity for a sufficiently large number of countries is only available in a predicted form and it is predicted by migratory distance, the statistical information in both estimation strategies is identical.[16] This is, econometrically, an identification condition. However, the economics' rationale, the interpretation of the results, and the fundamental theoretical idea are different. These theoretical differences are examined in more detail below.

Suppose that there is a positive effect of migratory distance on economic institutions and that there is also a positive and monotonic effect of genetic diversity on economic institutions. It is still possible to observe the humped-shaped effect observed by Ashraf and Galor (2013) and Faria et al.

[16] The second-stage point estimates are mathematically identical because the predicted genetic diversity lies in the space spanned by the migratory distance. However, the coefficients of the first stages may differ numerically and the correct standard errors may differ as well.

(2016) without assuming the negative association either between genetic diversity and development or between genetic diversity and institutions for high levels of diversity. This is because as migratory distance increases, genetic diversity also changes, and the effect is not necessarily constant, and it is indeed, theoretically, non-linear. As the migratory distance increases beyond a certain threshold, the genetic diversity of the subpopulations of migrants decline even more rapidly[17], and it is this increasing homogeneity which becomes unfavorable for institutions and economic development.

For example, once the subpopulations of migrants reached a certain level, say beyond Anadyr (Russia) close to the Siberia region, or even after crossing the Bering land bridge, then the genetic drift starts playing a role and the sub-populations of migrants become homogenous more rapidly. The route from Addis Ababa to Cairo, and then to any part of Europe or the Middle East takes between two to six thousand kilometers. In contrast, the full route from Ethiopia to Egypt, to Russia, to Canada, to Panama, and finally to Brazil, takes about 25 thousand kilometers. If during the last 10 thousand kilometers of this journey the genetic diversity declined more rapidly with the distance, then the favorable and declining positive effect of additional distance migrated on early rules and norms does not compensate for the negative and increasing effect of declining genetic diversity. The marginal effect of distance becomes negative because the genetic diversity effect dominates the distance effect, which was always assumed to be positive.

The idea here is that institutions are shaped by the culture, which in turn has been determined by the experience of thousands of years of changing conditions, much of which is captured by migratory distance. As groups of people migrate, they face new challenges and perils and new weather conditions that must be overcome. As they face new and changing conditions, they need to interact among themselves and possibly interact with other groups and set up rules and norms that will allow them to survive under these new situations and possibly anticipate future risks and perils. If they do not adapt to the changing conditions, it is unlikely they will survive. The societies that we observe today are a self-selected sample of only those that were able to make it. Therefore, the norms and rules evolved into a culture which ultimately led to rules of the game and institutions that are positive for the subpopulations of migrants and reflect their experience and their interactions under different circumstances. In a process of adaptation to constantly changing conditions, it is primarily the

[17] This is true under the assumption of no mutations or natural selection. When the populations become more homogenous, the genetic drift adds to the regular effect of subsets of migrating populations. This is because the genetic drift in an inbreeding population follows a Markovian process that ultimately leads to a dichotomous representation of the alleles (either 0 percent or 100 percent) in the population.

observed migratory distance and not necessarily the observed genetic diversity that is positively associated with the institutions and the culture of the society.

The above argument is consistent with a positive effect of genetic diversity on both economic institutions and productivity. Complementarities associated with increased diversity may facilitate specialization, technological innovation, and knowledge creation. This was acknowledged by Ashraf and Galor (2013), and Faria et al. (2016) for societies with too little genetic diversity like those in Latin America. However, in my argumentation above, this is true for all levels of genetic diversity and not only for homogeneous societies as they claimed. They argue that too much genetic diversity hurts social capital. In contrast, I argue that it is isolation, i.e., the lack of interactions and the lack of exposure to changing conditions, that led these societies to the continuing stagnation in technology and culture for thousands of years. This argument explains why Papua New Guinea, for instance, despite having near-optimal levels of genetic diversity given the migratory distance of their early settlers, has stagnated both culturally and institutionally and indeed, as of today, it remains relatively isolated from the rest of the world.

Because the exodus was a slow process, and the migratory routes were different, the experiences and the adaptation processes were different for distinct subpopulations of migrants. Consider two groups that migrated the same distance, but one had more interactions with other groups than the other. Then the group with more interactions may have adapted differently despite both groups having the same migratory distance and therefore, the same predicted genetic diversity. For example, Switzerland and Guinea-Bissau have about the same level of predicted genetic diversity (73.61 for Switzerland and 73.29 for Guinea-Bissau). But the average economic freedom rating for Switzerland during 1985-2015 was 8.30 while for Guinea-Bissau it was 4.47. Rather than institutions reflecting solely, or even primarily, genetic diversity, it is more plausible that the process of migration and more and different interactions with other populations contributed to cultural differences that play a role in the shaping of institutions, including those of Switzerland and Guinea-Bissau. Of course, under this theory, migratory distance and genetic diversity are only aspects of a broader migratory process characterized by interactions and experiences that shaped the culture of the early tribes.

The shape and location of continents may also have played a role in the development of institutions. The experiences faced by early tribes that migrated west and south of Ethiopia to populate Sub-Saharan Africa are inexorably different than the accumulation of experiences of the tribes that migrated north to populate Europe and Asia. The former tribes became relatively isolated in a large geographic area with a north-south axis which reduced the likelihood of trade and technological exchange with other tribes. In contrast, the latter tribes faced geographic conditions that facilitated more frequent interactions with other tribes which eventually led them to specialize and trade, increasing the extent of their market and facilitating the adoption of a culture, and more complex institutions, that would allow them to take advantage of this increased market size. Laitin et al. (2012) provide evidence that the axis orientation of the continents, as hypothesized by Jared Diamond, contributed to the persistent linguistic diversity in Africa. As the European and Asian tribes migrated even further to populate the Americas after crossing the Bearing Strait, their own experiences continue to increase, but their interactions with others declined because they were not many with whom to interact. Without the need for exchange across tribes, complex institutions became less necessary.

3.5.4. Falsification Tests

This section presents empirical results that provide intuition about the validity of the instrumental variables discussed above. For the instrumental variables to be valid, they need to be orthogonal (i.e., uncorrelated) with the structural error term. This condition is mathematically equivalent to saying that, after controlling for the endogenous variable, the instrument has no additional effect on the dependent variable. In other words, the instrument affects the dependent variable only through the endogenous variable, but not directly. This section will provide a series of tests and regressions to capture the rationale above[18].

Table 3.10 presents falsification tests. Panel A is for economic institutions and ancestry unadjusted genetic diversity as a potential instrument. In columns 1 to 3, the dependent variable is per capita GDP in 2015. In column 1, both the linear and quadratic terms of genetic diversity are significantly associated with per capita GDP. The linear term is positive, and the quadratic term is negative, suggesting a humped-shape effect. This is basically a duplication of the results of Ashraf and Galor (2013). Column 2 adds the summary EFW rating in 2015. If the effect of genetic diversity on per capita GDP is indirect, through economic freedom, then genetic diversity in column 2 should be insignificant. Indeed, column 2 shows that both the linear and quadratic terms of genetic diversity are statistically insignificant. Column 3, instead of the summary EFW rating, uses the legal system (area 2 of EFW) as the main measure of economic institutions. Again, genetic diversity is statistically

[18] These tests are not formal validity tests (or exogeneity tests) for the instruments. The exclusion restriction assumption cannot be verified using state-of-the-art econometric techniques. However, it can be refuted or "falsified" using a number of intuitive econometric tests. These tests are only meant to provide intuition regarding the validity of the instruments.

insignificant after controlling for area 2 of EFW. This suggests that the significant effect found in the reduced form (column 1) is indeed through a channel of economic institutions.

Columns 4 and 5 reverse the roles of EFW and per capita GDP. In column 4, when the dependent variable is EFW, genetic diversity is statistically significant (both terms). In column 5, the per capita GDP is added to the equation as a regressor. If indeed genetic diversity is a valid and strong instrument for EFW, it should remain statistically significant. Indeed, after controlling for per capita GDP in column 5, genetic diversity is still significantly associated with EFW. It is important to compare and contrast this result with that of column 2, in which per capita GDP was the dependent variable and genetic diversity ceased to be significant once the summary EFW index is a regressor, but the reverse is not true. This is exactly the pattern of results necessary to reassure our intuition about the instrumental variable.

Columns 6 and 7 are like columns 4 and 5 except that the legal system (area 2 of EFW) is the dependent variable and main institutional variable. In column 6, genetic diversity is significant. In column 7, after controlling for per capita GDP, genetic diversity is still significant. This indicates that genetic diversity is strongly associated with the legal structure directly, after controlling for per capita GDP. But the results of column 3 indicated that the reversed was not true, genetic diversity was insignificant when per capita GDP was the dependent variable after controlling for the quality of the legal system. Overall, the results of Table 3.10, panel A (columns 1 to 7) validate our intuition that ancestry unadjusted predicted genetic diversity is a valid instrument for clusters of economic institutions.

Panels B and C of Table 3.10 do the same experiments, or falsification tests, using the political measures and their instruments. Panel B is for settler mortality rates and panel C is for early disease environment. The results are equally surprising in both panels B and C. In column 1, as expected, both instruments, settler mortality rates and early disease environment, are negative and significantly associated with per capita GDP in 2015. However, after controlling for democracy in 2015 in column 2, and executive constraints in 2015 in column 3, the instruments remain significant at the 1 percent level. This is an indication that these instruments have a direct impact on development, beyond the hypothesized indirect impact through their corresponding political institutions. In other words, this is an indication that they are not valid instruments because they are failing the falsification tests.

Columns 4 and 5 reversed democracy with per capita GDP. When democracy is the dependent variable, as expected, both the settler mortality rate and early disease environment are negative and statistically significant. However, after controlling for per capita GDP in column 5, they are insignificant, indicating that their correlation with the endogenous variable ceased after controlling for per capita GDP. Columns 6 and 7 do the same thing with executive constraints in 2015. When constraint on the executive is the dependent variables in column 6, the instruments are significant. But when per capita GDP is added as a regressor, while early disease environment remained marginally significant, the settler mortality rate is insignificant.

In summary, the results of panels B and C suggest that settler mortality rates and early disease environment are not strongly correlated with political institutions and they are strongly correlated with per capita GDP even after controlling for their corresponding measures of political institutions. This pattern is consistent with the view that settler mortality rate and early disease environment are neither a valid nor a strong instrument.

Appendix C shows an additional set of falsification tests. In general, the results were satisfactory using the measures of economic institutions. Using as instrumental variables either the ancestry unadjusted predicted genetic diversity in both linear and quadratic form, or the migratory distance from East Africa in both linear and quadratic form, the following specific measures of economic institutions yield successful results in the falsification tests: Average summary EFW rating during 1985-2015, average area 2 of EFW (legal system) during 1985-2015, average risk of expropriation during 1985-1995, as used by Acemoglu et. al. (2001), and the index of social infrastructure as used by Hall and Jones (1999). The results were unsatisfactory for the following measures of political institutions: The average combined democracy score from polity IV during 1985-2015, the average executive constraint during 1985-2015, the executive constraint at the year of independence as used by Acemoglu et al. (2001), and the average strong democracy during 1985-2015. These results are presented in Tables C.15 to C.17 of Appendix C.

Overall, the falsification tests strongly suggest that either the ancestry unadjusted predicted genetic diversity or the migratory distance from East Africa are good instruments (valid and strong) for economic institutions. Unfortunately, the evidence presented here also suggest that either the experienced settler mortality rates or the anticipated settler mortality rates (i.e. the early disease environment) are poor instruments (invalid and relatively weak) for political institutions.[19]

[19] The falsification tests also suggested that the instrumental variables were invalid for poverty rates.

3.5.5. Implausible Instrumental Variables

This section explores what would happen if implausible instrumental variables were added to the matrix of instruments. For example, if horse races were performed in two-stage least squares (2SLS), the matrix of excluded instruments would contain both the instruments for economic and political institutions. If any of the instrumental variables fails to satisfy the exclusion restriction (the validity condition), then all the coefficients in the second stage are potentially biased and inconsistent. Table 3.11 presents intuition regarding that possibility. Panel A of Table 3.11 presents results using simultaneously genetic diversity and early disease environment, panel B shows results using both genetic diversity and settler mortality rates, and panel C uses current (ancestry adjusted) human genetic diversity as used by Ashraf and Galor (2013).

In all panels, column 1 presents the reduced form. In this equation, the candidates for instruments seem to be directly correlated with the dependent variable, per capita GDP in 2015. In columns 2 and 3, after controlling for the summary EFW rating and area 2 of EFW, respectively, while genetic diversity is insignificant (both terms), the early disease environment and the settler mortality rates remained significant suggesting that they still have a direct effect on per capita GDP and suggesting that they do not satisfy the exclusion restriction. In panel C, it is revealing that current genetic diversity is correlated with 2015 per capita GDP even after controlling for EFW, but recall from Table 10 that this was not the case for ancestry unadjusted genetic diversity. This indicates that pre-colonial genetic diversity acts as a valid instrument for economic institutions, but contemporary genetic diversity does not.

In Table 3.11, columns 4 and 5, the summary EFW rating is the dependent variable, and in columns 6 and 7, area 2 of EFW is the dependent variable. In columns 4 and 6, all the candidates for instrumental variables are generally significant. After controlling for per capita GDP in columns 5 and 7, it is revealing that early disease environment is still significantly correlated with both the summary EFW rating and the area 2 of EFW. This indicates that this measure not only is directly correlated with political institutions but also with economic institutions. Similarly, in panel B, the settler mortality rate is significantly correlated with area 2 of EFW even after controlling for per capita GDP, suggesting that there is more than one channel through which this potential instrument impacts comparative economic development.

This section showed that implausible instrumental variables do not pass the intuition bar of the falsification tests. In addition, this section suggests that the colonial instruments proposed by

Acemoglu et al. (2001) and later refined by Auer (2013), affect economic development through multiple channels of not only political institutions but also, economic institutions. While the previous section showed evidence that the colonial instruments directly impacted per capita GDP (Table 3.10), this section provides evidence that these instruments also impacted economic institutions (Table 3.11), which in turn have a causal impact on comparative economic development, as the next section will show.

3.5.6. Economic Institutions and Per Capita GDP. Instrumental Variable Analysis

Having explored the validity of the instruments, this section will use the ancestral instruments as an exogenous source of variation in economic freedom. If the identification strategy employed here is correct, the results will have a causal interpretation. Table 3.12 presents the results when the dependent variable is the per capita GDP in 2015 (in log form) and the main independent variable is the average economic freedom from 1985 to 2015. Panel A shows the second stage results. Panel B shows the first stage results using as instruments the ancestry unadjusted predicted genetic diversity in both linear and quadratic form, as used by Faria et al. (2016). Panel C shows the first stage results using as instruments the linear and quadratic terms of the migratory distance from Addis Ababa, Ethiopia. For both panels B and C, the second stage results are numerically identical, so I present the results only once, in panel A.

Column 1 of Table 3.12 shows that, without further controls, the average summary EFW rating during 1985-2015 has a coefficient of 1.03, significant at the 1 percent level. Since this is a log-linear regression, the interpretation of this coefficient is that, on average, a unit increase in the average EFW during 1985-2015 is associated with a causal increase of 180 percent in per capita GDP in 2015 (the exponential of 1.03 is equal to 2.8). As expected from the results in Table 10, the Hansen over-identification restriction (OIR) test is passed with a p-value of 0.772 suggesting the instruments (genetic diversity both in a linear and quadratic form) are not invalid. Moreover, other additional specification tests for weak instruments, under-identification, and robust inferences, are all passed. Column 2 of Table 3.12 adds the main geographic disadvantage measure to the equation. In this case, EFW is insignificant but all the specification tests detect that the system is under-identified and that the instruments are weak in this specification. Under weak IVs, the variance of the 2SLS estimator is too large and the results can behave erratically. Thus, estimates from column 2 are not reliable.

Following Faria et al. (2016) column 3 adds the absolute value of latitude and column 4 adds the ethnolinguistic fractionalization.

Interestingly, after controlling for the standardized geographic disadvantage index, latitude enters positive and significant at the 1 percent level. This indicates that for levels of per capita GDP, the geographic disadvantage index does not capture geographical aspects that latitude does. In other words, latitude is still statistically significant above and beyond the three Sachs' variables expressed in the univariate disadvantage index. This may provide justification for why latitude has been widely used in the literature as a geographical control. Despite being a very crude measure of climate and location, it enters positive and significant, indicating that countries in temperate zones tend to have higher income levels.

In column 4 of Table 3.12, ethnolinguistic fractionalization is insignificant. In columns 3 and 4, the coefficients for the average EFW during 1985-2015 were 0.53 and 0.55, respectively. These coefficients indicate that, after controlling for geography (in column 3) and then also for ethnolinguistic fractionalization (in column 4), a 1-unit increase in the average EFW summary rating during 1985-2015 is associated with a causal increase in per capita GDP of 69.9 percent (column 3) and 73.3 percent (column 4). The specification tests for columns 3 and 4 are passed, suggesting that these are valid specifications.

Columns 5 and 6 perform additional falsification tests. In column 5, the instruments are added in both linear a quadratic form. Reassuringly they are not statistically significant, indicating that, when EFW is a regressor, they do not affect per capita GDP directly. In column 6, EFW is the dependent variable and per capita GDP is now a regressor. In this equation, both the linear and quadratic forms of the ancestral instruments are statistically significant, indicating that they are correlated with EFW above and beyond their impact on per capita GDP. The falsification tests for columns 5 and 6 are presented for migratory distance from Addis Ababa, Ethiopia (the instrument used in panel C), but as argued above, the results are identical using genetic diversity predicted with migratory distance (the instrument used in panel B). Overall, the evidence indicates that the identification strategy is correct and that the second-stage coefficients of EFW have a causal interpretation.

3.5.7 First-Stage Analysis and Policy Implications

Exhibit 3.12, Panels B and C show the first stage results using genetic diversity and migratory distance, respectively. The results are numerically equivalent for all the relevant statistics, such as the F-test for the joint significance of the excluded instruments.[20] It is expected that the results of all these tests will be numerically identical because the statistical information is the same when using either migratory distance or genetic diversity predicted with migratory distance. Mathematically, both variables lie in the same space spanned by migratory distance. However, the interpretation of the results is different.

The original results of Ashraf and Galor (2013) have a direct policy implication. Their results imply that there is an optimal contemporary genetic diversity for the per capita GDP in 2000. According to their table 6 (page 36) this optimal genetic diversity would be between 71.2 and 71.5 percent. They also claim that there was an optimal precolonial genetic diversity for the population density of 1500.[21] According to their table 1 (page 21) this optimal was between 68.3 and 69.9 percent. In turn, the first-stage results of Faria et al. (2016) may be misinterpreted as causal and therefore as having some policy implications, although in a much more indirect way. Their results suggest that there was an optimal pre-colonial genetic diversity for the development of current institutions. According to their table 2 (page 10), this number was between 65.3 and 65.5 percent. If the observed correlation between precolonial genetic diversity and current institutions persist over time, one could argue that an optimal level of current genetic diversity could potentially lead to a better quality of economic institutions in the future. This argument is misleading for at least two reasons. First, the first stages are never causal, they just show correlations. Second, it is not genetic diversity that was used but rather predicted genetic diversity using migratory distance.

In contrast, the first stages of this research, using migratory distance as the main instrument and the only exogenous source of variation, have no direct policy implication. This is a desirable feature. Because the migratory distance from East-Africa is essentially a geographic instrument, it cannot be altered or modified and therefore all policy implications are ruled out from the first stages. Therefore, it becomes clearer that the policy implications should come from the second stage relating the summary EFW rating with per capita GDP.

---

[20] The relevant referential distributions are not actually the usual Fisher-Snedecor F distribution, but rather the multivariate generalizations of Cragg and Donald (1993) and Kleiberbgen and Paap (2006), and the corresponding multivariate F test of excluded instruments of Angrist and Pischke (2009).

[21] According to Ashraf and Galor, population density is the relevant measure gauging comparative economic development of earlier periods rather than per capita GDP. But there is debate about this. See Acemoglu et. al. (2002) for a caveat in this interpretation. They argue that in a Malthusian society the population density merely reflects the "excess" population at a given point in time and that this excess will be naturally corrected according to the Malthusian theory. Therefore, it is not as good as a measure as urbanization in 1500.

3.5.8 The Generally Weak Relationship between Migratory Distance and Genetic Diversity

This subsection will provide additional empirical evidence suggesting that it is a better idea to use migratory distance from Addis Ababa, Ethiopia, rather than genetic diversity predicted with it. The fundamental argument to use predicted genetic diversity using migratory distance is that the correlation between observed diversity, when available, and migratory distance is strong. But this is not generally the case. The strong association is mostly driven by countries in Latin America. This subsection will show evidence consistent with this case.

Table 3.13 shows the 53 Ethnic groups as used by Ashraf and Galor (2013). Their data come originally from the HGDP-CEPH Human Genome Diversity Cell Line Panel. They argue that these are the most reliable and consistent data for genetic diversity among indigenous populations from around the world. This analysis uses these same data. These 53 ethnic groups span only 21 countries, and there are only four observations in Latin America spanning only three countries, Mexico, Colombia, and Brazil. Table 3.13 shows, for each ethnic group, the observed genetic diversity and the migratory distance from Addis Ababa using five obligatory intermediate waypoints that capture paleontological and genetic evidence on prehistoric human migration patterns[22]. The median migratory distance in this sample of 53 ethnic-groups is 6.48 thousand kilometers, and that corresponds to the ethnic group of Burusho, in Pakistan.

Table 3.14 shows that the correlation between the migratory distance and the observed genetic diversity using these 53 ethnic groups is high (-0.9265) and highly statistically significant. Column 1 shows the corresponding r-squared of 0.8584. Column 2 shows that migratory distance is still statistically significant at the 1 percent level after controlling for latitude. This strong association is at the heart of using predicted genetic diversity with migratory distance.

However, column 3 shows that the r-squared goes down to 29 percent when using the first half of the sample, that is, the 27 observations with a migratory distance less than or equal to the median (or say less than 6.5 thousand kilometers). After controlling for latitude in column 4, migratory distance is statistically insignificant predicting observed genetic diversity.

[22] The five waypoints, as in Ashraf and Galor (2013), are Cairo (Egypt), Istanbul (Turkey), Phnom Penh (Cambodia), Anadyr (Russia), and Prince Rupert (Canada).

In contrast, for the second half of the sample, that is for the 26 observations with a migratory distance larger than 6.5 thousand kilometers, the r-squared remained high at 83 percent, and migratory distance remained significant even after controlling for latitude in column 6.

Table 3.14, Panel B shows similar results using country-level regressions instead of ethnic-group-level regressions. Despite the fewer observations, the results are essentially the same. Using the full sample of 21 countries, observed diversity seems to be strongly associated with migratory distance with an R-squared of 94 percent, but mostly Latin American countries drive this result. Splitting the sample into two halves according to the migratory distance, the r-squares go down to 36 percent in the first half and goes up to 97 percent in the second half. After controlling for latitude, the migratory distance is insignificant (and with the wrong sign) in the first half of the sample but still quite significant with a t-ratio of -14.44 in the second half of the sample (column 6).

These results indicate that the association between genetic diversity and migratory distance is only strong when the migratory distance is sufficiently large, but it is weak when the migratory distance is relatively small. Splitting the sample into halves, the relationship is week when the migratory distance is less than six and a half thousand kilometers, which comprises all of Africa, most of Europe, all the Middle East, and parts of Asia. Therefore, the interpretations of the genetic diversity theory from Ashraf and Galor (2013) and Faria et al. (2016) and even in part of this research, should be done with caution. The predicted genetic diversity is only a reliable measure of genetic diversity for about half of the countries. For the other half, it is a weak measure. This explains why so many heterogeneous countries in Africa, the Middle East, and Europe, have about the same level of predicted genetic diversity.

3.5.9. Migratory Distance and Continental Dummies. A Refinement

Given the theory outlined above and the results of the previous sub-section, it seems natural that the effect of migratory distance on economic freedom is a function of the geographic characteristics of the continent. These geographic characteristics include location, weather, land suitability, access to ocean, and axis (East-West versus North-South) orientation. This was an initial observation made out of Figure 1. If the theory outlined above is true, the observed correlation between migratory distance on economic institutions must be a function of the continental effects and in this way be consistent with the humped-shape relation documented in Figure 1.

Regression analysis is conducted to test this conjecture. The dependent variable is the average summary EFW rating during 1985-2015, and the independent variables are a set of interactions between migratory distance and continental dummies. Figure 3.3 shows the marginal effects (and 95 percent confidence intervals) of migratory distance on economic freedom, for Africa, Europe, Asia, Oceania, and the Americas. As expected, the marginal effects are consistent with the humped-shape relation described above. They are largest for Europe, lower for Asia, Africa and Oceania, and lowest for the Americas. But this suggests that there is nothing special about the humped-shape functional form between migratory distance (or genetic diversity) and economic institutions. It just reflects the shape of the world, its continents, and the relative amount of successful interactions that early civilizations from each continent had with other distant civilizations allowing them to increase the extent of their markets.

The regression analysis conducted above can be thought of as a refinement of the first-stage regressions of Table 3.12. Because of the theory outlined here, it is expected that this first-stage would yield even stronger first stages while maintaining the validity of the ancestral instruments. To explore if this is the case, Table 3.15 re-estimates column 4 of Table 3.12 using migratory distance interacted with the continents as the instrumental variables for economic institutions.

Column 1 of Table 3.15 shows the second stage results. The coefficient of 0.86 for the summary EFW index is larger than before: A unit increase in the average EFW during 1985-2015 is associated with a causal increase in per capita GDP of about 136 percent in 2015.

Column 2 of Table 3.15 shows the first stage results. The dependent variable is the average summary EFW index during 1985-2015. As expected, the F-test for the joint significance of the excluded instruments is large (4.437) and statistically significant. This result indicates that migratory distance interacted with the continental dummies, as an instrumental variable set, meet the strength condition.

Columns 3 and 4 of Table 3.15 are basic falsification tests. Column 3 adds per capita GDP as a regressor. The dependent variable is the same as in column 2, economic freedom. It is reassuring that the F-test for the joint significance of the excluded instruments is even larger than before (5.210) and statistically significant. This result confirms a strong correlation between the migratory distance interacted with the continental dummies, as an instrumental variable set, and economic institutions.

Column 4 of Table 3.15 switches the role of EFW and per capita GDP. If migratory distance interacted with the continental dummies is a valid set of instruments for economic institutions, then it is expected that their effect on per capita GDP is only through EFW. Therefore, if EFW is a regressor, the instruments should be insignificant. Indeed, the F-test for the joint significance of the excluded instruments is low (0.965) with a p-value of 0.445. This suggests that the effect of migratory distance interacted with the continental dummies on per capita GDP is insignificant once the economic institutions are held constant.

Table 3.15 confirms the previous finding that there is a causal impact from economic freedom to prosperity. By using a better instrument, migratory distance interacted with continental dummies; the estimated impact is slightly larger than before. The results are also in line with the prediction of the previous theory that interactions shape culture, and culture shapes institutions. The results are consistent with the idea that there is nothing special about the humped-shape unveiled by Ashraf and Galor (2013) and Faria and Montesinos (2016), but it reflects the geographic characteristics of the world, its continents, and the propensity for having more successful interactions and trade among early tribes.

3.5.10. Intuition Regarding the Exogeneity of the Ancestral Instruments

All that is needed for a good instrumental variable is to be an exogenous source of variation in the endogenous variable. In the case of this research, the endogenous variables are contemporary measures of institutions. The instrumental variables do not need to be (or claim to be) the only source of variation or even the most important source of variation. In the case of this research, both the ancestral instruments and the colonial instruments are important sources of variation. But the former seems to be exogenous while the latter seems to be endogenous. As argued by Paldam and Gunlach (2008) and partially documented here, it is hard to disentangle the effects of institutions on development because they are part of a "grand transition" in which causation runs both ways and therefore the evidence we observe is mixed. They argue that, according to the grand transition view, a "lucky spark" is needed to set the development process in motion.

This research is in line with Paldam and Gunlach (2008) but provides additional insight. Particularly since colonial times, a myriad of "lucky factors" (and some that are not so lucky) have influenced the pattern of development in a process of interaction with human-made choices that ultimately resulted in the current institutions. But along this process, interactions with the native population took place constantly. These interactions may be endogenous but the genetic composition of the native population (or their migratory distance) is not.[23]

In the case of non-colonies, it is easy to see that the culture of the native population may have influenced their current institutions. In the case of ex-colonies, it is not so clear, but it is still possible that the interactions between the colonizers and the native population shaped the culture and the institutions of the resulting colony. It is not just that the colonizers imposed their cultures and values. It is more likely that this was a process in which interactions took place, and the norms and values of the resulting colony were the results of a combination of these interactions with the native population and the original culture of the natives. The strong and robust correlation between the ancestral instruments and the current economic institutions is consistent with this view. See Figure 1.

But having observed the above correlation, it is unlikely that the ancestral instruments (the genetic composition of the native population or their migratory distance from East Africa) are directly affecting development beyond institutions. It is possible that the ancestral instruments affected the ancestral culture of the native populations, and through this channel, they affected current institutions, which in turn affects contemporary economic development. But it is unlikely that the ancestral instruments are affecting development directly because there is no connection between the ancestral characteristics of the native population and current economic development other than through their culture and possibly their interactions with the colonizers. Note that these interactions may themselves be endogenous (reinforcing the difficulty to use colonial instruments) but the genetic composition of the interacting parties, determined tens of thousands of years before the interaction took place, is not. See Figure 2 for a schematic illustration of this theory.

Overall, section 5 sheds light on the literature in several ways. Rather than using genetic diversity alone as previous studies have done, here I argue that it is a combination of migratory distance and genetic diversity that affected the current economic institutions. I theorized that the interplay between these two ancestral instruments shaped the culture of ancient civilizations. In turn, this culture and the interactions with the colonizers when they took place, shaped the current economic institutions. By exploiting an exogenous source of variation stemming from these ancestral instruments, this research unveils a positive, large in magnitude, and statistically significant channel of

[23] The decision to migrate west and south of Ethiopia as opposed to east and north (either through the Red Sea or through the Nile to cut through the Sahara Desert) can be considered as one of the earliest "lucky sparks" because the migrants had no way of foreseeing the potential opportunities of each route.

causation from clusters of economic institutions that protect property rights and promote economic liberalization, to contemporary economic development.

3.6. The Relationship between Economic and Political Institutions

The results of the last section uncovered new causal evidence that economic institutions cause prosperity. This evidence is consistent with multiple prior studies such as Berggren (2003), Gwartney et al. (2006), de Haan et al. (2006), Faria and Montesinos (2009), and Faria et al. (2016). But this evidence does not explain how the economic institutions are determined. One natural answer lies in the political process. Consistent with this view, Rode and Gwartney (2012) find that transitions from authoritarian regimes to political democracies are associated with economic liberalizations.

To further inquire into this question, this section will explore the relationship between economic and political institutions. Given the lack of an instrumental variable strategy to address this question, Granger causality tests will be employed. The idea of Granger causality is to evaluate if changes in economic institutions lead to subsequent changes in political institutions and, the other way around, if changes in political institutions lead to subsequent changes in economic institutions. Table 3.16 shows the relationship between economic and political institutions using the Granger causality idea. Columns 1 to 4 perform the analysis in levels and columns 5 to 8 perform the analysis in changes. The overall focus is in periods of 15 years and the lags will be of 5 years. For example, for the change analysis, the last period is 2000 -2015 and the lagged period is 1995-2010. The main measure of economic institutions is the summary EFW index and the main measure of political institutions is the combined democracy score from Polity IV.

The dependent variable in column 1 is the level of EFW in the years 2015, 2000, and 1985. The main independent variables are the levels of EFW and democracy 5 years prior. That is, in 2010, 1995, and 1980, respectively. The coefficient of lagged EFW is positive and highly statistically significant with a t-ratio of 32.99. This is expected, and it is an indication of persistence in economic institutions. The coefficient of lagged democracy is also positive and statistically significant with a t-ratio of 3.62. This indicates that previous levels of democracy are positively associated with economic freedom even after controlling for previous levels of the summary EFW index.

In column 2, the dependent variable is now the level of democracy in the years 2015, 2000, and 1985. The independent variables are the same as in column 1, the levels of EFW and democracy 5 years prior. The coefficient for lagged democracy is positive and highly significant with a t-ratio of

30.55. Again, this is expected and merely reflects a high persistence in democracy. But the coefficient for lagged EFW is insignificant. This indicates that after controlling for the level of democracy today, the level of economic freedom today is not significantly associated with the level of democracy 5 years in the future. Taken together, the results from column 1 and 2 suggest that levels of democracy Granger-cause the levels of economic freedom but not the other way around.

Columns 3 and 4 do the same analysis of columns 1 and 2 but include the four additional years 2010, 2005, 1995, and 1990. With a higher statistical power derived from a larger number of observations, the evidence points to the same conclusion as in columns 1 and 2: The level of democracy Granger causes the level of economic freedom but the level of economic freedom does not Granger cause the level of democracy.

Columns 5 to 8 turn to the changes. In column 5, the dependent variable is the change in the summary EFW rating during 2000-2015 and during 1985-2000. The independent variables are the changes in the summary EFW rating and democracy during 1995-2010 and during 1980-1995. That is, the 15-year change in each variable, lagged 5 years. As expected, the lagged change in EFW is positive and significantly associated with the change in EFW. But the lagged change in democracy is also positive and significantly associated with the change in EFW. This suggests that past changes in democracy predict subsequent changes in economic freedom. This is the idea behind Granger causality. In column 6, now the dependent variable is the change in democracy during the same two periods: 2000-2015 and 1985-2000. The independent variables are again the 15-year changes in each variable, lagged 5 years. In this case, lagged democracy is positive and highly statistically significant, as expected. But lagged EFW is insignificant suggesting that increases in economic freedom do not Granger cause increases in democracy.

Columns 7 and 8 are like columns 5 and 6 but include the additional periods 1995-2010 and 1990-2005. In column 7, the change in summary EFW rating is the dependent variable. In this case, both lagged changes in EFW and democracy are positive and statistically significant. This is consistent with the idea that movements toward democracy Granger cause movements toward economic liberalization. In column 8, the dependent variable is now the 15-year change in democracy. In this case, the lagged changes in democracy are significant and positive but the lagged changes in EFW are not.

The results above were also verified using 10-year changes and 5-year changes instead of 15-year changes for the independent variables, and using also 10-year lags and 15-year lags instead of 5-year lags. In all cases, the evidence suggests that both levels and changes in democracy are respectively associated with subsequent levels and changes in economic freedom. This evidence is consistent with the view that some portion of the economic institutions is determined within the domain of the political process.

3.7. Conclusions and Summary of Key Points

The goal of this chapter was to analyze the relative merits of economic and political institutions on comparative economic development as measured by levels and changes of per capita GDP and poverty rates. The chapter also provides insights into the relationship between democracy and economic freedom. The following is a summary of the key points:

Preliminary correlation analysis indicates that at least ten of the most used institutional variables in the literature are indeed measuring different aspects of the institutional spectrum as some of their correlations are low. The correlation between the most recent democracy measure by Acemoglu et al. (2019) and the summary EFW rating was 0.40 in 2010, and the correlation was even lower (0.32) with area 2 of EFW, a measure of the quality of the legal system.

Even after taking averages over extended periods of 30 years, the correlation between the summary EFW rating and the dichotomous democracy variable used by Acemoglu et al. (2019) is 0.46. This democracy variable, in turn, has a correlation of 0.92 with the combined democracy score from Polity IV. The relatively low correlation between measures of economic and political institutions is a sign that they capture different institutional elements.

Democracy is a blunt concept, and there is more measurement error in the middle range of the political spectrum. To alleviate this problem, a refined measure of democracy was constructed. The binary measure is equal to one when the combined polity score is equal to 8, 9, or 10, and when both the political rights and civil liberties from Freedom House indicate a rating of "free" or "partially free." Reassuringly, the strong democracy binary indicator was highly correlated with the rule of law measure, a correlation of 0.80.

Using a base sample of 135 countries with continuous per capita GDP data available since 1970, all measures of institutions, both economic and political measures, were strongly correlated with levels of per capita GDP and poverty rates in 2015. However, after controlling for geography, only the measures of economic institutions and the strong democracy measure remained significant and with their expected sign for both levels of per capita GDP and poverty rates. In OLS horse races, economic institutions are associated with higher levels of per capita GDP and lower poverty rates, and only the strong democracy measure remained positive and significant for the levels of per capita GDP. However, some measures of democracy are indeed negatively associated with per capita GDP after controlling for rule of law.

Regression analysis indicates that changes in economic institutions are positively and significantly associated with subsequent growth rates of per capita GDP, and that the levels of economic institutions are positively associated with the reduction in poverty rates. Movements toward democracy are not found to impact the growth of per capita GDP directly. Paradoxically, however, there is weak evidence that democratization is associated with increases in poverty rates.

Instrumental variable analysis is necessary to have estimates with causal interpretation. Ancestral and colonial instruments were candidates for the analysis. The ancestral candidates were the migratory distance from Addis Ababa, and the genetic diversity predicted using migratory distance. The colonial candidates were the settler mortality rate and the early disease environment. Falsification tests indicate that only the ancestral instruments were valid instruments for economic institutions, and no valid instrument is available for political institutions. The results of the instrumental variable analysis indicate that economic freedom has a positive and statistically significant impact on per capita GDP. The estimated average impact of a unit increase in EFW enhances per capita GDP by an estimated 70 percent to 136 percent.

A new theory is provided to explain the observed hump-shaped correlation between the ancestral instruments and current economic institutions. In contrast with previous theories that rely only on genetic diversity, the new theory is based on a combination of both migratory distance and genetic diversity. Migratory distance increased the potential for exposure, experiences, interactions, trade, and the extent of the market of ancient civilizations. Therefore, it fosters specialization and technological change, as well as norms and rules developed to take advantage of those opportunities. But when the migratory distance is too large, genetic diversity starts to decline more rapidly, increasing the vulnerability to new changing conditions and reducing the gains from specialization, knowledge creation, and innovation, as well as reducing the incentive to set up norms and rules that permit greater gains from the division of labor. As opposed to previous theories, there is not an intermediate optimal genetic diversity.

Empirical evidence is provided suggesting that genetic diversity predicted with migratory distance has too much measurement error when the migratory distance is low. The association between the two measures drops from 86 percent to 29 percent when using half of the ethnic-group-level observations that are closest to Africa. But the association remained strong (83 percent) when using half of the sample closest to America. After controlling for latitude, the association disappeared in the first half while it remained intact in the second half. These empirical results call for caution when using predicted genetic diversity and call for a better theoretical argument linking migratory distance with economic development.

A separate theoretical explanation is provided for the validity of the ancestral instruments. The theory, summarized in Figure 2, states that the ancestral instruments (migratory distance and genetic diversity) affected the early norms and culture of the ancient civilizations and through this channel, it affected current institutions which in turn affects contemporary economic development. But it is unlikely that the ancestral instruments are affecting development directly because there is no connection between the ancestral characteristics of the native population and current economic development other than through their culture and possibly their interactions with the colonizers.

Finally, this chapter provides evidence about the relationship between political and economic institutions. Using Granger causality tests in both levels and changes, the evidence suggests that political institutions predate economic institutions but not the other way around. That is, there is evidence that political institutions Granger cause economic freedom, but there is no evidence indicating that economic freedom Granger causes political institutions.

Table 3.1: Main variables, definitions, and sources

Variable	Definition	Source
EFW	The Economic Freedom of the World (EFW) Index is a comprehensive measure of the degree to which the policies and institutions of a country are supportive of personal choice, voluntary exchange, market allocation of goods and services, free trade, and protection of individuals and their property from aggression by others. The summary index is based on ratings ranging from zero to ten for 42 different components which are classified in 5 separate areas and then averaged. Higher ratings are indicative of more economic freedom.	Gwartney et al. (2018).
efm30	Average EFW for the last 30 years for the years ending in zero or five. In 2015, this variable was the average EFW for the period 1985-2015. A minimum of five (out of the seven possible) observations is required to calculate this average. The rationale for this calculation is to measure economic institutions over an extended period. Therefore, this calculation follows a large and growing literature. For example, Connors (2011) used the average EFW for an extended period of 25-years (1980-2005) to measure the impact of institutions on levels and reductions of poverty rates.	Gwartney et al. (2018) and own calculation.
Area 2 (EFW)	Area 2 of EFW measures the integrity of the legal system and the protection of property rights. This variable is the average of nine different components: Judicial independence, impartial courts, protection of property rights, military interference in rule of law and politics, the integrity of the legal system, legal enforcement of contracts, regulatory costs of the sale of real property, reliability of police, and business costs of crime. These components are scaled to range from zero to ten and then averaged to obtain the area 2 rating of EFW. Higher ratings are indicative of a legal system consistent with the principles of economic freedom.	Gwartney et al. (2018).
a2m30	Average Area 2 of EFW for the last 30 years. In 2015, this variable is the average of Area 2 of EFW for the period 1985-2015. A minimum of five (out of the seven possible) observations is required to calculate this average.	Own calculation.
Rule of Law (WGI)	"Rule of law captures perceptions of the extent to which agents have confidence in and abide by the rules of society, and in particular the quality of contract enforcement, property rights, the police, and the courts, as well as the likelihood of crime and violence." (Kauffman and Kraay, 2019). The variable is standardized and ranges from minus 2.5 to plus 2.5. Higher numbers reflect closer adherence to the rule of law.	Kauffman and Kraay (2019). World Governance Indicators (WGI). The World Bank Group.
rlm30	Average Rule of Law (WGI). Since the original variable started in 1996, this variable is the average for the years 1996, 2000, 2005, 2010, and 2015. A minimum of three (out of the five possible) observations are required to calculate this average.	Kauffman and Kraay (2019), and own calculation.

Table 3.1 – Continued

Variable	Definition	Source
Democracy (Polity IV)	"The POLITY score is computed by subtracting the AUTOC score from the DEMOC score; the resulting unified polity scale ranges from +10 (strongly democratic) to -10 (strongly autocratic). Marshall, Gurr, and Jaggers (2016). This variable is the revised combined polity score which has been modified to make it suitable for econometric analyses.	Marshall, Gurr, and Jaggers (2018). The Polity IV Project.
polm30	Average Democracy (Polity IV) for the last 30 years. In 2015, this variable is the average of the revised combined polity score for the period 1985-2015. A minimum of five (out of the seven possible) observations is required to calculate this average.	Own calculation.
Political Rights (FH)	The political rights variable is the average of 10 political rights indicators grouped into three subcategories: Electoral Process, Political Pluralism and Participation, and Functioning of Government. This variable ranges from 1 (most free) to 7 (least free).	Freedom House (2019).
prm30	Average Political Rights for the last 30 years. In 2015, this variable is the average of the Freedom House Political Rights variable for the period 1985-2015. A minimum of five (out of the seven possible) observations is required to calculate this average.	Own calculation.
Civil Liberties (FH)	The civil liberties variable is the average of 15 civil liberties indicators grouped into four subcategories: Freedom of Expression and Belief, Associational and Organizational Rights, Rule of Law, and Personal Autonomy and Individual Rights. This variable ranges from 1 (most free) to 7 (least free).	Freedom House (2019).
clm30	Average Civil Liberties for the last 30 years. In 2015, this variable was the average of the Freedom House Civil Liberties variable for the period 1985-2015. A minimum of five (out of the seven possible) observations is required to calculate this average.	Own calculation.
Political Freedom (FH)	The political freedom variable is the average of political rights and civil liberties from Freedom House. This variable has been inverted so that it ranges from 1 (least free) to 7 (most free).	Own calculation, and following Faria et al. (2014).
pfm30	Average Political Freedom for the last 30 years. In 2015, this variable is the average of the Political Freedom variable (which ultimately comes from Freedom House) for the period 1985-2015. A minimum of five (out of the seven possible) observations is required to calculate this average.	Freedom House and own calculation.

Table 3.1 – Continued

Variable	Definition	Source
Democracy (ANRR)	A dichotomous measure of democracy as used by Acemoglu, Naidu, Restrepo, and Robinson (2019). It classifies a country as democratic if both Freedom House assigns a "free" or "partially free" and Polity IV assigns it a positive score. It fills any missing values using the classifications provided by Cheibub, Gandhi, and Vreeland (2010) or Boix, Miller, and Rosato (2012).	Acemoglu et al. (2019)
dem30	Average of Acemoglu's et al. (ANRR) primary democracy variable for the last 30 years. In 2010, this variable was the average of the ANRR democracy variable for the period 1980-2010. A minimum of five (out of the seven possible) observations is required to calculate this average. Note that Acemoglu's sample spans from 1960 to 2010.	Acemoglu et al. (2019) and own calculation.
Extreme Poverty Rate	Percentage of the total population living on less than $1.90 a day at 2011 international prices. Missing values for this variable were filled using linear interpolation in the log-odds-ratio and an iterative autoregressive algorithm based on the adjacent poverty rate and contemporaneous under-5 mortality rate. See Appendix A for details.	Own calculation (See Appendix A) based on World Bank (2019) and Connors and Montesinos (2018).
Per capita GDP (MDP)	Per capita Gross Domestic Product (in 2011 PPP dollars).	Maddison Project Database (2018), Penn World Table, and World Bank (2019).
Malaria Ecology	Malaria ecology is a purely climatological variable indicating the ecological conditions for the prevalence of malaria. The malaria ecology index ranges from 0 (least-favorable environment for malaria) to 31 (most-favorable environment for malaria). That is, higher numbers of this variable indicate a higher geographic (climatological) disadvantage for economic development.	Gallup, Sachs, and Mellinger (1999), Sachs (2003), and Sachs (2012).
Distance to Major Markets	Minimum air distance in thousands of kilometers to New York, Rotterdam, or Tokyo. Higher numbers indicate a more considerable geographic disadvantage.	Gallup, Sachs, and Mellinger (1999), Sachs (2003), and Sachs (2012).
Coastal Population	The proportion of the population of the country living within 100 kilometers of ice-free coasts. Smaller numbers indicate a more substantial geographic disadvantage.	Gallup, Sachs, and Mellinger (1999), Sachs (2003), and Sachs (2012).
Geographic Disadvantage	Standardized Geographic Disadvantage Index. This measure was constructed by first standardizing, and then adding, the three key Sachs variables (population within 100 km of ocean coast, distance to major markets, and malaria ecology) in such a way that higher numbers indicate a higher geographic disadvantage for each of the variables. The final sum was then standardized to have zero mean and a standard deviation of 1.	Gallup, Sachs, and Mellinger (1999), Sachs (2003), Sachs (2012), and own calculations.

Table 3.1 – Continued

Variable	Definition	Source
Migratory Distance	Prehistoric migratory distance from Addis Ababa (Ethiopia) to contemporary geographic coordinates using the great circle (or geodesic) distances. Following the out of Africa hypothesis, the calculation is subject to obligatory intermediate waypoints in the possible patterns of human migration: Cairo (Egypt), Istanbul (Turkey), Phnom Penh (Cambodia), Anadyr (Russia) and Prince Rupert (Canada). See Ashraf and Galor (2013), for details. This variable is measured in thousands of kilometers and ranges from 0 (Ethiopia) to 26.77 (Uruguay).	Ashraf and Galor (2013).
Genetic Diversity	Predicted Genetic Diversity using Migratory Distance from East Africa. This variable is ancestry unadjusted, and therefore it has the interpretation of the predicted genetic diversity of the pre-colonial populations, or say, in the year 1500. Genetic diversity is measured by geneticists using an index of "Expected Heterozygosity," which is the probability that two randomly selected individuals differ from one another with respect to a given set of genes. See Ashraf and Galor (2013) for details.	Ashraf and Galor (2013).
Genetic Diversity (Ancestry Adjusted)	A measure of Contemporary Genetic Diversity. This measure is constructed by adjusting the pre-colonial predicted genetic diversity of pure ethnic groups by post-1500 population flows. The weighting uses the share of a country's population in 2000 that descended from the population of every other country in 1500 which is available from the World Migration Matrix, 1500-2000 from Putterman and Weil (2010). See Ashraf and Galor (2013) for details.	Ashraf and Galor (2013).
Log Settler Mortality Rates	The natural logarithm of the mortality rates experienced by soldiers, bishops, and sailors who stationed in the colonies between the seventeenth and nineteenth centuries. The source of these data is Curtin (1995) but they were assembled, organized, and popularized by Acemoglu et al. (2001).	Curtin (1995) and Acemoglu et al. (2001).
Ethno-Linguistic Fractionalization	This is a measure of the probability that two individuals randomly selected from the population either speak a different language or are from a different race. This measure is computed in practice as the average of five different indices of ethnolinguistic fragmentation. I used this variable in the same form as did Easterly and Levine (1997), La Porta et al. (1999), Acemoglu et al. (2001), Faria and Montesinos (2009), and Faria et al. (2016), among others.	Easterly and Levine (1997) and multiple others in the literature.
Early Disease Environment (EDE)	This is the natural logarithm of the anticipated (or potential) probability of death for European males in the age cohort of soldiers. This measure is calculated using the settler mortality rate and geographic characteristics such as malaria mortality, latitude, rainfall, temperature, and sailing distance. The standardized measure was proposed by Raphael Auer.	Auer (2013).

Table 3.2: Pairwise correlation between economic and political institution variables, 1980-2015

Panel A: Full Period 1980-2015

	(1) EFW	(2) Area 2 (EFW)	(3) Rule of Law (WGI)	(4) Demo-cracy (Polity IV)	(5) Exec. Cons. (Pol. IV)	(6) Poli-tical Rights (FH)	(7) Civil Liber-ties (FH)	(8_ Poli-tical Free-dom (FH)	(9) Demo-cracy (ANRR)	(10) Strong Demo-cracy
(1)EFW	1.00									
(2) Area 2 (EFW)	0.72	1.00								
(3) Rule of Law (WGI)	0.74	0.91	1.00							
(4) Democracy (Polity IV)	0.48	0.47	0.45	1.00						
(5) Exec. Const.(Pol. IV)	0.50	0.50	0.50	0.95	1.00					
(6) Political Rights (FH)	-0.48	-0.56	-0.64	-0.89	-0.86	1.00				
(7) Civil Liberties (FH)	-0.56	-0.63	-0.72	-0.85	-0.82	0.93	1.00			
(8) Pol Freedom (FH)	0.52	0.61	0.69	0.89	0.86	-0.98	-0.98	1.00		
(9) Democracy (ANRR)	0.41	0.41	0.39	0.91	0.88	-0.86	-0.80	0.85	1.00	
(10) Strong Democracy	0.51	0.65	0.72	0.64	0.64	-0.73	-0.78	0.77	0.57	1.00

Panel B: 2015

	(1)	(2)	(3)	(4)	(5)	(6)	(7)	(8)	(9)	(10)
(1) EFW	1.00									
(2) Area 2 (EFW)	0.78	1.00								
(3) Rule of Law (WGI)	0.76	0.92	1.00							
(4) Democracy (Polity IV)	0.39	0.33	0.45	1.00						
(5) Exec. Const.(Pol. IV)	0.44	0.36	0.46	0.96	1.00					
(6) Political Rights (FH)	-0.50	-0.55	-0.67	-0.87	-0.85	1.00				
(7) Civil Liberties (FH)	-0.57	-0.64	-0.76	-0.83	-0.82	0.95	1.00			
(8) Pol. Freedom (FH)	0.54	0.60	0.72	0.86	0.84	-0.99	-0.98	1.00		
(9) Democracy (ANRR)	0.40	0.32	0.36	0.88	0.87	-0.81	-0.75	0.80	1.00	
(10) Strong Democracy	0.50	0.65	0.73	0.57	0.57	-0.72	-0.78	0.76	0.49	1.00

Panel C: Means 1985-2015

	(1)	(2)	(3)	(4)	(5)	(6)	(7)	(8)	(9)	(10)
(1) EFW	1.00									
Area 2 (EFW)	0.82	1.00								
Rule of Law (WGI)	0.85	0.91	1.00							
Democracy (Polity IV)	0.54	0.55	0.60	1.00						
Exec. Const.(Polity IV)	0.58	0.60	0.65	0.97	1.00					
Political Rights (FH)	-0.62	-0.66	-0.75	-0.94	-0.93	1.00				
Civil Liberties (FH)	-0.69	-0.73	-0.81	-0.91	-0.91	0.97	1.00			
Political Freedom (FH)	0.66	0.70	0.78	0.93	0.93	0.99	-0.99	1.00		
Democracy (ANRR)	0.46	0.46	0.57	0.92	0.89	-0.90	-0.85	0.88	1.00	
Strong Democracy	0.68	0.77	0.80	0.71	0.73	-0.80	-0.83	0.82	0.62	1.00

Notes: All correlations, in both panels, are statistically significant at the 1 percent level. ANRR stands for Acemoglu, Naidu, Restrepo, and Robinson (2019). The correlation between Democracy (ANRR) and the other variables is for the year 2010.

Table 3.3: Descriptive statistics for the base sample of 135 countries

Panel A: 1985	N	Simple Mean	Median	Standard Deviation	Min.	Max.
EFW	108	5.26	5.13	1.30	1.81	8.68
Area 2 (EFW)	105	4.43	4.20	1.87	1.34	7.81
Rule of Law (WGI)		(No Rule of Law data from WGI prior to 1996)				
Democracy (Polity IV)	124	-0.85	-6.00	7.77	-10.00	10.00
Executive Constraints (Polity IV)	118	3.69	3.00	2.37	1.00	7.00
Political Rights (FH)	133	4.08	5.00	2.23	1.00	7.00
Civil Liberties (FH)	133	4.23	5.00	2.03	1.00	7.00
Political Freedom (FH)	133	3.85	3.50	2.09	1.00	7.00
Democracy (ANRR)	133	0.39	0.00	0.49	0.00	1.00
Strong Democracy	124	0.24	0.00	0.43	0.00	1.00
Extreme Poverty Rate ($1.90 a day)	133	28.08	13.30	30.64	0.06	97.07
Per capita GDP (2011 PPP $)	135	$13,301	$6,178	$22,390	$280	$194,482
Panel B: 2000						
EFW	112	6.60	6.72	1.05	3.84	8.95
Area 2 (EFW)	112	5.25	5.15	1.89	1.50	9.01
Rule of Law (WGI)	135	0.05	-0.15	1.02	-2.01	1.99
Democracy (Polity IV)	126	3.67	6.00	6.31	-10.00	10.00
Executive Constraints (Polity IV)	119	4.94	5.00	1.95	1.00	7.00
Political Rights (FH)	135	3.39	3.00	2.16	1.00	7.00
Civil Liberties (FH)	135	3.48	3.00	1.70	1.00	7.00
Political Freedom (FH)	135	4.57	4.50	1.89	1.00	7.00
Democracy	134	0.66	1.00	0.48	0.00	1.00
Strong Democracy	126	0.31	0.00	0.46	0.00	1.00
Extreme Poverty Rate ($1.90 a day)	133	22.11	9.53	25.94	0.00	94.86
Per capita GDP (2011 PPP $)	135	$16,061	$7,738	$20,838	$502	$128,455
Panel C: 2015						
EFW	135	6.80	6.90	0.93	2.96	8.97
Area 2 (EFW)	135	5.30	5.16	1.63	1.85	8.88
Rule of Law (WGI)	135	0.05	-0.15	1.00	-2.03	2.06
Democracy (Polity IV)	127	4.66	7.00	5.89	-10.00	10.00
Executive Constraints (Polity IV)	124	5.33	6.00	1.82	1.00	7.00
Political Rights (FH)	135	3.33	3.00	2.07	1.00	7.00
Civil Liberties (FH)	135	3.27	3.00	1.76	1.00	7.00
Political Freedom (FH)	135	4.70	5.00	1.88	1.00	7.00
Democracy	134	0.67	1.00	0.47	0.00	1.00
Strong Democracy	127	0.32	0.00	0.47	0.00	1.00
Extreme Poverty Rate ($1.90 a day)	133	12.73	1.90	19.27	0.00	71.25
Per capita GDP (2011 PPP $)	135	$19,515	$11,849	$21,802	$576	$156,029

Table 3.4: Institutions, per capita GDP, and extreme poverty. Univariate regressions

	(1)	(2)	(3)	(4)	(5)	(6)	(7)	(8)	(9)	(10)
Panel A: Dependent Variable is per Capita GDP (2011 PPP dollars)										
Institutional Variable:	efm30	a2m30	rlm30	polm30	xcm30	prm30	clm30	pfm30	dem30	SDem30
Coefficient	0.77***	0.80***	0.78***	0.37***	0.45***	-0.51***	-0.56***	0.53***	0.35***	0.62***
(t-stat)	(11.80)	(18.11)	(17.24)	(3.52)	(4.45)	(-6.67)	(-7.75)	(7.24)	(4.16)	(11.53)
Observations	112	108	135	126	121	135	135	135	134	126
R-squared	0.59	0.64	0.61	0.13	0.20	0.26	0.31	0.29	0.12	0.38
Panel B: Dependent Variable is Extreme Poverty ($1.90 a day in 2011 PPP dollars)										
Institutional Variable:	efm30	a2m30	rlm30	polm30	xcm30	prm30	clm30	pfm30	dem30	SDem30
Coefficient	-0.58***	-0.53***	-0.53***	-0.30***	-0.38***	0.39***	0.41***	-0.40***	-0.29***	-0.43***
(t-stat)	(-6.27)	(-6.64)	(-8.19)	(-3.86)	(-4.87)	(5.45)	(5.57)	(-5.56)	(-3.95)	(-7.63)
Observations	110	106	133	125	120	133	133	133	133	125
R-squared	0.33	0.28	0.28	0.09	0.14	0.15	0.17	0.16	0.09	0.19

Notes: Standardized beta coefficients reported; t statistics in parentheses. * $p<0.1$ ** $p<0.05$ *** $p<0.01$. The institutional variables are averages over 30 years requiring a minimum of 5 observations except for Rule of Law, which is required to have a minimum of 3 observations. The average economic freedom is efm30, the rule of law is rlm30, democracy (Polity IV) is polm30, the executive constraint is xcm30, political rights is prm30, civil liberties is clm30, political freedom is pfm30, democracy (ANRR) is dem30, and strong democracy is SDem30.

Table 3.5: Institutions, per capita GDP, and extreme poverty, after controlling for geography

	(1)	(2)	(3)	(4)	(5)	(6)	(7)	(8)	(9)	(10)
Panel A: Dependent Variable is per Capita GDP (2011 PPP dollars)										
Institutional Variable:	efm30	a2m30	rlm30	polm30	xcm30	prm30	clm30	pfm30	dem30	SDem30
Coefficient Institutions	0.56***	0.61***	0.56***	0.10	0.11	-0.22***	-0.29***	0.25***	0.07	0.36***
	(8.36)	(10.94)	(11.33)	(1.11)	(1.19)	(-2.69)	(-3.71)	(3.17)	(0.88)	(6.17)
Malaria Ecology	-0.27***	-0.25***	-0.30***	-0.45***	-0.42***	-0.40***	-0.40***	-0.40***	-0.44***	-0.39***
	(-4.27)	(-4.38)	(-5.83)	(-6.49)	(-5.67)	(-6.18)	(-6.43)	(-6.25)	(-6.56)	(-6.28)
Distance to Major Markets	-0.17***	-0.08	-0.09**	-0.26***	-0.25***	-0.21***	-0.18***	-0.20***	-0.25***	-0.15***
	(-3.29)	(-1.41)	(-1.99)	(-4.08)	(-4.03)	(-3.77)	(-3.66)	(-3.72)	(-3.91)	(-3.31)
Coastal population	0.06	0.16***	0.14***	0.22***	0.26***	0.21***	0.19***	0.20***	0.24***	0.19***
	(1.05)	(3.02)	(2.91)	(2.78)	(3.32)	(2.87)	(2.66)	(2.76)	(3.16)	(2.66)
Observations	112	108	135	126	121	135	135	135	134	126
R-squared	0.69	0.74	0.72	0.52	0.54	0.54	0.57	0.56	0.51	0.61

	(1)	(2)	(3)	(4)	(5)	(6)	(7)	(8)	(9)	(10)
Panel B: Dependent Variable is Extreme Poverty ($1.90 a day in 2011 PPP dollars)										
Institutional Variable:	efm30	a2m30	rlm30	polm30	xcm30	prm30	clm30	pfm30	dem30	SDem30
Coefficient Institutions	-0.25***	-0.22***	-0.19***	-0.02	-0.03	0.06	0.09	-0.07	0.00	-0.11**
	(-3.16)	(-2.87)	(-3.17)	(-0.36)	(-0.45)	(0.94)	(1.44)	(-1.18)	(0.08)	(-2.08)
Malaria Ecology	0.41***	0.44***	0.41***	0.47***	0.45***	0.45***	0.44***	0.45***	0.46***	0.44***
	(4.76)	(5.06)	(5.76)	(6.16)	(5.65)	(5.93)	(6.01)	(5.95)	(6.08)	(5.96)
Distance to Major Markets	0.18**	0.16*	0.23***	0.30***	0.30***	0.27***	0.26***	0.27***	0.29***	0.26***
	(2.49)	(1.95)	(3.03)	(3.73)	(3.65)	(3.47)	(3.42)	(3.44)	(3.68)	(3.45)
Coastal population	-0.15**	-0.18**	-0.20***	-0.22***	-0.22***	-0.22***	-0.22***	-0.22***	-0.24***	-0.20***
	(-2.21)	(-2.55)	(-3.29)	(-3.27)	(-3.40)	(-3.54)	(-3.45)	(-3.50)	(-3.63)	(-3.19)
Observations	110	106	133	125	120	133	133	133	133	125
R-squared	0.55	0.55	0.55	0.52	0.52	0.52	0.53	0.52	0.52	0.53

Standardized beta coefficients reported; t statistics in parentheses. * p<0.1 ** p<0.05 *** p<0.01.

Table 3.6: Horse races. Economic versus political institutions.

	(1)	(2)	(3)	(4)	(5)	(6)	(7)	(8)	(9)	(10)
Panel A: Dependent Variable is per Capita GDP (2011 PPP dollars)										
efm30	0.56***	0.52***	0.50***	0.56***	0.44***					
	(7.06)	(6.70)	(5.80)	(7.68)	(4.65)					
rlm30						0.62***	0.59***	0.68***	0.62***	0.62***
						(10.09)	(9.55)	(8.76)	(10.75)	(6.45)
polm30	-0.02					-0.14**				
	(-0.20)					(-2.10)				
xcm30		0.01					-0.14*			
		(0.13)					(-1.82)			
pfm30			0.10					-0.18**		
			(1.15)					(-2.14)		
dem30				-0.00					-0.15**	
				(-0.01)					(-2.34)	
SDem30					0.20**					-0.08
					(2.49)					(-0.86)
Malaria Ecology	-0.27***	-0.28***	-0.26***	-0.26***	-0.25***	-0.32***	-0.35***	-0.31***	-0.33***	-0.31***
	(-4.12)	(-4.03)	(-4.03)	(-4.02)	(-4.01)	(-6.07)	(-6.02)	(-5.92)	(-6.12)	(-5.88)
Distance to Major Markets	-0.17***	-0.18***	-0.16***	-0.17***	-0.13***	-0.12**	-0.13***	-0.10**	-0.10**	-0.12**
	(-3.22)	(-3.44)	(-3.16)	(-3.24)	(-2.63)	(-2.48)	(-2.68)	(-2.11)	(-2.11)	(-2.49)
Coastal Population	0.07	0.11*	0.06	0.06	0.09	0.14***	0.17***	0.15***	0.14***	0.13***
	(1.19)	(1.86)	(0.99)	(1.06)	(1.55)	(2.98)	(3.39)	(3.19)	(3.07)	(2.73)
Observations	106	103	112	111	106	126	121	135	134	126
R-squared	0.69	0.70	0.70	0.69	0.71	0.74	0.73	0.74	0.74	0.73

Standardized beta coefficients reported; t statistics in parentheses. * p<0.1 ** p<0.05 *** p<0.01.

Table 3.6 – Continued

	(1)	(2)	(3)	(4)	(5)	(6)	(7)	(8)	(9)	(10)
Panel B: Dependent Variable is Extreme Poverty ($1.90 a day in 2011 PPP dollars)										
efm30	-0.26***	-0.22**	-0.24**	-0.25***	-0.24**					
	(-3.00)	(-2.40)	(-2.60)	(-3.05)	(-2.39)					
rlm30						-0.23***	-0.18**	-0.25***	-0.23***	-0.24**
						(-3.34)	(-2.53)	(-3.50)	(-3.64)	(-2.41)
polm30	0.03					0.07				
	(0.38)					(1.31)				
xcm30		0.01					0.05			
		(0.08)					(0.75)			
pfm30			-0.02					0.09		
			(-0.18)					(1.25)		
dem30				0.00					0.08	
				(0.02)					(1.41)	
SDem30					-0.01					0.06
					(-0.12)					(0.73)
Malaria Ecology	0.42***	0.43***	0.41***	0.41***	0.41***	0.42***	0.43***	0.41***	0.42***	0.41***
	(4.66)	(4.48)	(4.63)	(4.61)	(4.69)	(5.82)	(5.66)	(5.74)	(5.85)	(5.74)
Distance to Major Markets	0.19**	0.20**	0.18**	0.18**	0.18**	0.25***	0.26***	0.23***	0.23***	0.25***
	(2.48)	(2.52)	(2.39)	(2.46)	(2.37)	(3.14)	(3.21)	(3.01)	(3.02)	(3.15)
Coastal Population	-0.15**	-0.16**	-0.15**	-0.15**	-0.15**	-0.19***	-0.20***	-0.20***	-0.20***	-0.18***
	(-2.18)	(-2.25)	(-2.25)	(-2.24)	(-2.13)	(-3.10)	(-3.11)	(-3.41)	(-3.38)	(-3.01)
Observations	105	102	110	110	105	125	120	133	133	125
R-squared	0.55	0.54	0.55	0.55	0.55	0.55	0.53	0.55	0.55	0.54

Standardized beta coefficients reported; t statistics in parentheses. * $p<0.1$ ** $p<0.05$ *** $p<0.01$.

Table 3.7: Changes in economic institutions, growth of per capita GDP, and changes in poverty rates

	(1)	(2)	(3)	(4)	(5)	(6)	(7)	(8)
					Panel Analysis 15-year periods			
	Period 1985-2000		Period 2000-2015		No Overlap	Overlap	No Overlap	Overlap
	Dep. Var. (Cols 1-6): Annual Growth Rate of Per capita GDP (15-Year Period)						Dep. Var. (Cols 7-8) Change in Pov. Rate (15-Year Period)	
Log Initial Per Capita GDP	-0.41**	-0.43*	-0.86***	-0.79***	-0.64***	-0.58***		
	(-2.09)	(-1.90)	(-3.80)	(-3.21)	(-3.86)	(-4.97)		
EFW 5-years prior to the beginning of the period	1.29***	0.71***	0.65**	0.86**	0.80***	0.77***	-1.94**	-1.50***
	(5.85)	(4.06)	(2.13)	(2.51)	(5.10)	(6.89)	(-2.53)	(-2.64)
Change in EFW 5-years prior to the period	1.97***	1.34***	0.28	0.69	1.14***	0.95***	0.87	-1.10
	(5.35)	(4.25)	(0.66)	(1.46)	(5.22)	(6.74)	(0.77)	(-1.43)
Change in EFW first 5-years of the period	1.23***	0.69**	1.39***	1.45***	0.86***	1.02***	-0.26	-0.55
	(3.28)	(2.36)	(2.88)	(3.26)	(3.61)	(7.19)	(-0.21)	(-0.69)
Change in EFW second 5-years of the period	1.47***	0.79***	0.23	0.70	0.74***	0.74***	-1.87*	-0.23
	(5.81)	(3.49)	(0.40)	(1.15)	(3.58)	(4.95)	(-1.66)	(-0.27)
Log Initial Population		0.14		0.28***	0.20***	0.21***	-0.73**	-0.72***
		(1.54)		(2.81)	(3.23)	(4.95)	(-2.23)	(-3.11)
Geographic Disadvantage Index		-0.39*		-0.19	-0.31**	-0.29***	2.05***	2.06***
		(-1.84)		(-0.85)	(-2.09)	(-2.95)	(2.70)	(3.77)
Change in Prime Age Population		0.12***		0.10**	0.12***	0.11***	-0.55***	-0.62***
		(2.76)		(2.50)	(4.45)	(6.15)	(-3.90)	(-5.90)
Net fuel Exports. Average		-0.02		0.02	-0.00	0.00	-0.07	-0.04
		(-1.29)		(1.32)	(-0.21)	(0.32)	(-1.14)	(-0.88)
Dummy for ME Oil Exporters		-0.93*		-3.88***	-2.17***	-1.77***	5.95	5.27**
		(-1.86)		(-3.14)	(-3.15)	(-3.89)	(1.63)	(2.05)
War on Soil		-1.30**		-5.85***	-3.54***	-3.14***	6.77	11.35**
		(-2.52)		(-17.36)	(-3.41)	(-3.87)	(1.22)	(2.49)
Dummy for the periods								
2000-2015					-0.05	0.07	-3.20**	-2.05*
					(-0.20)	(0.32)	(-2.40)	(-1.68)
1990-2005						-0.17		-0.64
						(-0.85)		(-0.56)
1995-2010						-0.11		-1.01
						(-0.52)		(-0.84)
Initial Poverty Rate							-0.39***	-0.38***
							(-11.41)	(-15.39)
Intercept	-3.13**	-0.18	5.24**	2.17	1.17	0.68	18.90***	16.09***
	(-2.11)	(-0.10)	(2.45)	(0.81)	(0.93)	(0.79)	(3.62)	(4.06)
Observations	102.00	95.00	112.00	108.00	203.00	411.00	201.00	407.00
R-squared	0.41	0.54	0.20	0.47	0.43	0.40	0.50	0.48

Notes: Robust t statistics in parentheses. * p<0.1 ** p<0.05 *** p<0.01. Seemingly Unrelated Regressions (SUR) used in panel analysis (Columns 5-8).

Table 3.8: Changes in political institutions, growth of per capita GDP, and changes in poverty rates

	(1)	(2)	(3)	(4)	(5)	(6)	(7)	(8)
					Panel Analysis 15-year periods			
	Period 1985-2000		Period 2000-2015		No Overlap	Overlap	No Overlap	Overlap
	Dependent Variable (Columns 1-6) Annual Growth Rate of Per capita GDP (15-Year Period)						Dep. Var. (Cols 7-8) Change in Poverty Rate (15-Year Period)	
Log Initial Per Capita GDP	0.08	-0.36	-0.62***	-0.60***	-0.58***	-0.52***		
	(0.40)	(-1.45)	(-4.18)	(-2.72)	(-3.90)	(-4.91)		
Democracy, 5-years prior to the beginning of the period	0.10***	0.05	0.04	-0.01	0.04*	0.03*	0.28**	0.29***
	(3.33)	(1.04)	(1.07)	(-0.26)	(1.71)	(1.89)	(2.33)	(3.20)
Change in Democracy 5-years prior to the period	0.10***	0.06	0.10*	0.01	0.04	0.03	0.15	0.46***
	(3.25)	(1.48)	(1.88)	(0.10)	(1.19)	(1.47)	(0.80)	(3.79)
Change in Democracy first 5-years of the period	0.01	-0.05	0.09	0.11	-0.01	-0.02	0.16	0.53***
	(0.19)	(-0.88)	(1.02)	(1.22)	(-0.21)	(-0.68)	(0.87)	(4.23)
Change in Democracy second 5-years of the period	-0.00	-0.02	0.03	-0.01	-0.04	-0.02	0.42**	0.51***
	(-0.07)	(-0.38)	(0.42)	(-0.23)	(-1.30)	(-0.70)	(2.42)	(3.73)
Log Initial Population		0.11		0.19*	0.14**	0.11**	-0.23	-0.29
		(1.00)		(1.86)	(1.97)	(2.38)	(-0.65)	(-1.15)
Geographic Disadvantage Index		-0.36		-0.36*	-0.33**	-0.38***	2.76***	2.91***
		(-1.47)		(-1.74)	(-2.08)	(-3.51)	(3.44)	(5.04)
Change in Prime Age Population		0.17***		0.11***	0.14***	0.14***	-0.48***	-0.60***
		(3.36)		(2.81)	(5.25)	(7.00)	(-3.49)	(-5.81)
Net fuel Exports. Average		-0.02		0.00	-0.01	-0.01	0.02	0.05
		(-1.18)		(0.12)	(-0.86)	(-0.65)	(0.43)	(1.28)
Dummy for ME Oil Exporters		-0.11		-2.91***	-1.08	-1.27**	6.84*	6.87***
		(-0.10)		(-2.65)	(-1.44)	(-2.42)	(1.91)	(2.65)
War on Soil		-2.18***		-6.47***	-3.63***	-3.00***	19.08***	20.40***
		(-4.72)		(-11.43)	(-3.76)	(-4.11)	(3.88)	(5.30)
Dummy for the periods								
2000-2015					0.56**	0.64***	-4.74***	-4.00***
					(2.38)	(2.87)	(-3.97)	(-3.42)
1990-2005						0.28		-1.71
						(1.27)		(-1.49)
1995-2010						0.54**		-2.62**
						(2.41)		(-2.23)
Initial Poverty Rate							-0.36***	-0.38***
							(-11.27)	(-16.51)
Intercept	0.63	3.74*	7.40***	6.69***	5.68***	5.15***	4.23**	4.36***
	(0.34)	(1.70)	(5.45)	(3.23)	(4.33)	(5.53)	(2.47)	(3.18)
Observations	122.00	109.00	126.00	121.00	230.00	459.00	230.00	459.00
R-squared	0.14	0.39	0.17	0.38	0.35	0.29	0.52	0.54

Notes: Robust t statistics in parentheses. * $p<0.1$ ** $p<0.05$ *** $p<0.01$. Seemingly Unrelated Regressions (SUR) used in panel analysis (Columns 5-8).

Table 3.9: Changes in economic and political institutions, growth of per capita GDP, and changes in poverty rates

	(1)	(2)	(3)	(4)	(5)	(6)	(7)	(8)
					Panel Analysis 15-year periods			
	Period 1985-2000		Period 2000-2015		No Overlap	Overlap	No Overlap	Overlap
	Dependent Variable (Columns 1-6) Annual Growth Rate of Per capita GDP (15-Year Period)						Dep. Var. (Cols 7-8) Change in Poverty Rate (15-Year Period)	
Log Initial Per Capita GDP	-0.64***	-0.59**	-0.81***	-0.70**	-0.69***	-0.59***		
	(-2.85)	(-2.29)	(-3.52)	(-2.58)	(-3.98)	(-4.94)		
EFW 5-years prior to the beginning of the period	1.16***	0.65***	0.48	0.88**	0.78***	0.79***	-2.47***	-1.87***
	(4.53)	(3.18)	(1.59)	(2.46)	(4.58)	(6.62)	(-2.91)	(-2.96)
Change in EFW 5-years prior to the period	1.91***	1.33***	0.03	0.71	1.02***	1.00***	0.93	-1.33
	(4.96)	(4.11)	(0.08)	(1.53)	(4.46)	(6.73)	(0.77)	(-1.57)
Change in EFW first 5-years of the period	1.14**	0.65**	1.30**	1.45***	0.96***	1.00***	-1.00	-0.86
	(2.56)	(2.04)	(2.46)	(2.89)	(3.75)	(6.73)	(-0.72)	(-1.00)
Change in EFW second 5-years of the period	1.20***	0.62**	0.11	0.82	0.58**	0.74***	-1.67	-0.49
	(4.63)	(2.40)	(0.15)	(1.14)	(2.53)	(4.78)	(-1.34)	(-0.54)
Democracy, 5-years prior to the beginning of the period	0.05	0.06	0.04	-0.04	0.02	0.01	0.25*	0.18*
	(1.65)	(1.53)	(0.73)	(-0.76)	(0.69)	(0.61)	(1.78)	(1.76)
Change in Democracy 5-years prior to the period	0.03	0.06	0.11*	-0.02	0.01	0.02	0.17	0.23*
	(0.88)	(1.45)	(1.83)	(-0.28)	(0.44)	(1.03)	(0.92)	(1.76)
Change in Democracy first 5-years of the period	0.02	0.01	0.07	0.05	0.01	-0.01	0.13	0.35**
	(0.43)	(0.21)	(0.66)	(0.57)	(0.15)	(-0.42)	(0.66)	(2.47)
Change in Democracy second 5-years of the period	-0.05	-0.01	-0.00	-0.04	-0.04	-0.01	0.43**	0.39***
	(-0.85)	(-0.22)	(-0.04)	(-0.65)	(-1.03)	(-0.53)	(2.06)	(2.68)
Log Initial Population		0.18		0.29**	0.23***	0.24***	-0.66*	-0.69**
		(1.59)		(2.58)	(3.28)	(4.97)	(-1.70)	(-2.48)
Geographic Disadvantage Index		-0.20		-0.16	-0.20	-0.21**	2.01**	2.02***
		(-0.91)		(-0.73)	(-1.29)	(-2.13)	(2.47)	(3.47)
Change in Prime Age Population		0.14***		0.11***	0.13***	0.13***	-0.50***	-0.61***
		(3.22)		(2.68)	(4.59)	(6.58)	(-3.35)	(-5.42)
Net fuel Exports. Average		-0.01		0.02	-0.00	0.00	-0.06	-0.02
		(-0.39)		(1.03)	(-0.05)	(0.50)	(-0.94)	(-0.52)
Dummy for ME Oil Exporters		-0.13		-4.54***	-2.27***	-2.23***	9.57**	7.67**
		(-0.14)		(-3.54)	(-2.83)	(-4.11)	(2.21)	(2.46)
War on Soil		-1.16**		-6.22***	-3.36***	-2.96***	8.03	11.98**
		(-2.01)		(-9.03)	(-3.25)	(-3.71)	(1.41)	(2.57)
Dummy for the periods								
2000-2015					-0.08	0.04	-2.97**	-1.39
					(-0.31)	(0.18)	(-2.07)	(-1.07)
1990-2005						-0.23		-0.51
						(-1.11)		(-0.42)
1995-2010						-0.14		-0.55
						(-0.64)		(-0.43)
Initial Poverty Rate							-0.39***	-0.38***
							(-11.14)	(-15.05)
Intercept	-0.33	1.36	5.80**	1.26	1.53	0.53	20.29***	16.70***
	(-0.16)	(0.61)	(2.59)	(0.46)	(1.11)	(0.56)	(3.63)	(3.92)
Observations	95.00	88.00	106.00	102.00	190.00	384.00	190.00	384.00
R-squared	0.44	0.58	0.22	0.50	0.47	0.44	0.51	0.49

Notes: Robust t statistics in parentheses. * $p<0.1$ ** $p<0.05$ *** $p<0.01$. Seemingly Unrelated Regressions (SUR) used in panel analysis (Columns 5-8).

Table 3.10: Institutions and instrumental variables. Falsification tests

Panel A: Economic Institutions and Ancestry Unadjusted Genetic Diversity (FMMN 2016)

	(1)	(2)	(3)	(4)	(5)	(6)	(7)
	2015 per capita GDP			Economic Freedom		Legal System	
Genetic Diversity	185.35***	69.47	25.91	163.71***	92.11**	297.85***	130.97**
	(4.06)	(1.44)	(0.63)	(3.90)	(2.27)	(4.32)	(2.45)
Gen. Div. (Squared)	-140.35***	-53.64	-22.67	-122.50***	-68.28**	-219.84***	-93.47**
	(-4.15)	(-1.49)	(-0.74)	(-3.97)	(-2.29)	(-4.31)	(-2.34)
Econ. Freedom (EFW)		0.71***					
		(4.92)					
Leg Sys (EFW Area 2)			0.54***				
			(12.08)				
Log per capita GDP					0.39***		0.90***
					(8.91)		(11.22)
Intercept	-51.18***	-17.71	-0.51	-47.30***	-27.52**	-94.66***	-48.57***
	(-3.36)	(-1.13)	(-0.04)	(-3.34)	(-2.02)	(-4.09)	(-2.74)
Observations	135.00	135.00	135.00	135.00	135.00	135.00	135.00
R-squared	0.12	0.36	0.54	0.12	0.36	0.12	0.54

Panel B: Political Institutions and Settler Mortality Rates (AJR 2003)

	(1)	(2)	(3)	(4)	(5)	(6)	(7)
	Per capita GDP			Democracy (Polity)		Executive Constraints	
Log Settler Mort. Rate	-0.66***	-0.58***	-0.57***	-1.22**	-0.20	-0.46***	-0.15
	(-7.47)	(-5.89)	(-5.60)	(-2.64)	(-0.36)	(-2.89)	(-0.77)
Democracy (Polity)		0.05**					
		(2.09)					
Executive Constraints			0.13*				
			(1.88)				
Log of per capita GDP					1.59**		0.49**
					(2.59)		(2.10)
Intercept	11.86***	11.25***	10.78***	10.32***	-8.38	7.35***	1.65
	(28.22)	(20.41)	(13.90)	(4.59)	(-1.15)	(9.59)	(0.60)
Observations	73.00	69.00	67.00	69.00	69.00	67.00	67.00
R-squared	0.48	0.51	0.52	0.09	0.16	0.12	0.17

Panel C: Political Institutions and Early Disease Environment (Auer 2013)

	(1)	(2)	(3)	(4)	(5)	(6)	(7)
	Per capita GDP			Democracy (Polity)		Executive Constraints	
Colony × EDE	-1.00***	-0.96***	-0.92***	-1.91***	-1.37	-0.76***	-0.56**
	(-9.23)	(-8.53)	(-7.87)	(-3.56)	(-1.59)	(-4.56)	(-2.27)
Democracy (Polity)		0.02					
		(0.86)					
Executive Constraints			0.07				
			(1.18)				
2015 per capita GDP					0.54		0.21
					(0.87)		(1.17)
Intercept	9.43***	9.33***	9.06***	5.23***	0.19	5.54***	3.58**
	(99.99)	(62.28)	(26.29)	(9.66)	(0.03)	(34.10)	(2.16)
Observations	122.00	121.00	119.00	121.00	121.00	119.00	119.00
R-squared	0.38	0.38	0.38	0.06	0.07	0.11	0.12

Notes: Institutions and per capita GDP are in 2015. Robust t-statistics are in parentheses. * $p<0.1$ ** $p<0.05$ *** $p<0.01$. Colony × EDE is the interaction between a colonial dummy and Early Disease Environment.

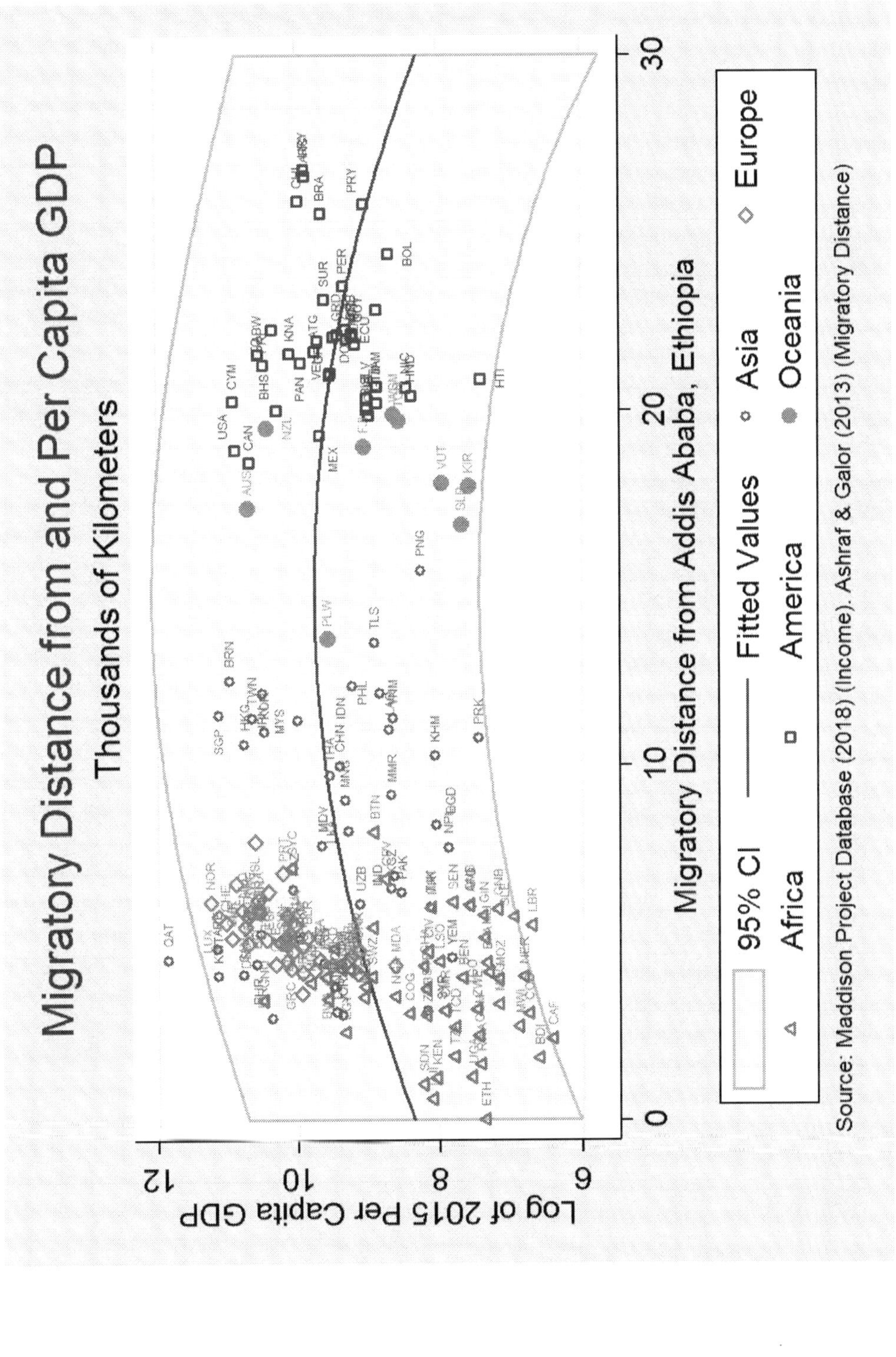

Figure 3.1: Prehistoric migratory distance, genetic diversity, and comparative economic development
Panel A: Ancestral migratory distance and 2015 per capita GDP

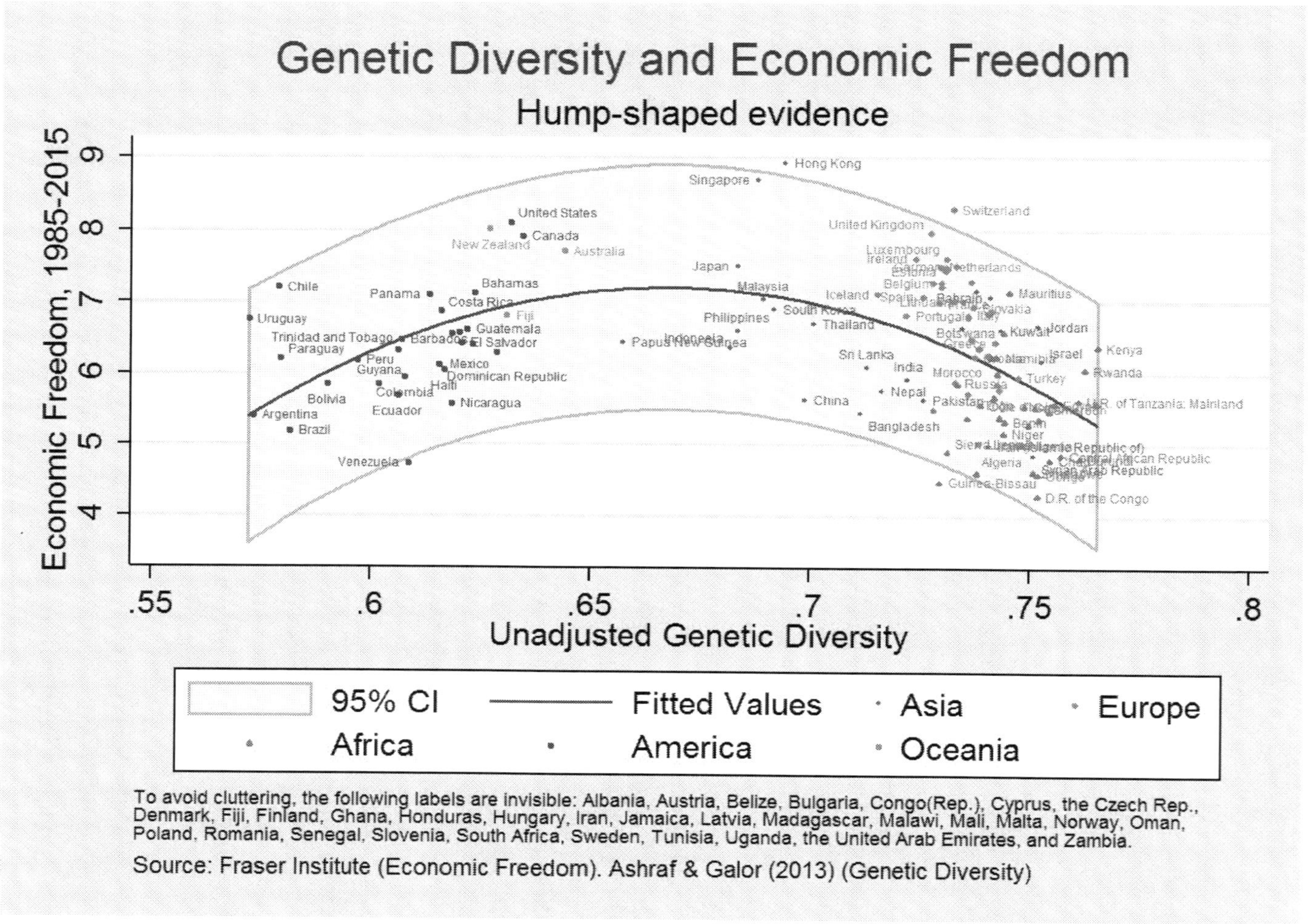

Figure 3.1 – Continued

Panel B: Ancestry unadjusted predicted genetic diversity and contemporary economic institutions

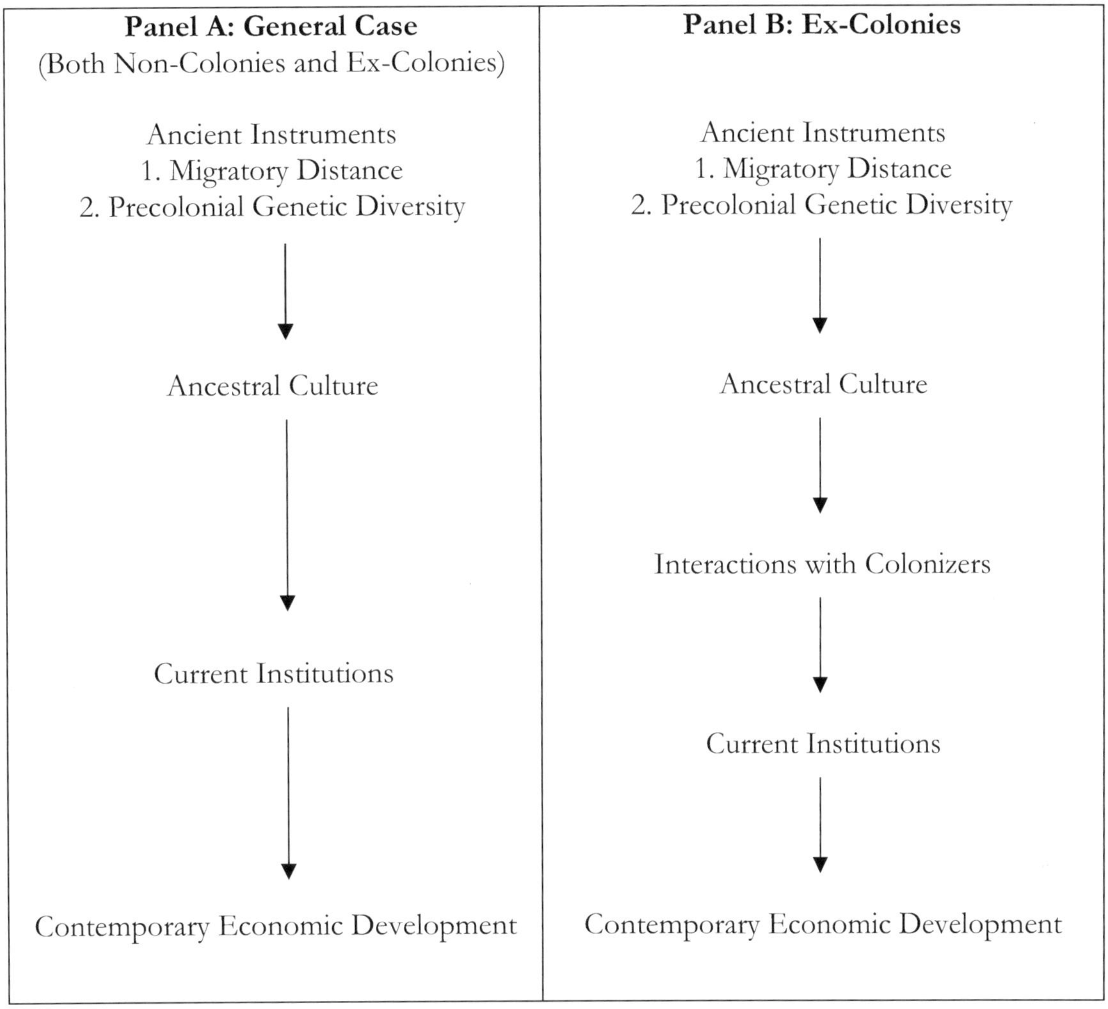

Figure 3.2: Schematic representation of the ancestral channel of economic development

Table 3.11: Economic institutions in 2015 and implausible instrument variables

Panel A: Early Disease Environment

	(1)	(2)	(3)	(4)	(5)	(6)	(7)
		Per capita GDP		Economic Freedom		Legal System	
Genetic Diversity	113.82***	50.80	17.18	143.30***	108.15***	230.78***	144.24***
	(2.82)	(1.17)	(0.43)	(3.79)	(2.75)	(4.04)	(2.83)
Genetic Diversity Squared	-83.53***	-37.22	-14.41	-105.30***	-79.51***	-165.06***	-101.55***
	(-2.79)	(-1.15)	(-0.48)	(-3.78)	(-2.75)	(-3.91)	(-2.67)
EDE × Colonial Dummy	-0.99***	-0.75***	-0.49***	-0.54***	-0.23**	-1.20***	-0.45***
	(-7.56)	(-5.27)	(-3.59)	(-5.89)	(-2.33)	(-8.32)	(-2.84)
Economic Freedom (EFW)		0.44***					
		(3.45)					
Legal Sys. (Area 2 of EFW)			0.42***				
			(7.72)				
Log of per capita GDP					0.31***		0.76***
					(5.52)		(7.32)
Intercept	-29.00**	-10.81	2.21	-41.38***	-32.42**	-74.54***	-52.49***
	(-2.15)	(-0.76)	(0.17)	(-3.23)	(-2.45)	(-3.90)	(-3.11)
Observations	122.00	122.00	122.00	122.00	122.00	122.00	122.00
R-squared	0.41	0.49	0.60	0.29	0.38	0.37	0.57

Panel B: Log Settler Mortality Rates

	(1)	(2)	(3)	(4)	(5)	(6)	(7)
Genetic Diversity	65.34*	45.75	30.93	114.85**	98.29*	132.14*	83.35
	(1.71)	(1.28)	(0.89)	(2.16)	(1.87)	(1.87)	(1.29)
Genetic Diversity Squared	-52.96*	-38.14	-27.57	-86.96**	-73.53*	-97.55*	-58.00
	(-1.85)	(-1.42)	(-1.05)	(-2.21)	(-1.89)	(-1.86)	(-1.20)
Log Settler Mortality Rate	-0.48***	-0.43***	-0.30***	-0.25***	-0.13	-0.67***	-0.31**
	(-5.24)	(-4.76)	(-3.26)	(-2.88)	(-1.62)	(-4.86)	(-2.20)
Economic Freedom (EFW)		0.17					
		(1.59)					
Legal Sys. (Area 2 of EFW)			0.26***				
			(3.67)				
Log of per capita GDP					0.25**		0.75***
					(2.13)		(4.56)
Intercept	-8.64	-3.57	0.85	-29.70	-27.52	-36.45	-30.00
	(-0.68)	(-0.30)	(0.08)	(-1.66)	(-1.58)	(-1.55)	(-1.42)
Observations	73.00	73.00	73.00	73.00	73.00	73.00	73.00
R-squared	0.61	0.62	0.68	0.26	0.29	0.35	0.48

Panel C: Current (Ancestry Adjusted) Genetic Diversity

	(1)	(2)	(3)	(4)	(5)	(6)	(7)
Current Genetic Diversity	604.49***	423.81***	203.65*	267.68**	18.07	790.26***	254.26*
	(5.14)	(3.15)	(1.82)	(2.56)	(0.17)	(4.33)	(1.81)
Current Gen. Div. Squared	-432.59***	-301.88***	-149.03*	-193.64**	-15.01	-559.05***	-175.47*
	(-5.21)	(-3.16)	(-1.87)	(-2.60)	(-0.20)	(-4.32)	(-1.74)
Economic Freedom (EFW)		0.67***					
		(4.85)					
Legal Sys. (Area 2 of EFW)			0.51***				
			(10.56)				
Log of per capita GDP					0.41***		0.89***
					(9.16)		(10.57)
Intercept	-201.36***	-143.75***	-62.68	-85.35**	-2.20	-273.41***	-94.86*
	(-4.84)	(-3.06)	(-1.61)	(-2.34)	(-0.06)	(-4.26)	(-1.95)
Observations	128.00	128.00	128.00	128.00	128.00	128.00	128.00
R-squared	0.15	0.39	0.53	0.08	0.34	0.12	0.51

Notes: Institutions and per capita GDP are measured in 2015. Robust t-statistics are in parentheses. * $p<0.1$ ** $p<0.05$ *** $p<0.01$. Colony × EDE is the interaction between a colonial dummy and Early Disease Environment.

Table 3.12: Economic institutions and per capita GDP. Instrumental variable analysis

Panel A: Second Stage Results (columns 1-4) and Falsification Tests (columns 5-6)

	(1)	(2)	(3)	(4)	(5)	(6)
	Log of 2015 Per Capita GDP (Columns 1-5)					EFW
Average EFW, 1985-2015	1.03***	0.03	0.53**	0.55**	0.63***	
	(5.86)	(0.06)	(2.24)	(2.31)	(6.55)	
Geographic Disadvantage		-0.78***	-0.35***	-0.34***	-0.37***	0.06
		(-3.10)	(-3.06)	(-2.61)	(-3.47)	(0.59)
Absolute Value of Latitude			0.02***	0.02***	0.02***	0.00
			(3.46)	(3.17)	(3.51)	(0.54)
Ethno Linguistic Fractionalization				0.03	0.27	-0.06
				(0.09)	(0.74)	(-0.19)
Migratory Distance					-0.06	0.15***
					(-1.24)	(2.67)
Migratory Distance Squared					0.00	-0.01**
					(1.53)	(-2.52)
Log of Per Capita GDP, 2015						0.54***
						(6.84)
Intercept	2.85**	9.09***	5.47***	5.34***	4.92***	0.49
	(2.52)	(3.08)	(3.86)	(3.78)	(8.47)	(0.70)
Observations	112	112	112	112	112	112
Adjusted R-squared	0.599	0.494	0.723	0.724	0.734	0.639
P-value (Hansen J-OIR Test)	0.772	0.941	0.181	0.103		
P-value (Kleibergen-Paap F)	0.000	0.118	0.009	0.006		

Notes: The instruments used are either the ancestry unadjusted predicted genetic diversity in linear and quadratic form or the migratory distance from Addis Ababa in linear and quadratic form. In both cases, the second stages are the same (panel A). The corresponding first stages are in panels B and C. Robust t statistics in parentheses. * p<0.1 ** p<0.05 *** p<0.01.

Table 3.12 – Continued

Panel B: First Stage Results using Predicted Genetic Diversity

	(1)	(2)	(3)	(4)
	Average EFW, 1985-2015			
Genetic Diversity	224.04***	104.74*	122.88**	117.79*
	(4.73)	(1.91)	(2.23)	(1.90)
Genetic Diversity Squared	-168.29***	-78.55*	-93.37**	-89.71*
	(-4.82)	(-1.93)	(-2.27)	(-1.95)
Geographic Disadvantage		-0.42***	-0.20**	-0.22*
		(-5.85)	(-2.34)	(-1.93)
Absolute Value of Latitude			0.02***	0.02***
			(3.78)	(3.56)
Ethno Linguistic Fractionalization				0.13
				(0.34)
Intercept	-67.42***	-28.26	-34.15*	-32.47
	(-4.24)	(-1.55)	(-1.86)	(-1.58)
Observations	112	112	112	112
Adj.R-squared	0.224	0.371	0.449	0.450
F-value (Excluded IVs, Angrist-Pischke)	17.410	2.181	4.897	5.389

Panel C: First Stage Results using Migratory Distance

	(1)	(2)	(3)	(4)
	Average EFW, 1985-2015			
Migratory Distance	0.31***	0.14**	0.18**	0.18**
	(5.32)	(2.02)	(2.54)	(2.26)
Migratory Distance Squared	-0.01***	-0.01*	-0.01**	-0.01*
	(-4.82)	(-1.93)	(-2.27)	(-1.95)
Geographic Disadvantage		-0.42***	-0.20**	-0.22*
		(-5.85)	(-2.34)	(-1.93)
Absolute Value of Latitude			0.02***	0.02***
			(3.78)	(3.56)
Ethno Linguistic Fractionalization				0.13
				(0.34)
Intercept	4.93***	5.63***	4.88***	4.82***
	(20.81)	(19.71)	(14.11)	(14.07)
Observations	112	112	112	112
Adj.R-squared	0.224	0.371	0.449	0.450
F-value (Excluded IVs, Angrist-Pischke)	17.410	2.181	4.897	5.389

Notes: Robust t statistics in parentheses. * $p<0.1$ ** $p<0.05$ *** $p<0.01$. The identification condition between migratory distance and predicted genetic diversity implies that the maximizing value of the likelihood in panels A and B is invariant to the choice between these two sets of instruments. In other words, the statistical information in panels A and B is the same and, therefore, the second stage results corresponding to migratory distance and predicted genetic diversity are identical.

Table 3.13: Migratory distance and observed genetic diversity for the 53 ethnic groups from the HGDP-CEPH Human Genome Diversity Cell Line Panel, as used by Ashraf and Galor (2013)

Rank	Ethnic-Group	Country	Migratory Distance	Observed Genetic Diversity	Region
1	Mbuti-Pygmy	Zaire	1.34	0.75	Africa
2	Bantu-Kenya	Kenya	1.34	0.76	Africa
3	Biaka-Pygmy	Central Afr. Rep.	2.38	0.76	Africa
4	Bedouin	Israel	2.84	0.74	Middle East
5	Druze	Israel	2.89	0.72	Middle East
6	Palestinian	Israel	2.89	0.74	Middle East
7	Yoruba	Nigeria	3.63	0.76	Africa
8	San	Namibia	3.87	0.74	Africa
9	Bantu-SW	Namibia	3.95	0.76	Africa
10	Adygei	Russia	4.16	0.73	Europe
11	Bantu-SE	South Africa	4.31	0.77	Africa
12	Mozabite	Algeria	4.42	0.74	Middle East
13	Tuscan	Italy	5.12	0.74	Europe
14	Italian	Italy	5.25	0.73	Europe
15	Sardinian	Italy	5.31	0.72	Europe
16	Mandenka	Senegal	5.47	0.76	Africa
17	Makrani	Pakistan	5.70	0.74	Asia
18	Balochi	Pakistan	5.84	0.73	Asia
19	Brahui	Pakistan	5.84	0.73	Asia
20	French	France	5.86	0.73	Europe
21	Russian	Russia	5.96	0.73	Europe
22	Basque	France	6.01	0.72	Europe
23	Hazara	Pakistan	6.13	0.73	Asia
24	Pathan	Pakistan	6.18	0.73	Asia
25	Sindhi	Pakistan	6.20	0.74	Asia
26	Kalash	Pakistan	6.25	0.70	Asia
27	Burusho	Pakistan	6.48	0.73	Asia
28	Orcadian	UK	6.64	0.73	Europe
29	Uygur	China	7.07	0.73	Asia
30	Xibo	China	7.11	0.71	Asia
31	Tu	China	8.87	0.71	Asia
32	Naxi	China	9.13	0.69	Asia
33	Lahu	China	9.30	0.68	Asia
34	Yi	China	9.33	0.71	Asia
35	Dai	China	9.34	0.70	Asia
36	Tujia	China	9.83	0.70	Asia
37	Han-NChina	China	9.85	0.71	Asia
38	Mongola	China	9.87	0.71	Asia
39	Miao	China	9.88	0.70	Asia
40	Yakut	Russia	9.92	0.70	(Siberia)
41	Han	China	10.12	0.71	Asia
42	Daur	China	10.21	0.71	Asia
43	Cambodian	Cambodia	10.26	0.71	Asia
44	Oroqen	China	10.29	0.69	Asia
45	She	China	10.82	0.69	Asia
46	Hezhen	China	10.90	0.70	Asia
47	Japanese	Japan	11.76	0.70	Asia
48	Papuan	Papua New Guinea	14.84	0.67	New
49	Melanesian	Papua New Guinea	16.17	0.66	New
50	Pima	Mexico	18.02	0.60	Americas
51	Maya	Mexico	19.83	0.67	Americas
52	Colombian	Colombia	22.66	0.60	Americas
53	Karitiana	Brazil	24.18	0.55	Americas

Table 3.14: The association between observed genetic diversity and migratory distance

The dependent variable in both panels is the observed genetic diversity

Panel A: Ethnic-group level regression

	(1) Whole Sample	(2) Whole Sample	(3) 1st Half of the Sample	(4) 1st Half of the Sample	(5) 2nd Half of the Sample	(6) 2nd Half of the Sample
Migratory Distance	-0.76***	-0.76***	-0.53***	-0.19	-0.81***	-0.81***
	(-17.58)	(-17.18)	(-3.17)	(-0.98)	(-10.88)	(-8.23)
Absolute Latitude		-0.00		-0.06***		0.00
		(-0.17)		(-2.80)		(0.03)
Intercept	77.43***	77.51***	76.28***	76.40***	78.15***	78.10***
	(189.62)	(120.71)	(93.97)	(106.05)	(83.19)	(42.01)
Observations	53.00	53.00	27.00	27.00	26.00	26.00
R-squared	0.86	0.86	0.29	0.46	0.83	0.83

Panel B: Country-level regression

	(1) Whole Sample	(2) Whole Sample	(3) 1st Half of the Sample	(4) 1st Half of the Sample	(5) 2nd Half of the Sample	(6) 2nd Half of the Sample
Migratory Distance	-0.80***	-0.81***	-0.66*	0.22	-0.90***	-0.95***
	(-17.65)	(-17.17)	(-2.24)	(0.50)	(-15.61)	(-14.44)
Absolute Latitude		-0.01		-0.08**		-0.04
		(-0.68)		(-2.35)		(-1.49)
Intercept	78.04***	78.40***	77.13***	75.70***	79.75***	81.48***
	(161.03)	(109.61)	(63.31)	(64.97)	(93.30)	(57.80)
Observations	21.00	21.00	11.00	11.00	10.00	10.00
R-squared	0.94	0.94	0.36	0.62	0.97	0.98

Note: t statistics in parentheses * p<0.1 ** p<0.05 *** p<0.01.

Table 3.15: Economic institutions and prosperity, an IV approach using ancestral migratory distance interacted with the continent

	(1)	(2)	(3)	(4)
	Log Per Capita GDP, 2015	Average EFW, 1985-2015	Average EFW, 1985-2015	Log Per Capita GDP, 2015
Average EFW, 1985-2015	0.86***			0.57***
	(4.66)			(6.08)
Geographic Disadvantage	-0.21	-0.24**	-0.05	-0.25**
	(-1.64)	(-2.32)	(-0.48)	(-2.22)
Absolute Value of Latitude	0.01**	0.01	-0.00	0.02***
	(2.54)	(1.45)	(-0.14)	(3.14)
Ethnolinguistic Fractionalization	-0.01	0.29	0.10	0.22
	(-0.04)	(0.76)	(0.29)	(0.60)
Migratory Distance × Asia		0.09*	0.05	0.02
		(1.95)	(1.55)	(0.78)
Migratory Distance × Europe		0.14*	0.09	0.02
		(1.83)	(1.56)	(0.26)
Migratory Distance × Africa		-0.01	0.02	-0.06
		(-0.13)	(0.34)	(-0.91)
Migratory Distance × Americas		0.03**	0.01	0.01
		(2.12)	(1.22)	(0.71)
Migratory Distance × Oceania		0.09***	0.06***	-0.00
		(3.66)	(4.14)	(-0.02)
Log Per Capita GDP, 2015			0.50***	
			(5.73)	
Intercept	3.54***	5.34***	1.29*	5.04***
	(3.18)	(17.24)	(1.70)	(8.34)
Observations	112	112	112	112
R-squared	0.704	0.495	0.640	0.738
p-value (Hansen OIR Test)	0.537			
F-stat (Joint Signif. of IVs)		4.437	5.210	0.965
P-value (F-stat)		0.001	0.000	0.443

Note: Robust t statistics in parentheses. * $p<0.1$ ** $p<0.05$ *** $p<0.01$.

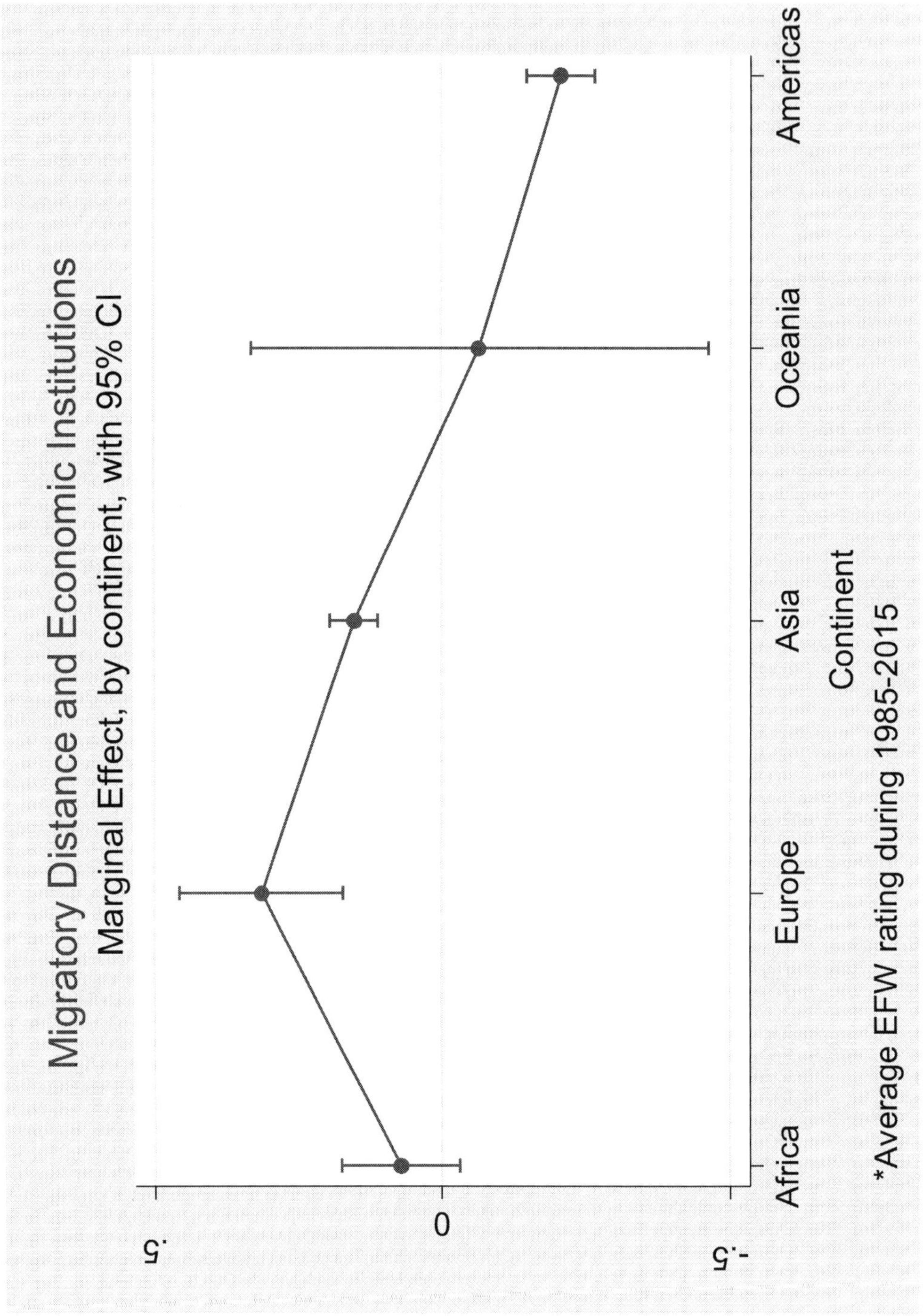

Figure 3.3: The average marginal effect of migratory distance on economic freedom, by continent

Table 3.16: The relationship between economic and political institutions. Granger causality tests

The dependent variables are the levels (columns 1-4) and 15-year changes of the institutional variable (cols 5-8)

The independent variables are 5-year lagged levels (cols. 1-4) and 5-year-lagged 15-year changes in the institutional variable (cols. 5-8)

	(1)	(2)	(3)	(4)	(5)	(6)	(7)	(8)
	Institutional Level				15-year change in Institutions			
	No Overlap		Overlapping Panels		No Overlap		Overlapping Panels	
(Regressors are 5-year lagged with respect to the dependent variable)	EFW(t)	Dem(t)	EFW(t)	Dem(t)	EFW(t)-EFW(t-15)	Dem(t)-Dem(t-15)	EFW(t)-EFW(t-15)	Dem(t)-Dem(t-15)
Democracy (t-5)	0.02***	0.84***	0.02***	0.81***				
	(3.62)	(30.55)	(7.42)	(42.12)				
EFW (t-5)	0.86***	0.20	0.80***	0.03				
	(32.99)	(1.36)	(48.33)	(0.25)				
Democracy(t-5)-Democracy(t-20)					0.04***	0.49***	0.04***	0.45***
					(2.99)	(6.46)	(5.07)	(8.59)
EFW(t-5)-EFW(t-20)					0.63***	-0.22	0.60***	-0.01
					(7.30)	(-0.70)	(12.82)	(-0.04)
Intercept	1.02***	-0.25	1.37***	1.25**	0.15*	1.26***	0.09	0.68**
	(6.62)	(-0.29)	(14.10)	(2.09)	(1.71)	(3.09)	(1.57)	(2.14)
Observations	325.00	325.00	753.00	752.00	202.00	202.00	409.00	408.00
R-squared	0.83	0.79	0.83	0.76	0.36	0.35	0.43	0.29
Does EFW Granger cause Democracy?		NO		NO		NO		NO
Does Democracy Granger cause EFW?	YES		YES		YES		YES	

Notes: Robust t statistics in parentheses. * p<0.1 ** p<0.05 *** p<0.01. Results strongly indicate that political institutions predate economic institutions. This table presents results using ordinary least squares. These results are robust to multiple estimation methods including panel vector autoregression (Abrigo and Love, 2016), seemingly unrelated regressions, three-stage least squares, Arellano-Bond dynamic panel data estimator, and the inclusion of fixed effects and year dummies.

CHAPTER 4

HUMAN CAPITAL AND ECONOMIC DEVELOPMENT

"The factors we have listed (innovation, economies of scale, education, capital accumulation, etc.) are not causes of growth; they are growth."
Douglas North.

4.1. Introduction

Human capital is an essential asset of any modern society. Well educated individuals generate ideas and make decisions that result in better technologies, more capital formation, and economic progress. An abundance of well-educated individuals implies high labor productivity and a greater ability to absorb advanced technology from developed countries. Human capital is also directly associated with social outcomes such as fertility rates, education of children, child mortality, and income distribution (Barro and Lee, 2010).

Human capital refers to the resources embedded in individuals. These include their health, education, talents, knowledge, experience, and cognitive skills. For many years, however, the economic profession has proxied human capital with literacy rates and measures of school attainment. See, for example, Blaug (1966), Mincer (1974), Heckman and Polachek (1974), Griliches (1977), Romer (1989), and Barro (1991).

Using school attainment as a proxy for human capital suffers from at least two fundamental shortcomings. First, heterogeneity in the quality of schooling leads to measurement error in this variable. One year of education in Singapore is not the same as one year of education in the Dominican Republic. In other words, schooling does not necessarily translate into learning. For example, the most recent World Bank learning report (World Bank 2018) documents that in Kenya, Tanzania, and Uganda, when grade 3 students were asked to read a sentence such as "The name of the dog is Puppy," three-quarters did not understand what it said. Similarly, "in rural India, just under three-quarters of students in grade 3 could not solve a two-digit subtraction such as 46 – 17, and by grade 5 half could still not do so."

Second, an essential part of human capital is built at home and has little to do with the educational attainment, either the years of schooling or enrollment rates. Following the works of Becker (1960) and Schultz (1961), the economic profession has recognized the importance of the "quality" aspect of human capital accumulation that occurs at home which is associated with increased spending of high-income families on their children. Due to the intangible and unobserved nature of this aspect of human capital, it is a challenge to quantify the full impact of human capital on economic development. With the recent application of large scale standardized international assessment projects, however, it is now possible to have a comparable, cross-country measure of learning outcomes and cognitive skills in fundamental areas such as mathematics, reading, science, and financial literacy.

The neoclassical model of Robert Solow considers human capital as one input in the aggregate production function. One strand of the literature of comparative economic development also sees human capital as a key driver of growth. For example, Glaeser et al. (2004) argue that during the colonization process, the colonizers did not bring with them just their institutions, but their human capital. They argue that differences in the initial endowment of human capital account for the divergent paths of the colonies.[24]

Human capital can also be considered an outcome (rather than input) of the development process. Douglas North argued that institutions are the fundamental cause of economic development and that the factors of production embodied in the Solow neoclassical model are only proximate (not fundamental) causes of growth. In other words, higher total factor productivity, more human capital, and more physical capital are not a valid explanation of the fundamental sources of prosperity but rather a redescription of prosperity. See North and Thomas (1973).

This chapter will explore the potential dual role of human capital for economic development. That is, the possibility that human capital can be simultaneously an input and output of the development process. If this is the case, the views of Glaeser and North outlined above would be complementary, leading to a positive feedback effect. The feedback would imply a virtuous cycle of economic development in which institutions lead to growth and expansion in human capital (consistent with North's views) and, in turn, human capital leads to more growth (consistent with Glaeser's views).

This chapter will also explore the impact of the quantity and quality of human capital on levels of per capita GDP. The "quantity" refers to measures of educational attainment such as the number of years of schooling and enrollment rates. The "quality" refers to measures of

[24] A similar argument is provided by Engerman and Sokoloff (2002, 2005).

actual learning or school achievement, such as the score on international assessment tests. In this case, it is convenient to explore not only the average achievement but the performance of the top students and its relationship with per capita GDP. Following Hanushek and Woessmann (2012), educational achievement is expected to trump attainment in explaining levels of per capita GDP.

Finally, this chapter will explore the determinants of educational achievement. Regardless of whether human capital is an input or output (or both) in the development process, understanding the determinants of learning is an important issue. This issue will be explored at the aggregate level and the individual level.

The rest of the chapter is organized as follows: The next section will describe the main data for the chapter with a focus on educational attainment. Section 4.3 will analyze the roles of school attainment on the levels of per capita GDP. Section 4.4 will focus on changes in school attainment and growth of per capita GDP. Section 4.5 will discuss the educational achievement data. Section 4.6 will discuss the determinants of learning at the aggregate and individual level, and section 4.7 will provide a summary of key points.

4.2. Educational Attainment Data

This section describes the main data and sources utilized in this chapter and uses the educational attainment data to answer the following questions: Can a society with high levels of human capital stagnate due to poor institutional quality? Conversely, what are the development prospects of countries with low education levels? Can a country with a poorly educated populace grow and develop if it gets the institutions right?

Table 4.1 presents a description and summary statistics of the main variables utilized in this chapter organized in six panels (A to F). The summary statistics are for the most recent year or period and include the number of observations, the sample means, standard deviation, minimum, and maximum.

Panels A, B, and C, of Table 4.1 show data from Barro and Lee (2013). There are 119 countries with available educational attainment data from the set of 135 countries for which the per capita GDP data exists continuously since 1970. The summary statistics for the Barro-Lee data are for this set of 119 countries in 2010, which is the most recent year in the Barro-Lee dataset.

Panel A of Table 4.1 shows the secondary school enrollment rate for the population aged 15-19, for the population over 25 years old, for the female population aged 15-19, and the 30-year average secondary school enrollment rate for the population over 25 years old. In 2010, the average enrollment rate for the population aged 15-19 was 63 percent, with a minimum of 10.6 percent (Liberia) and a maximum of 100 percent (Denmark).

Panel B of Table 4.1 presents the secondary school completion rate for the population aged 15-24, for the population over 25 years old, for the female population aged 15-24, and the 30-year average secondary school completion rate for the population over 25 years old. In 2010, the average school completion rate for the population aged 15-24 was 29.8 percent, with a minimum of 2.4 percent (the Republic of Congo) and a maximum of 72.2 percent (Mauritius).

Panel C of Table 4.1 displays the average years of schooling for the population aged 15-24, for the population over 25 years old, for the population aged 30-49, and the 30-year average secondary school completion rate for the population over 25 years old. In 2010, the years of schooling for the population aged 15-24 was 8.7 percent, with a minimum of 2.6 percent (Niger) and a maximum of 13.5 percent (Hong Kong, China).

Table 4.2 presents the average years of school attainment for the population over 25 years old in 1970, 1985, 2000, and 2010. Panel A of Table 4.2 shows the top 30 countries, and panel B shows the bottom 30 countries sorted according to the 1970 school attainment. The rank, among the 119 countries with data, is shown in parentheses. The last two columns of Table 4.2 show the 2015 per capita GDP (in 2011 PPP dollars) and the 2015 summary Economic Freedom of the World (EFW) rating.

While there is a clear upward tendency in the global school attainment, the persistence of the rankings is remarkable. For instance, the United States increased its ranking from 2nd in 1970 (with an average of 10.61 years of schooling) to 1st during 1985-2010 (with 13.42 years of schooling in 2010). No country in the sample of 119 countries moved up or down more than 40 ranking positions corresponding to about one-third of the sample. Among the top-30 group, panel A of Table 4.2 shows that whit the exception of Barbados, whose ranking moved from 10th in 1970 to 44th in 2010, no country increased or decreased its ranking by more than 21 positions. Among the bottom-30 group, panel B of Table 4.2 shows that Iran, Gabon, and Algeria showed the largest moves up in the rankings between 1970 and 2010, climbing up 38, 37, and 21 positions, respectively.

Panel A of Table 4.2 highlights in bold four former centrally planned countries: Hungary, Poland, Romania, and Bulgaria. These four countries enjoyed high levels of educational attainment back in 1970 but suffered from weak economic institutions under socialism. While their educational attainment did not change much and remained high during 1970-2010, their elevated human capital facilitated a more rapid adoption and assimilation of free-market reforms. By 2015, the summary EFW rating of these economies ranged from 7.19 to 7.71, and their per capita GDP ranged between $17,254 and $25,310. Two of these four economies, Romania and Bulgaria, are among the 20 fastest growing countries in the world during 2000-2015, with growth rates above 4 percent per year (Gwartney and Montesinos, 2018)[25]. Romania and Bulgaria, and the former socialist countries in general, are examples that a country can grow fast if it gets its institutions right, particularly if its population is educated[26].

Panel B of Table 4.2 highlights in bold four countries that are net fuel exporters: Algeria, Gabon, the Republic of Congo, and Iran. Among the bottom 30 group, three of these countries had the highest per capita 2015 GDP: Iran ($15,039), Gabon ($14,315), and Algeria ($13,024). These three countries also experienced the largest increases in educational attainment. Iran climbed up 38 positions, from 95th, corresponding to 1.17 years of schooling in 1970, to 57th, corresponding to 8.17 years of schooling in 2010. Similarly, Gabon climbed up 37 positions (from 102nd to 65th) and Algeria 21 (from 107th to 86th). These countries exemplify that fuel exports are an important factor driving up both the per capita GDP and the average educational attainment of the population.

The cases of Rwanda and Cambodia are also interesting. Their educational attainment did not improve much, but their institutions did. The average years of schooling (and ranking) in Rwanda was 0.69 (109th) in 1970 and 3.48 (110th) in 2010. The corresponding figure for Cambodia was 1.24 (93rd) in 1970 and 4.1 (103rd) in 2010. The 2015 summary EFW rating was 7.57 for Rwanda and 7.22 for Cambodia. Despite their low and stagnant educational attainment, the annual growth rate of per capita GDP of Rwanda and Cambodia during 2000-

[25] Gwartney and Montesinos (2018) provide a more extensive analysis of 25 former socialist economies after the collapse of the Soviet Union.

[26] Ireland and New Zealand, two countries with high educational attainment (see Table 4.2, panel A), also illustrate this point. Both countries adopted market reforms during 1984-1995 and experienced significant growth rates since 1985. The remote location of New Zealand partially explains its slightly slower growth rate relative to that of Ireland.

2015 was 5.21 percent and 5.84 percent, respectively. These two countries illustrate that it is possible to achieve high growth rates and start the development process with low educational attainment if the institutions are right.

However, no country in the sample was able to sustain low levels of education with increasing income per capita. This fact is consistent with the view that education is a normal good and a minimum level of income is necessary to afford the schooling. In the cases of Rwanda and Cambodia, their 2015 per capita GDP was still relatively low ($1,676 for Rwanda and $3,139 for Cambodia) to support high educational attainment. In the case of Botswana, however, its 2015 per capita GDP was $14,626 and its years of schooling increased from 1.34 (89th) in 1970 to 8.87 (49th), climbing up 40 positions, the largest increase in the sample.

In sum, the following key points are takeaways from the inspection of Table 4.2. First, countries can grow more rapidly if they have a highly educated population, and they also improve the quality of their economic institutions. Examples include New Zealand, Ireland, and the former socialist economies that undertook market reforms. Second, low-income countries can grow rapidly despite having low levels of educational attainment if their institutions are right. The cases of Rwanda and Cambodia are examples of this point. Finally, countries can increase their educational attainment more rapidly by increasing their per capita income first. This fact is consistent with the view that education is a normal good and an output of the development process. Examples are the oil-exporting countries and countries that have grown enough to achieve a minimum income, sufficiently above the subsistence level, such as Botswana. Consistent with this point, there are no cases of middle or high-income level countries that have grown substantially and whose educational attainment has declined or remained stagnant.

4.3 School Attainment and Levels of Per Capita GDP

This section will analyze the relationship between different measures of school attainment and income per capita. The goal is to first establish the correlation between the levels of school attainment and per capita GDP after possibly controlling for geography and economic institutions and then explore a causal relationship by updating the specification of Glaeser et al. (2004) with better data.

Table 4.3 examines this relation without controlling for economic institutions. The dependent variable is the natural logarithm of per capita GDP in 2015. The main independent variables are the secondary school enrollment rate in 2010 (column 1), the secondary school completion rate in 2010 (column 2), the mean years of schooling in 2010 (column 3), and the mean years of schooling during 1980-2010 (column 4). All the school attainment measures are for the population 25 years old or older. Columns 5 to 8 add the standardized geographic disadvantage index as a control variable.

All school attainment measures are positive and statistically significant at the 1 percent level. The t-ratios range from 7.66 (column 1) to 19.23 (column 3) and the r-squares range from 0.37 to 0.69, respectively. In column 3, the coefficient of 0.35 indicates that an additional year of schooling is associated with an average 42 percent increase in per capita GDP (0.42 = exp(0.35) – 1). After controlling for geography, all school attainment measures remain positive and significant at the 1 percent level, and the r-squares range from 0.58 (column 5) to 0.73 (column 7). The magnitude of the coefficients drops slightly, suggesting that the direct relationship between school attainment and the levels of per capita GDP is less strong and that part of it operates through geography. The coefficient of 0.27 in column 7 indicates that after controlling for geography, on average, one additional year of schooling is associated with a 31 percent increase in per capita GDP (0.31 = exp(0.27) – 1). The standardized geographic disadvantage index, as expected, is negative and significant in columns 5 to 8.

Table 4.4 explores the relationship between schooling and per capita income level after controlling for economic institutions. The measure used is the summary EFW rating, averaged over the years 1985-2015. Interestingly, all schooling variables remain positive and significant at the 1 percent level. As expected, the EFW summary rating is also positive and significant in all equations 1 to 8, and the standardized geographic disadvantage index is negative and significant in equations 5 to 8. The coefficient of 0.21 (column 7) indicates that after controlling for geography and economic institutions, one additional year of schooling is associated with an average increase of 23 percent in per capita GDP (0.23 = exp(0.21) – 1). The r-squared associated with this model is 79 percent.

Table 4.5 uses instrumental variable analysis. The identification strategy follows Glaeser et al. (2004). Using French legal origin as an instrument for years of schooling and settler mortality rate as an instrument for executive constraint, Glaeser et al. found that human capital mattered and that institutions were insignificant, leading them to conclude that the Europeans not only brought their institutions but also their human capital and it was the latter that cause development. However, settler mortality rates are not a good instrument for institutions, and executive constraints are not the best measure of institutions as it relates to economic development. Therefore, it would be interesting to update Glaeser's analysis using a larger sample of better quality data. Table 4.5 maintains legal origin as the instrument for educational attainment but uses the summary EFW rating as the measure of institutions. Following the analysis of chapter 3, the institutions are instrumented using migratory distance from East Africa interacted with continental dummies.

Panel A of Table 4.5 shows the second stage results in four columns which add successive control variables, one at a time: column 1, no additional controls; column 2 adds the standardized geographic disadvantage index; column 3 adds latitude, and column 4 adds ethnolinguistic fractionalization. As expected, economic freedom is positive and significant in all equations, indicating a direct causal channel linking economic institutions and the level of economic development. However, educational attainment is insignificant, reversing the argument provided by Glaeser et al. to one more supportive of economic institutions. These results remain robust if education in 1960 is an instrument and if the legal origin variable is used as a set of dummies for British, Germanic, and Scandinavian legal origin, instead of a single dummy for French legal origin. See Tables D.1 and D.2 of Appendix D for these results.

Panel B of Table 4.5 shows the first stages and falsification tests using the full set of controls as used in the last equation of Panel A. Column 1 shows the first stage for economic institutions while column 2 shows the first stage for years of schooling. Columns 3 to 6 show a series of falsification tests aimed to assess the validity and strength of the instruments.

Column 1 of Table 4.5 (panel B) shows that migratory distance interacted with continental dummies is significantly associated with economic institutions. Not only the individual coefficients are statistically significant, but the overall F-test for their joint significance is 4.38 with a p-value of virtually zero. However, French legal origin is also statistically significant, indicating that legal origin also affects economic institutions. Column 2 shows that the French legal origin dummy is significantly associated with the years of schooling with a t-value of 5.01 (and corresponding F-value of 25.11).

In panel B of Table 4.5, column 3 is like column 1 except that it adds per capita GDP as a control, and column 4 reverses the roles of economic institutions and per capita GDP. As expected, migratory distance interacted with the continental dummies is significant in column

3 (F-value of 4.44 and p-value of virtually 0) but not in column 4 (F-value of 0.59 and p-value of 0.71), indicating that its instrumental strength and validity could not be falsified. Columns 5 and 6 do the same thing with French legal origin. Column 5 is like column 2 except that it adds per capita GDP, and column 6 switches the roles of years of schooling and per capita GDP, making the latter the dependent variable. As expected, French legal origin is strongly associated with years of schooling, even after controlling for per capita GDP (column 5). However, it is only marginally significant with a p-value of 10 percent explaining per capita GDP after controlling for years of schooling (column 6). This last result hints at the invalidity of the French legal origin as an instrument (it barely passes the falsification test, at the margin).

Given the potential invalidity of French legal origin and the possibility of weak instruments, the overall results of table 4.5 need to be interpreted with caution. The main takeaway is that using a better measure of institutions than the one used by Glaeser et al. and using a larger sample, the results are indicative that economic institutions are indeed a crucial element for comparative economic development. The results do not necessarily invalidate the claim that the Europeans brought their human capital and that played a role in the divergent development paths. The high human capital of the settlers is consistent with institutions that protect property rights and that are generally consistent with economic freedom. But it is ultimately those institutions, and not the high human capital of those who enacted them, that led to the divergent comparative economic development paths.

4.4 Changes in School Attainment and Growth of Per Capita GDP

The previous section focused on the impact of levels of educational attainment on levels of per capita GDP. These results are interesting, but they reflect history in the sense that high-income countries historically developed educational systems supportive of higher enrollment rates. This section will focus on changes in educational attainment and subsequent growth rates of per capita GDP and vice-versa: growth rates and subsequent changes in educational attainment. Put another way, this section seeks to determine if there is a virtuous cycle of development that involves both human capital and growth of per capita GDP.

Table 4.6 explores if there is such a virtuous cycle. Two equations are estimated simultaneously: A growth equation (panel A) and a change in educational attainment equation (panel B). In panel A, the dependent variable is the growth rate of per capita GDP during periods of 15 years. In panel B, the dependent variable is the change in secondary school completion rate during the same periods of 15 years as in panel A.

Column 1 of Table 4.6 is for the period 1975-1990. The dependent variable in panel A is the annual growth rate of per capita GDP during 1975-1990, and in panel B it is the change in secondary school completion rate during the same period. The regressors in panel A are the initial (i.e., 1975) per capita GDP (in log form), the secondary school completion rate 15 years prior to the beginning of the period (i.e., 1960), and the change in secondary completion rate during the 15 years prior to the beginning of the period (i.e., during 1960-1975). The latter is the key variable of panel A. The regressors in panel B are the initial secondary school completion rate (i.e., 1975), the per capita GDP (in log form) 15 years prior to the beginning of the period (i.e., 1960), and the annual growth rate during the 15 years prior to the beginning of the period (i.e., during 1960-1975). The latter is the key variable of panel B.

In column 1 of Table 4.6, the change in the secondary school completion rate during 1960-1975 is positive and significant (with a t-ratio of 1.94) explaining the growth rate during 1975-1990 (panel A), and the growth rate during 1960-1975 is also positive and significant (with a t-ratio of 3.38) explaining the change in secondary completion rate during 1975-1990. The fact that positive changes in both variables are significantly associated with subsequent positive changes in the other variable is indicative of a virtuous cycle in which human capital is both an input and an output.

Column 2 of Table 4.6 is similar to column 1, except that the main period is 1995-2010. In column 2, the change in the secondary school completion rate during the 15 years before the period (i.e., during 1980-1995) is positive although not statistically significant (with a t-ratio of 1.43) explaining the growth rate during 1995-2010 (panel A). In turn, the growth rate during 1980-1995 is also positive but insignificant (with a t-ratio of 1.22) explaining the change in secondary completion rate during 1995-2010. Given the relatively smaller changes in secondary schooling during the most recent periods, the near-significant results could be an indication of low statistical power (or low capacity to correctly detect and reject a false null hypothesis). The negative and significant coefficients of initial per capita GDP in panel A and initial school attainment in panel B are indicative of conditional convergence. It is remarkable, however, that while there is evidence of conditional convergence in both panels, the coefficient of secondary school completion rate in 1980 is positive and significant explaining the growth rate during 1995-2010, and the coefficient of per capita GDP in 1980 is positive and significant explaining the changes in secondary school completion rates during 1995-2010. This result indicates that countries with higher income levels experienced larger subsequent increases in their educational attainment, and countries with higher levels of educational attainment also achieved higher subsequent rates of economic growth.

Column 3 of Table 4.6 exploits the panel structure of the data to increase statistical power. It includes the two periods of columns 1 and 2, and three additional intermediate periods: 1980-1995, 1985-2000, and 1990-2005. In panel A, the coefficient for the change in secondary school completion rate during the 15 years before each period is 0.05 (significant at the 1 percent level with a t-ratio of 4.11). This coefficient indicates that a 20 point increase in the secondary school completion rate in any 15 years is associated with an average growth rate increase of 1 percent per year during the subsequent 15 years. In panel B, the coefficient of 0.72 associated with the annual growth rate during the 15 years before each period is also positive and statistically significant at the 1 percent level with a t-ratio of 3.92. Overall, the results are consistent with a virtuous cycle in which growth rates lead to subsequent increases in educational attainment and, in turn, increases in educational attainment lead to subsequent increases in growth of per capita GDP.

An increase in educational attainment also increases the opportunity costs of having children. Therefore, it is possible that the positive effect observed in panel A (column 3) of changes in school attainment and subsequent growth rates is merely due to a change in the demographics. To account for this, column 4 adds demographics in panel A. Specifically, column 4 of Table 4.6 (panel A) adds the change in the share of the total population in the prime working-age 25-59 during the 15 years corresponding to the dependent variable. If the effect of education on growth is entirely through changes in the demographic variable, the relevant coefficient of education should be insignificant once the demographics are in the model. In column 4, the coefficient for the change in secondary school completion rate during the 15 years before each period is 0.02 (statistically significant with a t-ratio of 2.15). This is a substantial decline from 0.05 in the previous column, suggesting that part (but not all) of the effect in column 3 was due to a change in the demographic composition of the population that occurs as a result of the increasing schooling.

Similarly, it is possible that countries that experienced high increases in educational attainment and subsequent growth rates also experienced high levels and large increases in the quality of their institutions. To account for this, column 5 adds the summary EFW index (both level at the beginning of the period and change during the period). Because the EFW data are more reliable and complete starting in 1980, column 5 was estimated only for the four periods 1980-1995, 1985-2000, 1990-2005, and 1995-2010. The results indicate that after controlling for economic institutions (column 5), the coefficient for the change in the secondary school completion rate is larger (coefficient of 0.03) and more significant (t-ratio of 2.74) than when the economic institutions are omitted (column 4).

Taken together, the results of Table 4.6 are consistent with a virtuous cycle of education and growth. Changes in educational attainment lead to changes in subsequent growth and, in turn, changes in growth lead to subsequent changes in educational attainment. Besides, the coefficients for the levels are also consistent with the virtuous cycle. High-income countries tend to have higher subsequent increases in educational attainment and, in turn, countries with high educational attainment tend to have higher subsequent growth rates. The results hold after controlling for the demographic composition of the population and the quality of economic institutions. The results are also robust (and even stronger) using the educational attainment of the female population instead of the total population. See Table D.3 of Appendix D.

It is interesting to further analyze the impact of educational attainment on growth after additionally controlling for an extended set of covariates. In particular, variables such as fuel exports, the size of the country, a dummy for Middle Eastern oil-exporting countries, or having a war on the soil, certainly affect economic development. In turn, the impact of education on growth might change after these variables are added to the model. The following analysis will confirm (or eliminate) this possibility. In this regard, this analysis can be considered an extension of the last regression of panel A of Table 4.6 (column 5).

Table 4.7 further explores the relationship between educational attainment and growth. The dependent variable is the annual growth rate of per capita GDP during 15-year periods: 1985-2000 (columns 1 and 3), 2000-2015 (columns 2 and 4), and a panel analysis including the periods 1985-2000, 1990-2005, 1995-2010, and 2000-2015 (column 5). In the base model, columns 1 and 2, the independent variables include initial per capita GDP, measures of level and change of educational attainment and economic freedom, and the standardized geographic disadvantage index. The level of educational attainment is measured by the years of schooling for the population 25 years old or older, at the beginning of the period. The change in educational attainment is measured by the change in the secondary school completion rate for the population aged 15-24 during the 15 years before the beginning of the period. In the most comprehensive model, columns 3 to 5, the independent variables also include the initial population, the change in the share of the population in the prime working-age 25-59 category, the net fuel exports, a dummy for Middle Eastern oil-exporting countries, and a dummy for having a war on the soil.

In column 1 of Table 4.7, the dependent variable is the growth rate during 1985-2000. The coefficient for the change in the secondary school completion rate during 1970-1985 was 0.04, marginally significant at the 10 percent level with a t-ratio of 1.75. The standard deviation for this variable is close to 10 (9.79). This indicates that one standard deviation increase in the secondary school completion rate is associated with about half a percent additional annual growth rate during 1985-2000. Both level and change of the summary EFW rating are positive and statistically significant at the 1 percent level. As expected, the standardized geographic disadvantage index and the initial per capita GDP are negative and significant.

Column 2 of Table 4.7 shows the results when the dependent variable is the growth rate during 2000-2015. In this case, both level and change in educational attainment are positive and significant. The coefficient for the years of schooling in 2000 is 0.2, statistically significant with a t-ratio of 2.53. This indicates that an additional 5 years of education for the general population over age 25 in 2000 is associated with an additional 1 percent annual growth rate during 2000-2015. The coefficient for the change in the secondary school completion rate during 1985-2000 was 0.03. In this period, the standard deviation of this variable was 13.5, indicating that a one standard deviation increase in the secondary school completion rate during 1985-2000 was associated with about 0.4 percent increase in the annual growth rate of per capita GDP during 2000-2015. In this period, as expected, the change in the summary EFW rating is positive and statistically significant, and the initial per capita GDP is negative and significant, indicating the presence of conditional convergence.

Columns 3 and 4 present the most comprehensive model for the periods 1985-2000 and 2000-2015, respectively. In both cases, the initial per capita GDP is negative and statistically significant, indicating conditional convergence after controlling for institutions. In turn, the coefficients for the level of EFW at the beginning of the period and the change during the period are both positive and statistically significant, as expected. The change in the share of the population in the prime working-age 25-59 category is positive and significant in both periods, the initial population is positive and significant in the second period, and the dummies for Middle Eastern Oil exporter and having a war on soil are negative and significant in the second period. All the schooling variables are positive, as expected, with t-ratios above 1.2, but only the initial level in 2000 was statistically significant in equation 4. This pattern of positive coefficients for all schooling variables (both level and change) with t-ratios ranging between 1 and 3, is suggestive of low statistical power and potential multicollinearity. To mitigate those problems and increase efficiency in the estimation, column 5 estimates a single panel equation using seemingly unrelated regressions.

Column 5 estimates the most comprehensive model for the periods 1985-2000, 1990-2005, 1995-2010, and 2000-2015. In this model, both level and change in educational attainment are positive and statistically significant. The coefficient for the years of schooling at the beginning of each period was 0.16 (t-ratio = 3.72). The sample standard deviation for this variable was a little over 3. This indicates that an increase of 3 years of education is associated with an increase in the annual growth rate of per capita GDP during the subsequent 15 years of about half a percent ($0.48 = 0.16 \times 3$). The coefficient for the change in the secondary school completion rate during the 15 years before each period is 0.02 (t-ratio = 2.51). The standard deviation for this variable for the whole period is 10.21. This indicates that an increase in the secondary school completion rate of 10.21 percentage points is associated with an additional 0.2 percent annual growth rate during the subsequent 15 years. This number is not inconsequential. But perhaps more importantly, it says that after considering all the other variables in the model, including the demographic and institutional changes during the period, the early increases in secondary school completion rates still have a positive and statistically significant direct effect on growth rates. The total effect (including the indirect effect through the demographics and possibly the institutions and other channels) may be much larger.

All the other control variables in column 5 of Table 4.7 have the expected sign. The initial per capita GDP is negative and significant at the 1 percent level, indicating conditional convergence. Both the level and the change in the summary EFW rating were positive and highly statistically significant. The coefficient for the level of the summary EFW index was 0.93 (t-ratio = 7.46) and for the change during the period was 0.78 (t-ratio = 5.74). The coefficients for the standardized geographic disadvantage index, the dummy for Middle Eastern oil-exporting countries, and the dummy for having a war on the soil were all negative and statistically significant. The coefficients for the initial population and the change in the share of the population in the prime working-age 25-59 category during the period were positive and statistically significant. The r-square for this model was 42 percent.

In sum, the results of this section indicate that both levels and changes in school attainment have an impact on the subsequent growth rate of per capita GDP, even after accounting for economic institutions and demographic changes taking place during the period, and other potential confounders. This finding is consistent with the idea that human capital is a relevant input in the growth process. In turn, this section also provides evidence that growth rates lead to future increases, and higher subsequent levels, of school attainment. This finding is consistent with the view that education is a normal good, and it is an outcome of the development process. Overall, the evidence suggests that human capital serves a dual role as input and output in the growth process, contributing to a virtuous cycle of economic development.

4.5 Educational Achievement Data

The previous section focused on educational attainment, primarily because of the absence of a more accurate measure of human capital for a sizeable number of countries and periods. This, however, is beginning to change. With the large scale projects on educational assessment, comparable measures of learning are now available. The largest of such projects is the Programme for International Student Assessment (PISA), conducted by the Organization of Economic Co-operation and Development (OECD). The 2015 assessment (Pisa Dataset, 2015) covered 71 countries, the largest coverage for any international assessment project.

PISA is a triennial survey of 15-year-old students around the world. The goal of the survey is to assess "the extent to which 15-year-old students, near the end of their compulsory education, have acquired key knowledge and skills that are essential for full participation in modern societies." (PISA 2015). The assessment focuses on science, reading and mathematics, and how well students can extrapolate from what they have learned and can apply the knowledge in unfamiliar settings, both in and outside of school. In 2015, over half a million student completed the assessment, representing a population of about 29 million 15-year-olds in the participating countries.

Table 4.8 lists the 71 countries that participated in PISA in 2015 according to their average score. Panel A of Table 4.8 lists the top 35 countries and panel B lists the bottom 36 countries. Table 4.8 also provides the top 95 percentile score, aggregate proxies for the average family size, education of the parents, education of the population, the summary EFW rating (average during 1985-2015), and the per capita GDP in 2015. The average family size is proxied by the population under age 15 divided by the population in ages 30-49 (the adult age group most likely to have children in the under age 15 category). The average educational attainment of the parents is proxied by the years of schooling for the population in ages 30-49, and the educational attainment of the population is proxied by the years of schooling for the population 25 years old and older. The ranking of each variable, among the set of 71 countries, is provided in parentheses.

Panel A of Table 4.8 shows that the country with the highest 2015 average PISA score was Singapore with an average score of 551.6. Singapore also leads the list of countries with the highest scores, with a top 95 percentile score of 703.3. Singapore is the only country with an average score above 550 and a top 95 percentile score above 700. Following Singapore, Hong Kong had an average score of 532.6 and a top 95 percentile score of 662.9. In the bottom of the list is the Dominican Republic (panel B of Table 4.8) with an average score of 339.0 and a top 95 percentile of 469.8. The top 95 percentile score in the Dominican Republic was 81.8 points lower than the average score in Singapore. To complement Table 4.8, it is useful to see the summary statistics in panel D of Table 4.1. The average cross-country PISA score was 461.1, with a standard deviation of 50.8. This indicates that the average score in Singapore was about 1.8 standard deviations above the world average, while the average score in the Dominican Republic was about 2.4 standard deviations below the world average.

In Table 4.8, the high correlation between the average PISA score and the top 95 percentile is expected and almost evident by inspection (a correlation of 0.97). In turn, it is noticeable a correlation between the average PISA score and the other variables: family size (-0.53), education of the parents (0.67), education of the population (0.41), economic freedom (0.67), and per capita GDP (0.61). It is remarkable the high correlation between PISA scores and economic freedom. For example, the two countries (Hong Kong and Singapore) with the highest economic freedom ratings also have the highest average PISA scores. However, it is also remarkable the low correlation between PISA scores (a measure of educational achievement, or learning) and the measures of educational attainment of Barro-Lee previously used in this chapter. For example, the country with the highest educational attainment (the U.S.) is in the 30th position in terms of its educational achievement.

Table 4.9 examines the educational achievement and attainment as determinants of per capita GDP. The dependent variable is the log of per capita GDP in 2015. In column 1 of

Table 4.9, the independent variables are the average 2015 PISA score and average years of schooling during 1985-2010 for the population aged 25 and over. The former is significant at the 1 percent level, and the latter is insignificant. This indicates that once educational achievement is taken into consideration, educational attainment is insignificant. A remarkable aspect of this regression is that the scores were in 2015 for 15-year-olds that did not contribute to the 2015 GDP. Their parents contributed to both the country's GDP and their children's human capital. As a result, the 2015 scores of the 15-year-olds, which proxies the human capital of their parents, are a better predictor of the 2015 per capita GDP than the educational attainment of the general population. The r-square for this regression is 0.36.

Column 2 of Table 4.9 replaces the average PISA score by the top 95 percentile score. The pattern is similar to that of column 1: The PISA top 95 percentile achievement is positive and significantly associated with per capita GDP, while educational attainment of the population is insignificant. The r-square for this regression was 0.40, slightly higher than in column 1 when the average PISA score was employed, indicating that the top 95 percentile PISA score is an even better predictor of income than the average scores.

Columns 3 and 4 of Table 4.9 replace the educational attainment variable with economic institutions. The r-squares of these equations climbed up to 0.66 and 0.70. Both the summary EFW rating (average during 1985-2015) and PISA scores (both average and top 95 percentile) were statistically significant at the 1 percent level in both equations. The standardized coefficients for EFW are 0.43 in equation 3 and 0.42 in equation 4. The standardized coefficient for the average PISA score was 0.46 (column 3), and for the top 95 percentile was 0.51 (column 4). Therefore, on average, a one standard deviation increase in the average summary EFW rating, in the average PISA score, and the top 95 percentile PISA score, is associated with a respective increase in the 2015 per capita GDP of 75, 82, and 94 percent.[27]

The previous section showed evidence that educational attainment matters despite potentially large measurement error in the years of schooling variables or the enrollment and completion rates. The evidence suggested that educational attainment serves a dual role, both as an input and as an output of the development process. This section, in turn, showed evidence that learning (as measured by the educational achievement in the 2015 PISA scores) matters

[27] The 94 percent figure, for example, comes from the following calculation: The standard deviation of the dependent variable is about 1.3 (see Table 4.1) and the standardized coefficient for the 95 percentile score is 0.51. Therefore, a one standard deviation increase in the 95 percentile score is associated with an increase of $\exp(0.51\times1.3) - 1 = 94\%$.

even more, even after controlling for economic institutions. This is consistent with the idea that the PISA indirectly measures the human capital of the parents of the students who took the test with less measurement error than the educational attainment variables previously used in the literature. In other words, the PISA assessment is conducted for a representative sample of 15-year-old students who do not contribute to GDP, but they are indirectly providing a representative sample of the human capital of their parents. This evidence is in line with the findings of Hanushek and Woessman (2012) that cognitive skills in recent assessment tests outperform years of schooling in growth regressions.

This section also unveiled new evidence that the top 95 percentile performance in the PISA tests is even more strongly correlated with per capita GDP than the average PISA score. Following the rationale above, this would indirectly measure the human capital of the top 95 percentile of the parents, and perhaps even grandparents, across countries. It could be that the parents are entrepreneurs, academics, or highly motivated individuals who set up an environment for their children to thrive. The question of what determines the learning is of paramount importance in the future of comparative economic development. To next section will explore this question.

4.6 Determinants of Learning

This section will empirically test possible theoretical determinants of the PISA scores. Section 4.6.1 will perform an aggregate, country-level, analysis, and section 4.6.2 will perform an individual-level analysis.

4.6.1 Aggregate Analysis

Table 4.10 presents a country-level analysis of the determinants of learning, as measured by the average 2015 PISA score (columns 1, 3, and 5) and the top 95 percentile score (columns 2, 4, and 6). The scores are the average of the math, reading, and science scores. Disaggregated analyses by math, reading, and science are in Tables D.4., D.5., and D.6. of Appendix D.

The independent variables are the educational attainment of the parents, the family size, the income per capita, and the institutional economic environment during the lifetime of the student. A great deal of the learning, education, motivation, personality traits, aspirations, and other characteristics, occurs at home. Therefore, the educational attainment of the parents is a key element of the educational achievement of the students. The average educational attainment of the parents is measured, at the aggregate level, as the average years of schooling for the population aged 30-49 in 2010 (the latest year for which this variable is available). To understand why this age bracket in 2010, recall that the PISA students were 15-year olds in 2015. Consider parents giving birth around 2000 when they were between 20 and 39 years old. By 2010, they will be 30-49 years old. By 2015, the moment of the PISA test, they will be around 35-54 years old. The years of schooling for the population age 30-49 in 2010 has a mean of 8.5 years and a standard deviation of 3.3. See Table 4.1.

Consistent with the work of Gary Becker, and in the same spirit that a great deal of the learning occurs at home, family size is also a crucial determinant of human capital. Larger family sizes are expected to be associated with a large number of children and a reduced level of investment per child. This chapter uses the ratio of the total population under age 14 to the total population in ages 30-49 to proxy for the average family size at the aggregate level. The larger this ratio, the larger the number of kids per adult, and according to Becker's views, the smaller investment in human capital per child. Therefore, this variable is expected to have a negative coefficient.

The next two independent variables are the per capita GDP level in 2010, and the summary EFW rating averaged during 2000-2015, the lifespan of the students taking the PISA assessment test. These two variables are expected to be positively associated with student scores for different reasons. Per capita GDP, as a measure of wealth, proxies for the availability of educational resources that facilitate the learning process. The summary EFW rating, which measures the institutional economic environment, proxies for the motivation that the students have regarding their future career and earning prospects, as well as the expectation to keep what they will earn.

Column 1 of Table 4.10 includes the aggregate proxies for the education of the parents, family size, and per capita income in the model. As expected, the years of schooling for the population in ages 30-49 is positive and significant, and the family size is negative and significant. Both variables are statistically significant at the 1 percent level. The log of per capita GDP is positive but insignificant. This model explains 60 percent of the cross-country variation in the average PISA scores.

Column 2 of Table 4.10 uses the top 95 percentile score as the dependent variable. In this case, the r-square is 69 percent, indicating that the model explains more of the variation in the top scorers than the variation in the average PISA score. As in column 1, the years of schooling for the population 30-49 and the family size are both statistically significant at the 1 percent level, and their coefficients have the expected signs (positive for the former and negative for the latter). Again, per capita GDP is positive, but not statistically significant.

Columns 3 and 4 of Table 4.10 add the summary EFW rating, averaged annually during the period 2000-2015. In both cases, both EFW and the years of schooling variable are positive and significant, family size is negative and significant, and per capita GDP is insignificant. The r-squares are 0.65 in column 4 (average PISA score) and 0.71 in column 5 (top 95 percentile PISA score).

Finally, columns 5 and 6 remove per capita GDP from the model. As expected, economic freedom and years of schooling of the parents are both positive and significant, and the family size variable is negative and significant. All variables are statistically significant at the 1 percent level in this model, and the r-squares are 0.65 (column 5) and 0.70 (column 6).

The results of this analysis indicate that, at least at the aggregate level, there is evidence that there are at least three pillars for achievement: Parents (education of the parents), home (size of the family), and the environment (the institutional climate). Other variables that were analyzed and found to be insignificant after controlling for these three pillars, include the education of the grandparents, education of the population age 15-24, and education of the total population. These results are robust to a disaggregation of the scores by sub-areas of the test (reading, math, and science). The results for these sub-areas are in Appendix D. See Tables D.4 to D.6.

4.6.2 Individual-Level Analysis

One advantage of the PISA assessment test is the availability of individual-level data. This level of disaggregation opens a wider set of empirically testable hypotheses about the determinants of educational achievement. The student questionnaire employed in PISA 2015 provides additional key information. At the individual level, it is possible to obtain information about the student's parents, the home, and their teachers.

The main dependent variable in this section is the test score of the student.[28] Almost half a million (458,035) students took the test, and the average score was 462.7 with a standard deviation of 96.1. The minimum test score was 94.1, and the maximum was 802.6. See Table 4.1, panel F.

The main independent variables cover four dimensions: (1) Parent's relevant characteristics (education and wealth). (2) Home environment. (3) Student characteristics (4) Teacher/School characteristics. These four key dimensions alone explain about 30 percent of the variation in the 2015 PISA scores.

A natural and important parental determinant of the student's achievement is the parent's education. In this analysis, the variable PARED (Years of Education, Parents) refers to the highest number of years of education between the father and the mother of the student. This variable ranges from 3 to 18, with a mean of 13.2 and a standard deviation of 3.2.

The second important parental characteristic is family wealth. This variable is an index of the family wealth possessions (WEALTH) based on the specific items available at home. The WEALTH family index includes the following items: (1) A room of your own, (2) A link to the internet, (3) Televisions, (4) Cars, (5), Rooms with a bath or shower, (6) Cell phones with Internet access (e.g., smartphones), (7) Computers (desktop computer, portable laptop, or notebook), (8) Tablet computers (e.g. iPad®, BlackBerry®, PlayBook™), (9) E-book readers (e.g. KindleTM, Kobo, Bookeen), and (10) three country-specific wealth item. This index was computed by PISA using Item Response Theory and has a sample mean of -0.33 and a standard deviation of 1.28, ranging from -7.64 to 4.71. Higher values of this index indicate higher family wealth.

For the home environment, this analysis uses the number of books at home. A series of dummies capture the following seven categories: Between 0 and 10 books (20 percent of the sample), between 11 and 25 (20 percent), between 26 and 100 (28 percent), between 101 and 200 (15 percent), between 201 and 500 (11 percent), and more than 500 (6 percent). The omitted category is 0-10 books at home. Having books at home provides a stimulating intellectual environment. This environment encourages children to read more and sparks their intellectual curiosity. Therefore, this variable is expected to be a robust determinant of learning.

[28] Technically, because different individuals took different tests, PISA gives plausible values which are random samples of the conditional distribution of proficiency of the student obtained using Item Response Theory (IRT). See the PISA Technical Report (2015). The score for the student is obtained by averaging the plausible values for the three main sections: math, reading, and science.

For the student characteristics, this analysis uses the student grade level, and the students' expected occupational status at age 30. The grade level indicates the relative grade of the student for the country's modal grade i (value of 0). This variable ranges from -4 to +3, but most students are in the range ±1. A total of 70.95 percent of the students were in the modal grade (GRADE = 0). A total of 15.46 percent of students were 1 grade below the modal grade (GRADE = -1) while 8.76 percent were 1 grade above the modal grade (GRADE = +1). The remaining 4.83 percent of the students were outside the ±1 range.

In the student questionnaire, students were asked to write down their expected occupation at age 30 and a brief description of the job to which they aspire. The responses were coded according to the International Standard Classification of Occupations (ISCO) into four-digit codes, which were converted to the International Socio-Economic Index of occupational status (Ganzeboom et al., 1992; and Ganzeboom and Treiman, 2003). The resulting variable is the student's expected occupational status at age 30 (BSMJ, using the PISA nomenclature). This index ranges from 10 to 89, with higher values indicating a higher occupational status. The sample mean was 61.12, with a standard deviation of 17.54. See Table 4.1.

For the teacher/school characteristics, this analysis uses two main variables capturing the teacher instruction and the disciplinary climate. The teacher instruction is proxied by the teacher-directed science instruction (TDTEACH) variable. This variable captures how often the following things happen in the classroom: (1) The teacher explains scientific ideas, (2) A whole class discussion takes place with the teacher, (3) The teacher discusses the questions of the students, and (4) The teacher demonstrates an idea. The answers to those questions were added and standardized in the index of teacher-directed instruction (TDTEACH). Higher values of this index indicate a higher involvement and commitment of the teacher to explain ideas, discuss concepts with the students, and clarify their questions.

The disciplinary climate variable is measured by the disciplinary climate in science classes index (DISCLISC). This index measures the extent to which the following things happen in the classroom: (1) Students do not listen to what the teacher says, (2) there is noise and disorder, (3) the teacher has to wait a long time for students to quiet down, (4) students cannot work well, and (5) students do not start working for a long time after the lesson begins. The answers to those questions were added and standardized in an index of disciplinary climate (DISCLISC). Higher values of this index indicate a more peaceful and disciplined classroom.

Table 4.11 presents an individual-level analysis using this information. The dependent variable is the PISA score. Column 1 presents the results using the independent variables described above, except the two teachings variables, which are included in column 3. Columns 2 and 4 are like columns 1 and 3, but they restrict the sample to students having a grade level of GRADE = -1, 0 (modal), +1. That is, columns 2 and 4 exclude students with grade level below -1 or above +1 who could be potential outliers. The r-squares for the four models in columns 1 to 4 are 0.29, 0.25, 0.30, and 0.26, respectively.

As expected, all independent variables in Table 4.11 have coefficients that are positive and highly statistically significant in all models (columns 1 to 4). The years of education of the parents (highest of the two parents) has a coefficient ranging from 1.69 (t = 36.07) in column 1 and 1.91 (t=36.80). The standard deviation (S.D.) of this variable is about 3.2. Therefore, a one standard deviation increase in the years of schooling of the parents (about 3.2 years) is associated with an estimated score increase ranging from 5.4 (column 1) to 6.1 (column 4).

The wealth variable has a coefficient that is larger in magnitude and even more statistically significant than the parents' education. The coefficients range from a minimum of 7.47 (t = 61.29) in column 2 to a maximum of 8.39 (t = 67.10) in column 3. The standard deviation of this variable is about 1.28. This indicates that a one standard deviation increase in the wealth of the student's family is associated with a score increase ranging between 9.56 (column 2) and 10.74 (column 3).

The number of books at home is one of the most relevant variables in the model, both in terms of the magnitude, partial explanatory power, and statistical significance. For example, in column 1, students who reported having between 201 and 500 books at home had an average score 93.98 points higher than those who had between 0 and ten books at home (omitted category), after controlling for the other variables. The t-ratio for this variable was 175.97 (and it was even higher in columns 3 and 4). Considering the standard deviation of this dummy variable (of about 0.31), the standardized coefficient of this variable is about three times larger in magnitude than the wealth variable and about six times larger than the years of education of the parents. This indicates that the intellectual environment at home, as measured by the number of books, is the most important variable explaining the educational achievement of the students taking the PISA assessment.

The next variable is the grade level, which is considered a control variable in this model. It is expected that students above (below) the modal grade will perform better (worse) than those in the country modal grade for the age of the student. The coefficient of this variable ranges from 29.21 (t = 144.86) in column 1 to 21.64 (t = 73.39) in column 4. As expected, the coefficient and magnitude of this variable drops in columns 2 and 4 when the sample is restricted to students with grade levels ranging between -1 and +1. However, the coefficients and significance of the other variables remain qualitatively similar after holding the grade level constant or restricting the sample to the three central grade levels.

The next relevant student variable is the expected occupational status at age 30. The coefficients of this variable range from 0.75 (t=9510) in column 2 to 0.63 (t=77.55) in column 3. The standard deviation for this variable is about 17.54. Therefore, a one standard deviation increase in this variable is associated with a score increase of between 13.16 points (column 2) and 11.05 points (column 3). Following the books at home, this variable is the second most significant and largest in magnitude variable explaining the PISA scores.

The final two variables relate to the teacher-directed instruction and disciplinary climate in the classroom. These two variables have a mean of zero and a standard deviation of one, so the interpretation of the magnitude is straightforward. The teacher-directed instruction variable has coefficients of 3.87 (t=27.46) in column 3 and 3.85 (t=26.65) in column 4. In turn, the disciplinary climate variable has coefficients of 10.79 (t=73.37) in column 3 and 10.74 (t=71.47) in column 4. This indicates that both of these teaching variables matter, but the classroom/school disciplinary climate is about three times more relevant for the PISA scores, and it is almost as relevant as the wealth of the parents.[29]

Taken together, the results of Table 4.11 indicate that many factors play an important role in the performance of the students. The evidence suggests that the home factors are of paramount importance, followed by the students expected occupational status 15 years down the road, the order/discipline climate in the classroom, and the wealth and education of the parents.

Of course, many other variables could also significantly affect the PISA scores, including the family size, the number of siblings, the marital status of the parents, the education of the grandparents, involvement in school activities, as well as regional or country-level variables such as the institutional environment. The data for most of these variables at the

[29] The disciplinary environment was originally envisioned as a variable referring to science classes. However, this variable proxies for the environment in other classes as well. This variable performs equally well when the dependent variable is the PISA score in the sub-areas of reading, math, and science.

individual level are unavailable or not comparable. However, data at the aggregate level could be utilized to approximate the average effect of these factors. The next table explores this possibility.

Table 4.12 starts with the individual-level specifications of columns 1 and 3 of Table 4.11 and adds some country-level measures, one at a time. The following three country-level measures are added: (1) The average family size as proxied by the total population under age 15 divided by the total population in ages 30-49, (2) The educational attainment of the grandparents as proxied by the average years of schooling for the population aged 30-49 in 1980, and (3) The strong democracy variable constructed in the previous chapter as a measure of a strong and stable democratic institutional environment.

Column 1 of Table 4.12 is the base specification. This column includes only individual-level variables and no country-level variables. This specification is identical to column 1 of Table 4.11 except that the sample is restricted to the 325,890 observations for which data are available in the following columns 2, 3, and 4. All the variables in column 1 are positive and highly statistically significant as they were in Table 4.11. The relative magnitude of the coefficients remains the same.

Column 2 of Table 4.12 adds the family size variable. As expected, the coefficient for this variable is negative (-38.81) and highly statistically significant (t-ratio = -59.62). The standard deviation for this variable is 0.22 (see Table 4.1). Therefore, a one standard deviation decrease in the family size is associated with an average increase in the PISA score of 8.54 points.

Column 3 of Table 4.12 adds a proxy for the educational attainment of the grandparents. As expected, the years of schooling for the population in ages 30-49 in 1980 is positive and highly statistically significant, with a coefficient of 7.33 and a t-ratio of 142.67. This variable has a standard deviation of about 2.83 (see Table 4.1). Therefore, a one standard deviation increase in the years of education of the grandparents (about 2.83 years) is associated with an average increase of 20.74 points in the PISA score of the grandchildren. This result suggests that the effect of the educational attainment of the grandparents is more than twice as large as the comparable effect of the family size.

Column 4 of Table 4.12 adds the strong democracy variable as a measure of democratic institutional quality. The coefficient for this variable is 22.59 (t-ratio = 56.57). The standard deviation for this variable is 0.45 (see Table 4.1). Therefore, the corresponding standardized coefficient for this variable is 10.16, which is slightly larger than the coefficient for family size but about half the magnitude of the coefficient associated with the education of the grandparents. The r-square of this model, which includes the three country-level aggregate measures, is 37 percent.

Columns 5 to 8 are like columns 1 to 4, except that the two standardized teaching variables (teacher-directed instruction and disciplinary climate) are included. All the variables in these models are highly statistically significant and have their expected signs. The r-square is 0.33 in models 5 and 6, 0.37 in model 7, and 0.38 in model 8. Note the significant increase in the r-square from model 6 (0.33) to model 7 (0.37) in which the educational attainment of the grandparents is included.

Overall, table 4.12 extends the individual-level analysis by adding variables that are aggregate in nature (such as the strong democracy variable) and by proxying variables for which data are unavailable at the individual level but which averages can be calculated at the aggregate level (such as the family size and the education of the grandparents). The explanatory power of the regressions increased substantially, reaching almost 40 percent, which is remarkably large for individual-level regressions. Moreover, Table 4.12 allows testing important hypotheses and their relative merits as determinants of learning. The evidence suggests that the education of the grandparents, the home environment, the motivation of the students, and the climate at school, as well as the wealth and education of the grandparents, are all factors of paramount importance as determinants of learning.

4.7 Summary and Conclusions

This chapter examined the relationship between human capital and economic development. The primary focus was to provide insight regarding the extent to which countries can grow and prosper by having a well educated population. The major findings are the following:

Countries can grow more rapidly if they have a highly educated population and they improve the quality of their economic institutions. The cases of New Zealand, Ireland, and the former Soviet economies that adopted market reforms illustrate this point.

Low-income countries can grow rapidly despite having low levels of educational attainment if their institutions are compatible with economic freedom. The cases of Rwanda and Cambodia are examples of this point.

Countries can increase their educational attainment more rapidly when their per capita income is increasing. Education, therefore, is found to be a normal good and an output of the development process. Examples are the oil-exporting countries and countries that have grown enough to achieve a per capita income well above the subsistence level, such as Botswana. There are no cases of middle or high-income level countries that have grown substantially and whose educational attainment has declined or remained stagnant.

On average, educational attainment is significantly associated with higher levels of per capita GDP even after controlling for economic institutions and geography. Depending on the specification, a unit increase in the 2010 mean years of schooling in the adult population of a country is associated with 23 percent to 31 percent higher 2015 per capita GDP. See Tables 3 to 5.

An instrumental variable analysis for human capital was performed following the identification strategy of Glaeser et al. (2004). Using a better measure of institutions (economic freedom) than the one used by Glaeser et al. and using a larger sample, the results suggest that economic institutions are indeed a more fundamental cause of comparative economic development than educational attainment.

Analysis of the changes in educational attainment and growth indicates that these two factors contribute to a virtuous cycle of economic development. Both levels and changes in school attainment have an impact on the subsequent growth of per capita income, even after accounting for economic institutions and demographic changes during the period, and other potential confounders. In turn, growth rates of per capita GDP lead to future increases, and higher subsequent levels, of school attainment. This implies that human capital serves a dual role, as input and output, in the growth process.

Even though educational attainment matters for growth, it is a poor measure of human capital. The PISA scores provide a more accurate measure of human capital than educational attainment. Therefore, the learning outcomes nearly always outperform the educational attainment in regressions where the dependent variable is per capita income or other indicators of development. This is consistent with previous evidence provided by Hanushek and Woesmann (2012). This chapter also finds that the top 95 percentile scores outperform the average achievement score in nearly all income regressions.

Aggregate level analysis indicates that the years of schooling of the parents, the family size, and economic freedom, are all important determinants of learning. These variables explain 65 percent of the variation in the cross-country average PISA scores, and 70 percent of the variation in the top 95 percentile scores. See Table 4.9.

Individual-level analysis indicates that the home intellectual environment as measured by the number of books at home is one of the most important single variables explaining learning at school. Other key explanatory variables included the grade level, the expected occupational status of the student at age 30, the wealth and education of the parents, and the climate of teaching at school. These variables explained about 30 percent of the variation in the individual scores, using over 300,000 observations. See Table 4.11.

The individual-level analysis can be enhanced and complemented by using aggregate measures such as the institutional environment, and proxies for the average family size and the education of the grandparents. These additional variables increased the model's explanatory power of individual PISA scores to about 40 percent. See Table 4.12.

Table 4.1: Description of the variables, and summary statistics for the most recent year or period

Variable Description	Obs	Mean	SD	Min	Max
Panel A: School Enrollment Variables. Source: Barro and Lee (2013)					
Secondary School Enrollment Rate, Population in Ages 25 to 99	119	39.2	18.8	3.1	86.5
Secondary School Enrollment Rate, Population in Ages 15 to 19	119	63.0	26.4	10.6	100.0
Sec. School Enrollment Rate, Female Pop. in Ages 15 to 19	119	63.6	26.6	9.7	100.0
30-Year Average Sec. School Enrollment Rate, Pop. Age 25+	119	28.3	15.8	1.8	65.3
Panel B: School Completion Variables. Source: Barro and Lee (2013)					
Secondary School Completion Rate, Population in Ages 25 to 99	119	23.2	13.7	1.2	60.4
Secondary School Completion Rate, Population in Ages 15 to 24	119	29.8	16.5	2.4	72.2
Sec. School Completion Rate, Female Pop. in Ages 15 to 24	119	30.7	17.1	1.2	75.7
30-Year Average Sec. School Completion Rate, Pop. Age 25+	119	15.4	10.6	0.8	52.2
Panel C: Average Years of Schooling Variables. Source: Barro and Lee (2013)					
Average Years of Schooling, Total Population, Age 25+	119	7.8	3.0	1.2	13.4
Average Years of Schooling, Population in Ages 15 to 24	119	8.7	2.4	2.6	13.5
Average Years of Schooling, Population in Ages 30 to 49	119	8.5	3.3	1.4	13.7
30-Year Average Years of Schooling, Population Age 25+	119	6.0	2.8	0.8	12.5
Panel D: Learning (Achievement Variables). Source: Programme for International Student Assessment (PISA)					
Average PISA Score, 2015	71	461.1	50.8	339	552
Average PISA Reading Score, 2015	71	459.4	51.0	346.5	535.1
Average PISA Science Score, 2015	71	464.2	49.1	331.6	555.6
Average PISA Math Score, 2015	71	459.6	54.2	327.7	564.2
Top 95 percentile PISA Score, 2015	71	608.1	54.1	469.8	703
Top 95 Percentile PISA Reading Score, 2015	71	609.1	52.3	471.1	686.5
Top 95 percentile PISA Science Score, 2015	71	611.4	56.3	460.8	712.5
Top 95 percentile PISA Math Score, 2015	71	603.8	56.4	445.8	710.8

Table 4.1 – Continued

Description of the variables, and summary statistics for the most recent year or period

Variable Description	Obs	Mean	SD	Min	Max
Panel E: Other Country-Level Variables. Various Sources (Previous Chapters)					
30-Year Average EFW Summary Rating	106	6.3	1.0	4.3	8.9
Standardized Geographic Disadvantaged Index	119	0.0	1.0	-1.7	2.7
Absolute Value of Latitude	119	25.1	16.7	1.0	65.0
Ethnolinguistic Fractionalization	119	0.3	0.3	0.0	0.9
French Legal Origin (Source: Glaeser et al. 2004)	116	0.5	0.5	0.0	1.0
Migratory Distance from Addis Ababa (Thousands of Km)	119	9.5	7.4	1.2	26.8
Log Per Capita GDP in 2011 PPP dollars	119	9.3	1.3	6.4	11.8
Annual Growth Rate of Per Capita GDP	119	2.5	2.1	-3.1	8.6
Share of Pop. in the Prime Working-Age 25-59 Category	118	0.4	0.1	0.3	0.7
15-Year Change in the Share of Pop. in the Prime Age Group	119	4.7	4.7	-4.9	20.2
Panel F: Individual-Level Variables. Source: Programme for International Student Assessment (PISA), 71 countries covered in 2015.					
PVPisa (Pisa Avg. Score: Reading, Math, and Science)	458,035	462.7	96.1	94.1	802.6
PARED (Years of Education, Parents)	439,361	13.40	3.20	3	18
WEALTH	442,735	-0.33	1.28	-7.64	4.71
Number of Books at Home (Between 0 and 10)	440,645	0.20	0.40	0	1
Number of Books at Home (Between 11 and 25)	440,645	0.20	0.40	0	1
Number of Books at Home (Between 26-100)	440,645	0.28	0.45	0	1
Number of Books at Home (Between 101-200)	440,645	0.15	0.35	0	1
Number of Books at Home (Between 201-500)	440,645	0.11	0.31	0	1
Number of Books at Home (More than 500)	440,645	0.06	0.24	0	1
GRADE	456,484	-0.17	0.70	-4	3
Students' Expected Occupational Status at Age 30 (BSMJ)	365,021	61.12	17.54	10	89
Teacher-Directed Instruction (TDTEACH)	380,503	0.04	1.01	-2.45	2.08
Disciplinary Climate (DISCLISC)	392,560	0.02	0.98	-2.42	1.88
Average Family Size (Population 00-14 / Population 30-49)	458,162	0.64	0.22	0.25	3.13
Years of Schooling, Population Age 30-49, in 1980	437,267	7.18	2.83	0.01	12.66
Strong Democracy, 2000-2015	441,195	0.64	0.45	0	1

Table 4.2: Average years of school attained, population over 25, and economic development

Panel A: Top 30 countries according to the years of schooling in 1970.

Country	Years of Schooling, Pop. 25+ (Rank in parentheses) 1970	1985	2000	2010	Per Capita GDP 2015	EFW Summary Rating 2015
New Zealand	10.69 (1)	11.52 (2)	11.6 (3)	11.3 (19)	33,445	8.48
United States	10.61 (2)	12.14 (1)	12.93 (1)	13.42 (1)	52,591	7.94
Switzerland	9.76 (3)	10.37 (5)	10.29 (16)	13.42 (2)	61,476	8.36
Australia	9.35 (4)	11.02 (3)	11.26 (5)	11.77 (12)	44,336	8.00
Canada	8.66 (5)	9.83 (8)	10.98 (9)	12.56 (5)	42,844	7.92
Norway	8.27 (6)	9.67 (9)	11.21 (7)	11.8 (11)	76,305	7.62
Israel	8.27 (7)	10.41 (4)	11.8 (2)	12.76 (3)	31,729	7.45
Netherlands	8.03 (8)	9.91 (7)	10.98 (8)	11.6 (13)	48,463	7.73
Sweden	7.96 (9)	10.05 (6)	11.42 (4)	11.89 (10)	43,464	7.64
Barbados	7.83 (10)	7.35 (29)	8.68 (38)	9.32 (44)	10,030	6.51
Hungary	**7.82 (11)**	**8.81 (12)**	**11.24 (6)**	**12.14 (8)**	**23,539**	**7.19**
Germany	7.71 (12)	7.55 (25)	10.51 (14)	12.69 (4)	46,426	7.67
Austria	7.63 (13)	8.41 (15)	9.04 (32)	9.89 (34)	44,845	7.62
United Kingdom	7.54 (14)	8.39 (17)	9.86 (20)	12.32 (6)	38,749	8.02
Belize	7.22 (15)	7.35 (28)	10.1 (18)	11.59 (14)	8,157	6.81
Belgium	7.19 (16)	8.58 (13)	10.2 (17)	10.78 (24)	39,531	7.42
Japan	7.08 (17)	9.25 (10)	10.73 (12)	11.52 (16)	36,030	7.46
Ireland	7.01 (18)	9.25 (11)	10.84 (10)	12.2 (7)	53,372	8.25
Poland	**6.94 (19)**	**8.28 (18)**	**10.42 (15)**	**11.42 (18)**	**25,310**	**7.37**
Iceland	6.51 (20)	7.96 (22)	9.45 (26)	10.59 (28)	40,572	7.25
Romania	**6.05 (21)**	**8.41 (16)**	**10.02 (19)**	**10.81 (23)**	**20,549**	**7.71**
Greece	6.04 (22)	7.27 (32)	8.57 (41)	10.26 (32)	24,545	6.43
Argentina	5.92 (23)	7.45 (27)	8.55 (42)	9.48 (42)	19,316	4.98
Luxembourg	5.85 (24)	8.58 (14)	9.68 (21)	11.22 (20)	67,804	7.62
Chile	5.8 (25)	7.23 (33)	8.75 (37)	9.71 (38)	21,340	7.77
Denmark	5.79 (26)	8.02 (21)	10.73 (11)	11.53 (15)	44,939	7.74
Trinidad and Tobago	5.7 (27)	7.54 (26)	9.17 (31)	10.37 (29)	30,892	6.49
Bulgaria	**5.5 (28)**	**8.17 (19)**	**9.35 (27)**	**11.45 (17)**	**17,254**	**7.40**
Finland	5.4 (29)	7.33 (30)	9.32 (29)	10.21 (33)	37,920	7.67
Sri Lanka	5.33 (30)	6.93 (34)	9.65 (23)	9.76 (36)	10,734	6.63

Note: The ranking is based on the 119 countries with available educational attainment data from the set of 135 countries in the main sample.

Table 4.2 – Continued

Panel B: Bottom 30 countries according to the years of schooling in 1970.

Country	Years of Schooling, Pop. 25+ (Rank in parentheses) 1970	1985	2000	2010	Per Capita GDP 2015	EFW Summary Rating 2015
Pakistan	1.31 (90)	2.09 (103)	3.27 (102)	4.45 (97)	5,056	5.91
Cameroon	1.29 (91)	2.79 (90)	4.84 (85)	5.96 (87)	2,754	5.82
India	1.24 (92)	2.39 (97)	4.41 (92)	5.39 (92)	5,639	6.61
Cambodia	1.24 (93)	2.52 (93)	3.22 (105)	4.1 (103)	3,139	7.22
Malawi	1.2 (94)	2.08 (104)	3.05 (107)	4.29 (100)	960	5.77
Iran	**1.17 (95)**	**3.21 (86)**	**6.22 (66)**	**8.17 (57)**	**15,039**	**5.39**
Bangladesh	1.16 (96)	2.4 (96)	3.69 (99)	4.91 (94)	3,068	6.35
Rep. of Congo	**1.15 (97)**	**3.24 (84)**	**5.44 (79)**	**5.67 (88)**	**4,526**	**4.82**
Myanmar	1.12 (98)	2.26 (101)	3.1 (106)	4.09 (104)	5,834	5.32
Uganda	1.05 (99)	2.27 (100)	3.86 (95)	5.42 (91)	1,883	7.33
Egypt	1.03 (100)	2.97 (89)	4.75 (88)	6.55 (80)	11,236	5.76
Tunisia	1 (101)	2.62 (92)	4.9 (84)	6.58 (78)	10,608	6.32
Gabon	**1 (102)**	**3.25 (83)**	**6.15 (68)**	**7.57 (65)**	**14,315**	**5.81**
Liberia	0.99 (103)	2.03 (105)	3.46 (100)	4.09 (105)	798	6.87
Haiti	0.9 (104)	2.2 (102)	3.75 (97)	4.74 (95)	1,649	6.57
Mozambique	0.88 (105)	0.83 (117)	0.91 (119)	1.24 (119)	1,277	5.60
D.R. of the Congo	0.82 (106)	1.65 (108)	3.29 (101)	3.61 (108)	836	5.78
Algeria	**0.78 (107)**	**2.51 (95)**	**4.84 (86)**	**5.98 (86)**	**13,024**	**4.83**
Côte d'Ivoire	0.76 (108)	1.69 (107)	3.25 (104)	4.22 (102)	3,473	5.93
Rwanda	0.69 (109)	1.51 (110)	2.27 (113)	3.48 (110)	1,676	7.57
Burundi	0.67 (110)	1.32 (112)	1.84 (116)	2.68 (115)	723	5.89
Benin	0.63 (111)	1.09 (115)	2.57 (110)	3.3 (112)	2,141	5.78
Sierra Leone	0.58 (112)	1.25 (113)	2.3 (112)	3.06 (113)	1,033	5.78
Central African Republic	0.57 (113)	1.49 (111)	2.86 (109)	3.57 (109)	605	4.61
Morocco	0.57 (114)	1.62 (109)	3.26 (103)	4.24 (101)	7,577	6.33
Togo	0.48 (115)	2.37 (98)	3.98 (93)	4.33 (98)	1,482	5.66
Gambia	0.43 (116)	0.95 (116)	1.99 (114)	2.82 (114)	1,948	7.24
Niger	0.41 (117)	0.55 (118)	1.1 (117)	1.45 (118)	895	5.71
Nepal	0.25 (118)	1.24 (114)	2.37 (111)	3.31 (111)	2,607	6.50
Mali	0.2 (119)	0.54 (119)	1.01 (118)	1.5 (117)	1,563	5.81

The ranking is based on the 119 countries with available educational attainment data from the set of 135 countries in the main sample

Table 4.3: Measures of school attainment and level of per capita GDP

	(1)	(2)	(3)	(4)	(5)	(6)	(7)	(8)
	Dependent Variable is the Log of Per Capita GDP in 2015							
Secondary School Enrollment Rate, 2010	0.04***				0.02***			
	(7.66)				(4.72)			
Secondary School Completion Rate, 2010		0.06***				0.04***		
		(9.87)				(7.63)		
Years of Schooling, 2010			0.35***				0.27***	
			(19.23)				(10.80)	
Mean Years of Schooling, 1980-2010				0.36***				0.27***
				(17.42)				(10.88)
Standardized Geographic Disadvantage Index					-0.64***	-0.57***	-0.32***	-0.38***
					(-8.38)	(-7.14)	(-3.92)	(-4.82)
Intercept	7.70***	7.84***	6.57***	7.13***	8.34***	8.34***	7.14***	7.65***
	(35.10)	(45.30)	(38.91)	(46.16)	(41.68)	(57.48)	(32.61)	(44.19)
Observations	119	119	119	119	119	119	119	119
R-squared	0.37	0.47	0.69	0.65	0.58	0.63	0.73	0.71

Robust t statistics in parentheses. * $p<0.1$ ** $p<0.05$ *** $p<0.01$

Table 4.4: Measures of school attainment, economic institutions, and level of per capita GDP

	(1)	(2)	(3)	(4)	(5)	(6)	(7)	(8)
	Dependent Variable is the Log of Per Capita GDP in 2015							
Economic Freedom Index, 1985-2015	0.77***	0.69***	0.40***	0.44***	0.60***	0.53***	0.34***	0.37***
	(9.18)	(7.92)	(4.08)	(4.56)	(6.82)	(6.35)	(3.84)	(3.81)
Secondary School Enrollment Rate, 2010	0.02***				0.02***			
	(4.89)				(3.77)			
Secondary School Completion Rate, 2010		0.04***				0.03***		
		(7.13)				(6.69)		
Years of Schooling, 2010			0.25***				0.21***	
			(8.74)				(6.29)	
Mean Years of Schooling, 1980-2010				0.25***				0.20***
				(8.58)				(6.13)
Standardized Geographic Disadvantage Index					-0.36***	-0.34***	-0.24***	-0.28***
					(-4.65)	(-4.48)	(-3.14)	(-3.62)
Intercept	3.61***	4.15***	4.78***	5.04***	4.89***	5.26***	5.46***	5.77***
	(6.84)	(7.92)	(10.18)	(9.54)	(8.87)	(10.01)	(12.08)	(10.82)
Observations	106	106	106	106	106	106	106	106
R-squared	0.67	0.69	0.76	0.73	0.73	0.75	0.79	0.77

Robust t statistics in parentheses. * $p<0.1$ ** $p<0.05$ *** $p<0.01$

Table 4.5: School attainment, economic institutions, and per capita GDP. Instrumental variable analysis

Panel A: Second Stage Results

	(1)	(2)	(3)	(4)
	Dep Var: Log of Per Capita GDP in 2015			
Economic Freedom Index, 1985-2015	0.83***	0.60**	0.62**	0.67***
	(3.17)	(2.38)	(2.48)	(2.58)
Mean Years of Schooling, 1980-2010	0.13*	0.09	0.02	0.01
	(1.66)	(1.33)	(0.29)	(0.12)
Geographic Disadvantage Index		-0.33***	-0.29***	-0.26**
		(-3.36)	(-2.98)	(-2.04)
Absolute Value of Latitude			0.02***	0.02***
			(2.90)	(2.77)
Ethnolinguistic Fractionalization				-0.14
				(-0.36)
Intercept	3.47***	5.09***	5.00***	4.84***
	(2.94)	(4.22)	(4.15)	(3.95)
Observations	104.00	104.00	104.00	104.00
R-squared	0.69	0.74	0.73	0.73
p-value (OIR Test)	0.02	0.17	0.62	0.61
F(Weak Id. Kleibergen-Paap)	1.36	1.34	1.35	1.04

Instruments used: Migratory Distance interacted with continents and French legal origin
Robust t statistics in parentheses. * p<0.1 ** p<0.05 *** p<0.01

Table 4.5 – Continued

Panel B. First Stages and Falsifications Tests

	First Stages (Columns 1 and 2)		Falsification Tests (Columns 3 to 6)			
	(1)	(2)	(3)	(4)	(5)	(6)
	Econ. Freedom (EFW) 1980-2010	Years of Schooling 1980-2010	Econ. Freedom (EFW) 1980-2010	Log Per Capita GDP 2015	Years of Schooling 1980-2010	Log Per Capita GDP 2015
Geographic Disadvantage Index	-0.26**	-0.62**	-0.08	-0.25**	-0.13	-0.22**
	(-2.39)	(-2.42)	(-0.69)	(-2.09)	(-0.60)	(-2.03)
Absolute Value of Latitude	0.01	0.05***	-0.00	0.02***	0.02	0.01*
	(1.06)	(3.37)	(-0.33)	(2.96)	(1.47)	(1.72)
Ethnolinguistic Fractionalization	0.33	0.68	0.20	0.09	0.35	0.07
	(0.79)	(0.85)	(0.57)	(0.22)	(0.48)	(0.18)
Migratory Distance × Africa	0.07	-0.18	0.08	-0.04	-0.18	0.05
	(0.94)	(-1.07)	(1.11)	(-0.60)	(-1.21)	(0.68)
Migratory Distance × Europe	0.18**	0.29*	0.13**	0.02	0.14	0.04
	(2.35)	(1.78)	(2.02)	(0.28)	(0.91)	(0.51)
Migratory Distance × Asia	0.11**	0.03	0.07**	0.02	-0.07	0.07*
	(2.41)	(0.42)	(2.08)	(0.66)	(-0.79)	(1.83)
Migratory Distance × Americas	0.04***	0.09***	0.02*	0.01	0.05	0.01
	(2.95)	(3.04)	(1.98)	(0.60)	(1.64)	(0.48)
Migratory Distance × Oceania	0.09***	0.21***	0.07***	0.00	0.15***	-0.01
	(3.91)	(3.49)	(4.22)	(0.12)	(3.28)	(-0.37)
French Legal Origin	-0.39**	-1.53***	-0.31**	0.05	-1.33***	0.28
	(-2.52)	(-5.01)	(-2.42)	(0.34)	(-4.70)	(1.65)
Log Per Capita GDP, 2015			0.47***		1.25***	
			(5.21)		(6.56)	
Econ. Freedom (EFW), 1980-2010				0.55***		
				(5.91)		
Years of Schooling (YS), 1980-2010						0.29***
						(7.43)
Intercept	5.17***	4.57***	1.31	5.28***	-5.59***	6.83***
	(15.15)	(6.80)	(1.60)	(9.35)	(-3.88)	(17.78)
Observations	104.00	104.00	104.00	104.00	104.00	104.00
R-squared	0.52	0.70	0.65	0.73	0.81	0.77
F-test (joint sig. of excluded IVs)	4.38	25.11	4.44	0.59	22.13	2.72
p-value (F-test)	0.00	0.00	0.00	0.71	0.00	0.10

Robust t statistics in parentheses. * $p<0.1$ ** $p<0.05$ *** $p<0.01$

Table 4.6: Changes in school attainment and growth. A virtuous cycle

	(1)	(2)	(3)	(4)	(5)
	Secondary School Completed (Age 15-24) Corresponds to the Total (Male + Female) Population (Columns 1 to 4)				
Panel A: Dependent Variable is the Annual Growth Rate, During 15-Year Periods					
Log Initial Per Capita GDP	-0.14	-0.71***	-0.17	-0.30***	-0.52***
	(-0.56)	(-3.73)	(-1.63)	(-3.09)	(-4.56)
Sec. School Completion Rate, 15-Year Prior to the Period	0.07***	0.05***	0.06***	0.05***	0.03***
	(2.67)	(2.95)	(5.93)	(5.87)	(3.36)
Change in Secondary Completion Rate (Previous 15 Years)	0.07*	0.03	0.05***	0.02**	0.03***
	(1.94)	(1.43)	(4.11)	(2.15)	(2.74)
Change in the Prime Working Age 25-59 Share, During the 15 years				0.27***	0.24***
				(10.84)	(9.61)
Initial EFW					0.85***
					(7.90)
Change in EFW, During the Period					0.72***
					(6.71)
Intercept	1.57	7.44***	2.02**	2.42***	-0.88
	(0.80)	(5.08)	(2.43)	(3.24)	(-1.08)
Panel B: Dependent Variable is the Change in Secondary School Completion Rate, During 15-Year Periods					
Initial Secondary School Completion Rate	0.03	-0.53***	-0.28***	-0.28***	-0.36***
	(0.34)	(-6.19)	(-7.58)	(-7.63)	(-7.90)
Log Per Capita GDP, 15-Year Before the Beginning of the Period	-1.09	6.08***	2.75***	2.66***	3.06***
	(-0.99)	(5.46)	(5.37)	(5.18)	(4.68)
Annual Growth Rate (Previous 15 Years)	1.41***	0.52	0.72***	0.82***	0.87***
	(3.38)	(1.22)	(3.92)	(4.41)	(3.52)
Intercept	12.16	-32.75***	-12.23***	-11.64***	-13.21**
	(1.48)	(-3.74)	(-3.10)	(-2.94)	(-2.57)
Observations	114.00	114.00	570.00	570.00	402.00
R-squared 1 (Growth Equation)	0.10	0.11	0.09	0.27	0.42
R-squared 2 (Change in Human Capital Equation)	0.14	0.28	0.11	0.11	0.14
Periods Included:	1975-1990	1995-2010	1975-1990 1980-1995 1985-2000 1990-2005 1995-2010	1975-1990 1980-1995 1985-2000 1990-2005 1995-2010	1980-1995 1985-2000 1990-2005 1995-2010

All equations, by column, were estimated simultaneously. * $p<0.1$ ** $p<0.05$ *** $p<0.01$

Table 4.7: Educational attainment and growth of per capita GDP

	(1)	(2)	(3)	(4)	(5)
	Dependent Variable is the Annual Growth Rate of Real Per Capita GDP During the Period				
	1985-2000	2000-2015	1985-2000	2000-2015	1985-2015 (Panel)
Log Initial Per Capita GDP	-1.06***	-1.12***	-0.91***	-1.10***	-1.03***
	(-3.42)	(-3.85)	(-2.95)	(-3.61)	(-7.26)
Initial Years of Schooling, Population 25+	0.16	0.20**	0.16	0.18**	0.16***
	(1.42)	(2.53)	(1.61)	(2.36)	(3.72)
Change in Sec. School Completion Rate, Pop. 15-24. (15 years prior)	0.04*	0.03**	0.02	0.02	0.02**
	(1.75)	(2.40)	(1.21)	(1.30)	(2.51)
Initial Summary EFW Rating	1.21***	0.39	0.87***	0.64**	0.93***
	(3.94)	(1.48)	(3.32)	(2.16)	(7.46)
Change in Summary EFW Ranting, During the Period	0.88***	0.85**	0.57**	0.88***	0.78***
	(2.91)	(2.35)	(2.08)	(2.80)	(5.74)
Standardized Geographic Disadvantage Index	-0.63**	-0.29	-0.39*	-0.32	-0.37***
	(-2.44)	(-1.18)	(-1.67)	(-1.31)	(-3.39)
Log of Population, Initial			0.12	0.20**	0.19***
			(1.22)	(2.07)	(3.92)
Change in Prime Age 25-29 Share, During the Period			0.21***	0.10**	0.14***
			(3.46)	(2.14)	(6.19)
Net Fuel Exports, Period Average			-0.00	0.02	0.01
			(-0.18)	(1.38)	(1.34)
Middle East Oil Exporter			-0.89	-3.11***	-1.86**
			(-0.96)	(-2.67)	(-2.43)
War on Soil			-0.76	-4.61***	-2.67***
			(-1.35)	(-10.02)	(-2.65)
Intercept	1.79	7.59***	1.93	5.38**	2.63**
	(0.67)	(3.16)	(0.83)	(2.05)	(2.13)
Number of Observations	103.00	115.00	96.00	112.00	401.00
Adjusted R-squared	0.40	0.29	0.52	0.45	0.42
Periods Included:	1985-2000	2000-2015	1985-2000	2000-2015	1985-2000 1990-2005 1995-2010 2000-2015

Robust t statistics in parentheses. * p<0.1 ** p<0.05 *** p<0.01

Table 4.8: 2015 PISA scores, family size, school attainment, and economic development

Panel A: Top 35 Countries According to the Average PISA Score in 2015. (Ranking in Parentheses)

Country	Average PISA Score (2015)	PISA Top 95% (2015)	Fam. Size (Pop. Age 00-14 / Pop. Age 30-49) (2010)	Years of Schooling, Pop.Age 30-49 (2010)	Years of Schooling, Pop.Age 25+ (1985-2010)	EFW Summary Rating (1985-2015)	Per Capita GDP (2011 PPP dollars) (2015)
Singapore	551.6 (1)	703.3 (1)	0.5 (53)	12.6 (16)	7.7 (47)	8.7 (2)	67,110 (6)
Hong Kong	532.6 (2)	662.9 (8)	0.36 (68)	12.7 (15)	9.2 (30)	8.9 (1)	46,504 (11)
Japan	528.9 (3)	670.1 (4)	0.47 (64)	13 (10)	10.4 (16)	7.5 (11)	36,030 (23)
Macao (China)	527 (4)	653.5 (17)	0.38 (67)	8.7 (55)	6.4 (56)		93,887 (2)
Estonia	524.3 (5)	662 (9)	0.58 (39)	12.9 (13)	10.8 (12)	7.4 (16)	25,790 (36)
Canada	523.3 (6)	667.5 (5)	0.59 (37)	13.3 (7)	11.1 (9)	7.9 (7)	42,844 (17)
Finland	522.7 (7)	663.4 (7)	0.65 (32)	11.8 (33)	8.8 (38)	7.5 (14)	37,920 (22)
South Korea	519.1 (8)	670.3 (3)	0.43 (66)	13.7 (1)	10.1 (18)	6.9 (30)	35,316 (24)
China	514.3 (9)	677.9 (2)	0.56 (43)	8 (61)	6.4 (55)	5.6 (58)	12,002 (62)
Slovenia	509.3 (10)	655.2 (14)	0.5 (54)	12.6 (16)	11.2 (7)	6.5 (40)	28,077 (31)
Ireland	509 (11)	645.7 (23)	0.72 (23)	13.1 (9)	10.7 (14)	7.6 (10)	53,372 (8)
Germany	508.1 (12)	660.7 (10)	0.49 (58)	13.3 (8)	10.2 (17)	7.5 (12)	46,426 (12)
Netherlands	507.9 (13)	660.3 (11)	0.63 (35)	12.3 (23)	10.7 (13)	7.5 (13)	48,463 (10)
Switzerland	506.3 (14)	658.6 (13)	0.5 (51)	13.7 (2)	10.9 (11)	8.3 (3)	61,476 (7)
New Zealand	505.9 (15)	667.1 (6)	0.77 (18)	12.2 (24)	11.5 (5)	8 (5)	33,445 (26)
Norway	504.5 (16)	653 (18)	0.65 (33)	11.8 (34)	11 (10)	7.3 (18)	76,305 (3)
Denmark	504.3 (17)	640.8 (30)	0.65 (34)	12.8 (14)	10.1 (20)	7.5 (15)	44,939 (13)
Poland	503.9 (18)	647.7 (21)	0.5 (52)	12.5 (19)	10 (21)	5.7 (57)	25,310 (37)
Belgium	502.5 (19)	654.5 (16)	0.63 (36)	12 (28)	9.9 (23)	7.3 (19)	39,531 (19)
Australia	502.3 (20)	659.8 (12)	0.68 (27)	12.1 (26)	11.3 (6)	7.7 (8)	44,336 (15)
Viet Nam	502 (21)	632 (33)	0.77 (17)	7.9 (63)	5.4 (61)		5,733 (69)
U.K.	499.9 (22)	654.8 (15)	0.65 (31)	13 (11)	10 (22)	8 (6)	38,749 (20)
Portugal	497 (23)	644.7 (25)	0.48 (60)	8.9 (52)	6 (58)	6.8 (35)	27,255 (32)
Sweden	495.8 (24)	650.3 (20)	0.66 (29)	12.5 (18)	11.2 (8)	7.2 (20)	43,464 (16)
France	495.7 (25)	652.6 (19)	0.7 (24)	11.9 (31)	8.8 (39)	7 (28)	38,448 (21)
Austria	492.2 (26)	646.9 (22)	0.5 (55)	10.8 (44)	9.1 (33)	7.3 (17)	44,845 (14)
Russia	491.8 (27)	629.6 (34)	0.58 (40)	13 (12)	10.1 (19)	5.9 (54)	23,118 (42)
Spain	491.4 (28)	627.8 (35)	0.47 (65)	11.3 (38)	8.3 (44)	7.1 (24)	33,376 (27)
Czech Rep.	490.8 (29)	644.6 (26)	0.49 (57)	13.5 (4)	12.1 (2)	6.9 (31)	30,410 (30)
United States	487.6 (30)	642 (29)	0.74 (21)	13.6 (3)	12.8 (1)	8.1 (4)	52,591 (9)
Latvia	486.8 (31)	617.5 (40)	0.55 (44)	11 (42)	8.9 (35)	7 (26)	22,724 (43)
Italy	485 (32)	632.5 (32)	0.48 (61)	11.3 (39)	8.2 (45)	6.8 (34)	34,673 (25)
Luxembourg	483.3 (33)	644.3 (27)	0.52 (49)	12 (29)	9.7 (27)	7.6 (9)	67,804 (5)
Iceland	480.9 (34)	633.2 (31)	0.77 (19)	11.5 (36)	9.2 (31)	7.1 (23)	40,572 (18)
Croatia	475.4 (35)	622.4 (38)	0.54 (46)	12.2 (24)	9.7 (26)	6.2 (47)	20,905 (46)

Table 4.8 – Continued

Panel B: Bottom 36 Countries According to the Average PISA Score in 2015

Country	Average PISA Score (2015)	PISA Top 95% (2015)	Fam. Size (Pop. Age 00-14 / Pop. Age 30-49) (2010)	Years of Schooling, Pop.Age 30-49 (2010)	Years of Schooling, Pop.Age 25+ (1985-2010)	EFW Summary Rating (1985-2015)	Per Capita GDP (2015)
Lithuania	475.4 (36)	622.8 (37)	0.54 (45)	12.3 (22)	9.4 (29)	7 (27)	25,279 (38)
Hungary	474.4 (37)	625.8 (36)	0.48 (62)	12.5 (19)	10.5 (15)	6.4 (43)	23,539 (40)
Israel	471.7 (38)	642.9 (28)	1.1 (3)	13.4 (5)	11.6 (4)	6.2 (48)	31,729 (28)
Malta	463.4 (39)	645.1 (24)	0.53 (48)	12.1 (27)	8.9 (34)	6.8 (36)	26,577 (33)
Slovakia	462.8 (40)	619.6 (39)	0.5 (56)	13.4 (6)	11.6 (3)	6.9 (29)	25,896 (35)
Greece	458.5 (41)	606.9 (42)	0.48 (63)	12 (30)	8.7 (40)	6.4 (41)	24,545 (39)
Kazakhstan	447.8 (42)	584.5 (46)	0.99 (6)	11.8 (32)	9.7 (25)		23,408 (41)
Chile	442.7 (43)	584 (47)	0.73 (22)	10.7 (46)	8.6 (41)	7.2 (21)	21,340 (45)
Malaysia	439.9 (44)	566.6 (53)	0.91 (11)	10.7 (45)	7.7 (46)	7 (25)	22,075 (44)
Bulgaria	439.6 (45)	607.9 (41)	0.48 (59)	11.3 (37)	9.5 (28)	5.9 (55)	17,254 (52)
Cyprus	437.5 (46)	595.5 (44)	0.58 (38)	12.4 (21)	9.2 (32)	6.8 (33)	25,903 (34)
Romania	437.5 (47)	582.5 (48)	0.51 (50)	11.8 (35)	9.7 (24)	5.8 (56)	20,549 (48)
United Arab Emirates	432.6 (48)	601.9 (43)	0.25 (70)	8.9 (53)	7.2 (51)	7.1 (22)	69,237 (4)
Uruguay	430 (49)	581.9 (49)	0.82 (14)	8.9 (54)	7.5 (49)	6.7 (37)	19,668 (49)
Turkey	424.8 (50)	559.7 (56)	0.89 (12)	7.1 (65)	5.2 (62)	6 (52)	20,808 (47)
Trinidad and Tobago	423 (51)	586.6 (45)	0.69 (25)	11.1 (41)	8.9 (37)	6.3 (44)	30,892 (29)
Argentina	422.2 (52)	560.2 (55)	0.95 (9)	10 (47)	8.5 (43)	5.4 (59)	19,316 (50)
Moldova	421.3 (53)	570.3 (51)	0.54 (47)	11.2 (40)	8.9 (36)		5,569 (70)
Montenegro	418.7 (54)	567.1 (52)	0.68 (28)				17,738 (51)
Costa Rica	415.8 (55)	539.1 (63)	0.79 (16)	8.4 (59)	7.2 (50)	6.9 (32)	13,568 (57)
Mexico	415.7 (56)	539.2 (62)	0.98 (7)	9.1 (50)	6.7 (53)	6.3 (45)	15,766 (53)
Thailand	415.3 (57)	552.5 (60)	0.57 (41)	8.5 (57)	5 (63)	6.7 (38)	13,938 (55)
Albania	415.2 (58)	558.2 (57)	0.66 (30)	10.9 (43)	8.5 (42)	6.2 (46)	10,947 (65)
Colombia	410.1 (59)	549.4 (61)	0.84 (13)	9.1 (50)	6.3 (57)	5.9 (53)	12,858 (60)
Qatar	407.3 (60)	581 (50)	0.28 (69)	8.6 (56)	6.4 (54)		13,9542 (1)
Georgia	405.4 (61)	564.2 (54)	0.69 (26)				10,198 (67)
Jordan	399 (62)	537 (64)	1.45 (1)	9.7 (48)	6.9 (52)	6.7 (39)	11,738 (63)
Indonesia	395.5 (63)	524.1 (67)	0.96 (8)	8 (62)	4.8 (64)	6.4 (42)	10,099 (68)
Brazil	395 (64)	555.6 (58)	0.75 (20)	8.5 (58)	5.4 (60)	5.2 (60)	15,377 (54)
Peru	393.6 (65)	532.8 (65)	1.03 (4)	9.4 (49)	7.6 (48)	6.2 (49)	11,215 (64)
Lebanon	376.4 (66)	553 (59)	0.93 (10)				12,665 (61)
Tunisia	371.4 (67)	502.2 (68)	0.81 (15)	7.4 (64)	4.6 (65)	6 (51)	10,608 (66)
Macedonia	368.9 (68)	524.9 (66)	0.56 (42)				13,586 (56)
Kosovo	362.4 (69)	486.2 (69)					
Algeria	361.7 (70)	483.2 (70)	1.02 (5)	6.9 (66)	4.3 (66)	4.6 (61)	13,024 (59)
Dominican Republic	339 (71)	469.8 (71)	1.19 (2)	8.1 (60)	6 (59)	6.1 (50)	13,382 (58)

Table 4.9. Average and top 95 percentile PISA scores, years of schooling, economic institutions, and per capita GDP

	(1)	(2)	(3)	(4)	(5)	(6)
	Dependent Variable: Log of Per Capita GDP, 2015					
Average PISA Score, 2015	0.47***		0.46***		0.33***	
	(3.65)		(4.44)		(2.74)	
Years of Schooling, Pop.25+, 1985-2010	0.19	0.10			0.20*	0.14
	(1.47)	(0.75)			(1.99)	(1.33)
Top 95 Percentile PISA Score, 2015		0.57***		0.51***		0.41***
		(4.39)		(5.41)		(3.58)
EFW Summary Rating, 1985-2015			0.43***	0.42***	0.42***	0.41***
			(4.22)	(4.47)	(4.14)	(4.36)
Observations	66.00	66.00	61.00	61.00	61.00	61.00
R-squared	0.36	0.40	0.66	0.70	0.68	0.71

Standardized beta coefficients. Robust t statistics in parentheses. * p<0.1 ** p<0.05 *** p<0.01"

Table 4.10. Determinants of learning, country-level analysis

	(1)	(2)	(3)	(4)	(5)	(6)
	Dep.Var: Aggregate PISA Score (Math, Reading, Science)					
	Average	Top 95%	Average	Top 95%	Average	Top 95%
Years of Schooling, Pop. Age 30-49, 2010	11.11***	12.24***	10.32***	11.13***	10.30***	11.38***
	(3.17)	(4.02)	(3.14)	(3.50)	(3.21)	(3.67)
Family Size, 2010	-63.17***	-74.91***	-63.86***	-76.62***	-63.40***	-82.12***
	(-2.90)	(-3.24)	(-2.91)	(-3.21)	(-3.09)	(-4.05)
Log Per Capita GDP, 2010	12.57	16.11	-0.55	6.62		
	(1.09)	(1.59)	(-0.04)	(0.60)		
EFW Summary Rating, 2000-2015			17.28***	14.11**	17.02***	17.20***
			(3.16)	(2.27)	(2.94)	(2.79)
Intercept	258.93**	365.19***	274.36**	371.58***	270.58***	416.78***
	(2.19)	(3.07)	(2.30)	(3.10)	(4.56)	(6.48)
Observations	66.00	66.00	65.00	65.00	65.00	65.00
R-squared	0.60	0.69	0.65	0.71	0.65	0.70

Robust t statistics in parentheses. * $p<0.1$ ** $p<0.05$ *** $p<0.01$

Table 4.11. Determinants of learning, individual-level analysis

	(1)	(2)	(3)	(4)
	Dep.Var: PISA Score (Math, Reading, Science)			
PARED (Years of Education, Parents)	1.69***	1.87***	1.77***	1.91***
	(36.07)	(38.07)	(35.34)	(36.80)
WEALTH	7.87***	7.47***	8.39***	8.07***
	(66.67)	(61.29)	(67.10)	(62.71)
Between 11 and 25 books at Home	17.63***	18.57***	16.17***	16.79***
	(42.15)	(42.55)	(36.07)	(36.13)
Between 26-100 books at Home	51.77***	52.95***	49.38***	50.28***
	(129.17)	(127.77)	(115.48)	(114.28)
Between 101-200 books at Home	71.56***	72.81***	69.30***	70.26***
	(149.18)	(147.95)	(136.68)	(135.58)
Between 201-500 books at Home	93.98***	95.22***	91.09***	92.04***
	(175.97)	(174.57)	(162.55)	(161.32)
More than 500 Books at Home	80.95***	82.81***	81.75***	83.17***
	(125.89)	(126.08)	(121.08)	(121.02)
GRADE	29.21***	23.84***	26.56***	21.64***
	(144.86)	(85.81)	(118.72)	(73.39)
Students' Expected Occupational Status at Age 30 (BSMJ)	0.71***	0.75***	0.63***	0.66***
	(93.25)	(95.10)	(77.55)	(79.32)
Teacher-Directed Instruction (TDTEACH)			3.87***	3.85***
			(27.46)	(26.65)
Disciplinary Climate (DISCLISC)			10.79***	10.74***
			(73.37)	(71.47)
Intercept	363.82***	358.78***	372.42***	368.32***
	(461.24)	(438.75)	(439.01)	(421.39)
Observations	356,012	340,056	310,117	298,338
R-squared	0.29	0.25	0.30	0.26

Notes: t statistics in parentheses, * $p<0.05$ ** $p<0.01$ *** $p<0.001$. The omitted category is 0-10 books at home

Table 4.12. Determinants of learning, individual-level analysis with country-level characteristics

	(1)	(2)	(3)	(4)	(5)	(6)	(7)	(8)
	Dependent Variable: Average PISA Score (Math, Reading, Science)							
PARED (Years of Education, Parents)	2.26***	2.19***	1.59***	1.68***	2.33***	2.24***	1.61***	1.68***
	(47.44)	(46.13)	(34.43)	(36.50)	(45.70)	(44.26)	(32.70)	(34.23)
WEALTH	6.91***	4.81***	1.06***	0.78***	7.37***	5.22***	1.47***	1.09***
	(58.39)	(39.15)	(8.65)	(6.41)	(58.77)	(40.16)	(11.40)	(8.52)
Between 11 and 25 books at Home	17.24***	16.69***	16.44***	16.70***	15.94***	15.30***	14.77***	15.05***
	(40.84)	(39.73)	(40.34)	(41.18)	(35.19)	(33.99)	(33.86)	(34.73)
Between 26-100 books at Home	51.56***	49.82***	45.55***	45.52***	49.41***	47.50***	42.84***	42.73***
	(126.99)	(123.06)	(115.63)	(116.11)	(114.11)	(110.04)	(102.11)	(102.52)
Between 101-200 books at Home	72.09***	70.03***	63.30***	62.83***	69.93***	67.64***	60.37***	59.75***
	(148.31)	(144.49)	(133.93)	(133.57)	(136.12)	(132.08)	(121.01)	(120.52)
Between 201-500 books at Home	94.88***	92.53***	83.97***	82.98***	91.96***	89.35***	80.20***	78.99***
	(175.33)	(171.44)	(159.34)	(158.14)	(162.06)	(157.93)	(145.27)	(143.90)
More than 500 Books at Home	82.94***	80.85***	73.42***	72.78***	83.75***	81.33***	73.27***	72.38***
	(126.99)	(124.28)	(115.94)	(115.47)	(122.24)	(119.21)	(110.42)	(109.76)
GRADE	32.12***	31.31***	27.65***	29.62***	29.68***	28.95***	25.79***	27.81***
	(158.15)	(154.61)	(139.54)	(147.95)	(131.11)	(128.45)	(117.48)	(126.03)
Students' Expected Occupational Status at Age 30	0.71***	0.77***	1.01***	1.02***	0.63***	0.68***	0.91***	0.92***
	(92.31)	(99.16)	(131.25)	(133.23)	(76.94)	(83.39)	(112.44)	(114.45)
Avg. Fam. Size (Population 00-14 / Population 30-49)		-38.81***	-29.35***	-24.88***		-39.48***	-29.11***	-24.24***
		(-59.62)	(-46.23)	(-39.08)		(-58.69)	(-44.38)	(-36.91)
Years of Schooling, Population Age 30-49, in 1980			7.33***	5.09***			7.37***	4.78***
			(142.67)	(78.76)			(136.51)	(69.54)
Strong Democracy, 2000-2015				22.59***				25.55***
				(56.57)				(60.57)
Teacher-Directed Instruction					3.44***	3.82***	4.69***	5.25***
					(24.15)	(26.97)	(34.13)	(38.43)
Disciplinary Climate in Classes					10.63***	10.25***	9.96***	10.21***
					(71.64)	(69.44)	(69.66)	(71.84)
Intercept	357.71***	381.07***	317.67***	314.24***	366.68***	391.03***	328.32***	325.87***
	(448.73)	(430.90)	(328.77)	(326.16)	(427.47)	(412.40)	(319.72)	(319.13)
Observations	325,890	325,890	325,890	325,890	283,172	283,172	283,172	283,172
R-squared	0.32	0.33	0.36	0.37	0.33	0.33	0.37	0.38

t statistics in parentheses, * p<0.05 **p<0.01 ***p<0.001. The omitted category is 0-10 books at home

CHAPTER 5

CONCLUSIONS

This dissertation evaluated the relative merits of geography, institutions, and human capital for economic development. Each of these three factors represents a fundamental hypothesis in the literature of comparative economic development. In this literature, the proponents of each theory tend to find empirical evidence consistent with their hypothesis and typically inconsistent with alternative theories. In contrast, this research finds evidence consistent with all three of these theories using an integrated approach, uniform data of better quality, and a consistent methodology. This research indicates that geography, institutions, and human capital all play an important role in the development process and that the three theories generally complement each other and each adds to our understanding of the development process.

Chapter two documents that geographic conditions such as distance to major world markets, hot and humid climates favoring an ecology for malaria, and isolation in the hinterlands with limited access to ocean coastlines are key disadvantages for economic development. An index of geographic disadvantage was constructed and utilized throughout the dissertation.

A balanced annual poverty dataset spanning 176 countries during 1970-2015 was built. This novel dataset was utilized in chapters two and three of this dissertation. Appendix A explains the methodology used to construct it.

The evidence indicates that geographic disadvantages have been a major deterrent to growth and development historically and that they still play a role, albeit to a lesser extent. In the most recent periods, most of the impact of geography on economic development is indirect, through a historically negative effect on economic institutions. Some of the most geographically disadvantaged countries are starting to grow, providing evidence of change, but they continue to lag behind less geographically disadvantaged developing countries in terms of the level of per capita GDP and progress against poverty.

The gains from reductions in transportation and communication costs have exerted a differential impact on developing economies. The volume of international trade is much smaller, and it has increased less, in the geographically disadvantaged countries than in the other developing and high-income countries. International trade plays a vitally important role in the modern growth process. The relatively slow growth of international trade in countries with the largest geographic disadvantages indicates that geography is continuing to impact the economic growth of these countries adversely.

However, because digital communication costs do not respect geographic barriers, the digital revolution is reducing the overall geographic disadvantages of the past. While the Industrial Revolution positively impacted about 15 percent of the world's population, the transportation and communication revolution has resulted in substantial income gains for an additional 70 percent of the world's population, and the digital revolution is exerting a positive effect on the rest of the world's population.

Chapter three explores the role of economic and political institutions for economic development. Economic institutions are more strongly associated with both levels of per capita GDP and reductions in poverty rates than political institutions. Similarly, changes in economic institutions are more strongly associated with growth rates and reductions in poverty rates than changes in political institutions, even after controlling for geographic disadvantages.

Instrumental variable analysis indicates a positive and significant channel of causation from economic institutions to levels of per capita GDP. A new instrumental variable is constructed based on the interaction of migratory distance and continental dummies. A new theory is provided directly linking ancestral migratory distance with pre-colonial culture, and through this channel, exogenously affecting the development of current economic institutions. Migratory distance interacted with the geographic characteristics of the continents (including their axial orientation and shape, as originally proposed by Jared Diamond) bent the nature of early economic interactions and trade among tribes for tens of thousands of years. The most successful cultures and attributes prevailed and had a lasting effect on pre-colonial and current norms and informal rules, and therefore had an exogenous effect on subsequent formal economic institutions.

Chapter three also provides evidence about the relationship between political and economic institutions. The evidence indicates that political institutions Granger cause, or predate, economic institutions but not the other way around. The findings suggest economic institutions are, at least partially, an outcome of the political process.

Chapter four explores the role of human capital. Theoretically, human capital can serve as input and output of growth. The empirical evidence is consistent with this dual role. Levels and changes of educational attainment are associated with subsequent increases in per capita GDP. In turn, increases in per capita GDP are associated with subsequent increases in educational attainment. The evidence is consistent with a virtuous cycle of economic development and human capital accumulation.

Some countries have been able to grow and start the development process, i.e. break out of the Malthusian trap, even with very low human capital levels. Examples of growth-triggering events include the improvement in the quality of economic institutions, oil shocks, and demographic shocks.

However, once the growth process surpasses a certain tipping point of development and the countries exit the Malthusian stage, a virtuous combination of economic growth, declining fertility rates, and increases in human capital, generally leads to a period of sustained growth. During this period, human capital is both a cause and a consequence of growth. When combined with high-quality economic institutions and external technological advances, the development process can accelerate with potentially no other limit than the technological frontier. Examples of this are the former socialist countries, which transitioned toward more inclusive economic institutions and have experienced remarkable growth rates. However, when combined with poor quality economic institutions, this process can decelerate, disappear, and potentially erase the gains made, if any. An iconic example of this is Venezuela, which has adopted less inclusive economic institutions. In this regard, economic institutions act not only as a cause but also as a catalyst for economic development.

The empirical evidence indicates that educational achievement outperforms educational attainment in income regressions. This finding is consistent with the idea that the former is a more accurate measure of the human capital of the population than the latter. In turn, the evidence suggests that the top 95 percentile score is an even better predictor of per capita GDP than the average achievement score.

An analysis of the determinants of learnings at the country-level indicates that the years of schooling of the parents, the family size, and the institutional environment during the lifetime of the students are all important predictors of learning, explaining up to 70 percent of the variation in aggregate scores. At the individual level, the number of books at home, the grade level, the expected occupational status of the student at age 30, the wealth and education of the parents, and the teaching environment at the school, are all key determinants of the cognitive skills PISA scores. These measures can explain almost 40 percent of the variation in individual-level scores.

APPENDIX A

POVERTY DATASET

The World Bank extreme and moderate poverty rates are the most commonly used measures of global poverty. They are defined as the percentage of a country's population living on $1.90 and $3.20 per day, respectively, in 2011 international dollars. These poverty lines were originally proposed by Ravallion, Datt, and van de Walle (1991) and successfully modified and improved over time.

The World Bank poverty rate data is a first step toward understanding recent global trends in poverty. However, when using the poverty rates for cross-country analysis one confronts a significant missing data problem. Because the rates are generated from household surveys which are difficult to conduct in developing countries, they are conducted sporadically. The irregularity of the data is an issue in regression analyses.

For example, from the base sample of 135 countries, a cross-country regression utilizing the poverty rates in 2015, 2000, and 1985 is limited by a sample size of 56, 29, and 9 observations, respectively. To overcome this problem, Pinkovskiy and Sala-i-Martin (2009) used National Accounts and additional household surveys to approximate income distributions and then generate poverty rates. However, the data they used do not come directly from the poor and consequently, their poverty estimates are much lower than those of the World Bank. Deaton (2005) and Deaton and Heston (2010) point out that the National Accounts of many developing countries are unreliable and that they show substantial discrepancies with local surveys of the poor.

Connors and Montesinos (2018) took a different approach based on two basic ideas. First, the best predictor of the poverty rate in country A in a particular year is the poverty rate of country A in adjacent years. That is, the basic assumption is that poverty rates change slowly for each country. Second, the poverty rate and the under-five mortality rate (per 1,000 live birth) are highly correlated. The sample correlation between these two measures is about 85 percent. However, the under-five mortality rate data are nearly complete. For example, from the base sample of 135 countries, a cross-country regression utilizing the under-five mortality rate can be estimated with 133 observations. The two missing observations are Hong Kong and Taiwan. Indeed, this variable is complete annually for 184 countries back to 1970.

The methodology presented in this appendix is similar to that employed by Connors and Montesinos (2018) but with two technical differences. First, a logistic transformation is employed to smooth out the poverty rate approximation near the extremes (0 and 100 percent). Second, linear interpolation in the space of log-odds ratio to better fit the actual World Bank poverty rate data. The results are very to those in Connors and Montesinos, except for developed countries with too low poverty rates (close to zero percent) and developing countries with too high poverty rates (close to 100 percent).

The basic model uses the World Bank´s poverty rate country i at time t expressed in decimal form. i.e., 0.3 instead of 30 (percent). Denote that poverty rate by $\boldsymbol{poverty_{it}}$. Let the log-odds ratio for the poverty rate (LORP) of country i at time t be

$$LORP_{it} = \log\left(\frac{poverty_{it}}{1 - poverty_{it}}\right) = \log(poverty_{it}) - \log(1 - poverty_{it})$$

Let $u5Mort_{it}$ be the under-five mortality rate for country i at time t. Then the basic model is shown in equation 1.

$$LORP_{it} = \alpha + \beta_1 u5Mort_{it} + \beta_2 LORP_{it-1} + \epsilon_{it} \tag{1}$$

where $LORP_{it-1}$ denotes the log-odds ratio for the poverty rate of country i at time $t-1$.

While there are 1,646 country-year observations for which both the poverty rate and the under-five mortality rate are available, there are only 863 country-year observations such that the poverty rate is also available in the prior year (so that it is available in two consecutive years). The r-square of this regression is 94.99 percent. After performing linear interpolation in the log-odds ratio, the number of observations increases to 1,110, and the r-square increases to 95.69 percent. These high r-squares indicate that the regression model in (1) is an excellent predictor of the log odd-ratios[30].

The fitted values from equation 1 can be used to predict $LORP_{it+1}$ and $LORP_{it-2}$, if any of them are missing. That is, the model can be used to complete missing values that are adjacent to the observed data. Then, the model can be re-estimated iteratively until there are no remaining

[30] Using the original poverty rate instead of the log odd-ratio (LORP), the r-square for the same 863 observations is lower (92.72 percent). In Connors and Montesinos (2018), the corresponding r-square was 0.91 using 529 poverty observations available at the time. These indicators indicate that the logistic transformed model is superior than the one employed by Connors and Montesinos (2018).

missing values. Although the in-sample r-square increases rapidly with each iteration, the structural r-square corresponding to the classification error of unobserved data ranges between 85 percent (corresponding to the model that only includes under-five mortality rates) and 95.69 percent (corresponding to the autoregressive model).

The iterative autoregressive logistic model described above is superior is based on the theory of alternating projection methods described by Escalante and Raydan (2011). By iteratively making orthogonal projections and updating the model, in the limit, the approximating solution converges to the expected value of the corresponding log odds ratio of the poverty rate.

Finally, to compute the poverty rate, the output of the model needs to be transformed back using the inverse logistic function. That is,

$$poverty_{it} = \frac{\exp(LORP_{it})}{1 + \exp(LORP_{it})} = \frac{1}{1 + \exp(-LORP_{it})} .$$

This methodology was utilized to estimate the poverty rates for 176 countries for the period 1970-2015. The results are illustrated in Figures A.1 and A.2.[31]

Figure A.1 shows the population-weighted poverty rates for the developing world, Asia, Latin America and the Caribbean, and Sub-Saharan Africa. The extreme ($1.90 a day) and moderate ($3.20 a day) are displayed in the form of a bar graph from 1970 to 2015.

In the developing world (the world excluding the 21 high-income countries), the moderate poverty rates have declined monotonically from 76 percent in 1970 to 29.2 percent in 2015, a reduction of almost 62 percent. The extreme poverty rates fell from 56.8 to 11.5 percent in the same period, a reduction of almost 80 percent. Most of this decline, however, was due to huge reductions in poverty rates in Asia. The moderate poverty rate in Asia declined from 86.0 to 27.7 percent during 1970-2015 (a reduction of about 68 percent) while the extreme poverty declined from 68.0 to 7.8 percent (a reduction of almost 90 percent) during the same period.

In Latin America and the Caribbean, during 1970-2015, the moderate and extreme poverty rates experienced respective declines of 78 percent (from 44.2 to 9.7 percent), and 85 percent (from 24.8 to 3.8 percent, respectively. However, the magnitude of the reductions was substantially smaller in Sub-Saharan Africa. In this region, the moderate poverty rates fell from 88.1 to 64.9

[31] The full dataset of estimated poverty rates including the thresholds $1.90, $3.20, and $5.50 a day, are available at www.hugomontesinos.com/research

percent (a decline of 26.3 percent) while the extreme poverty rates fell from 73.0 to 39.5 percent (a reduction of 45.9 percent) during 1970-2015.

It is remarkable that despite the large efforts aiming at the poverty reductions and a substantial amount of foreign aid during 1970-2015, Sub-Saharan Africa has experienced the slowest declines in poverty rates. Only about half a century ago, the poverty rates in Asia and Sub-Saharan Africa were approximately the same. By 2015, the extreme poverty rate in Africa is 5 times that of Asia (39.5 versus 7.8 percent).

Figure A.2 shows the annual poverty rates for selected populous countries from Asia (China and India), Africa (Nigeria and Ethiopia), and Latin America (Brazil and Mexico)[32]. Line graphs with circular dots show the estimated extreme ($1.90 a day) and moderate ($3.20 a day) poverty rate from 1970 to 2015. Slightly bigger square dots show the actual World Bank poverty rate (input of the model). These graphs help visualize, using a selected set of countries, what exactly the logistic iterative autoregressive model does.

[32] In 2015, the population of these countries (in millions) was 1,365 (China), 1,253 (India), 181 (Nigeria), 108 (Ethiopia), 207 (Brazil), and 118 (Mexico).

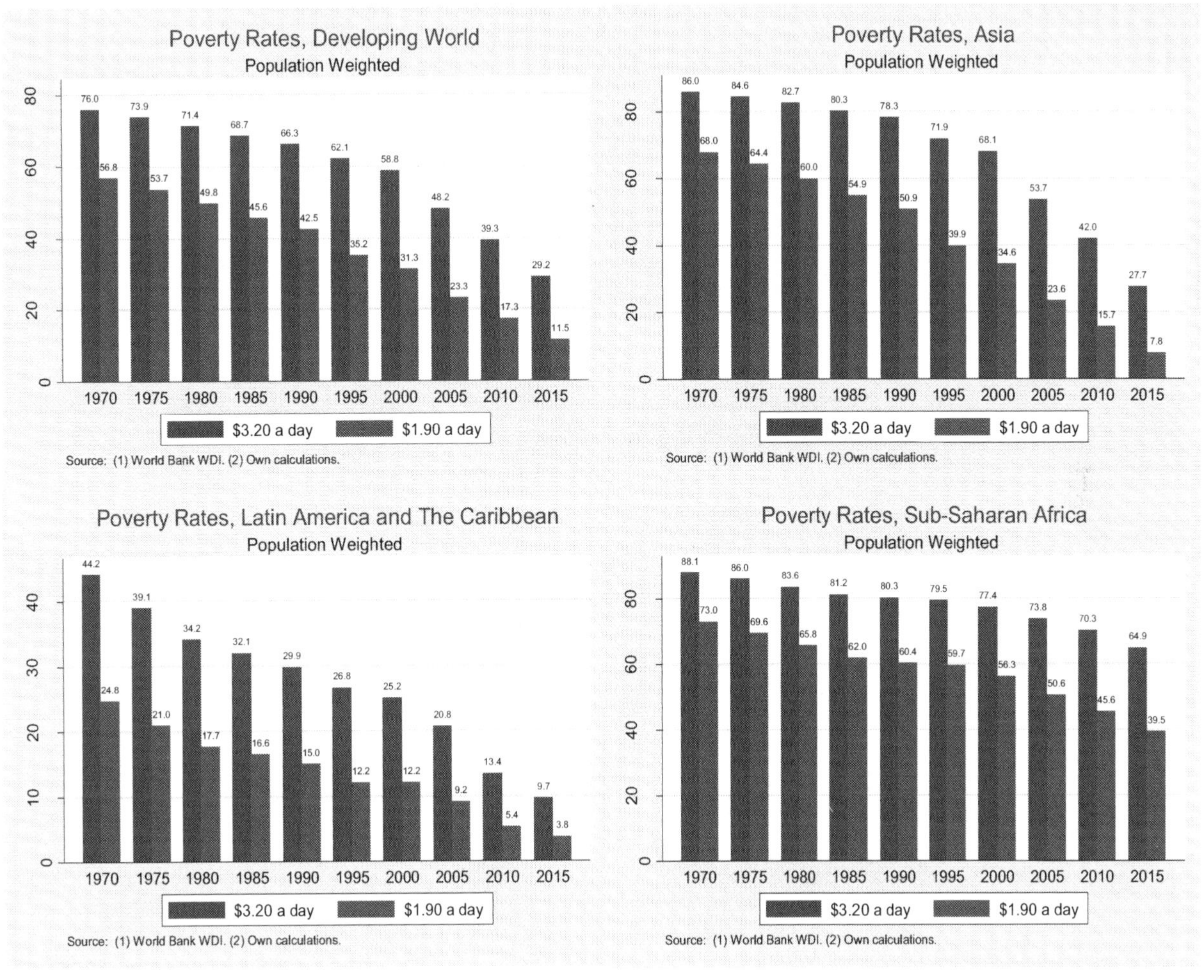

Figure A.1: The population-weighted average extreme ($1.90 a day) and moderate ($3.20 a day) poverty rate for the developing world, Asia, Latin America, and Sub-Saharan Africa, 1970-2015.

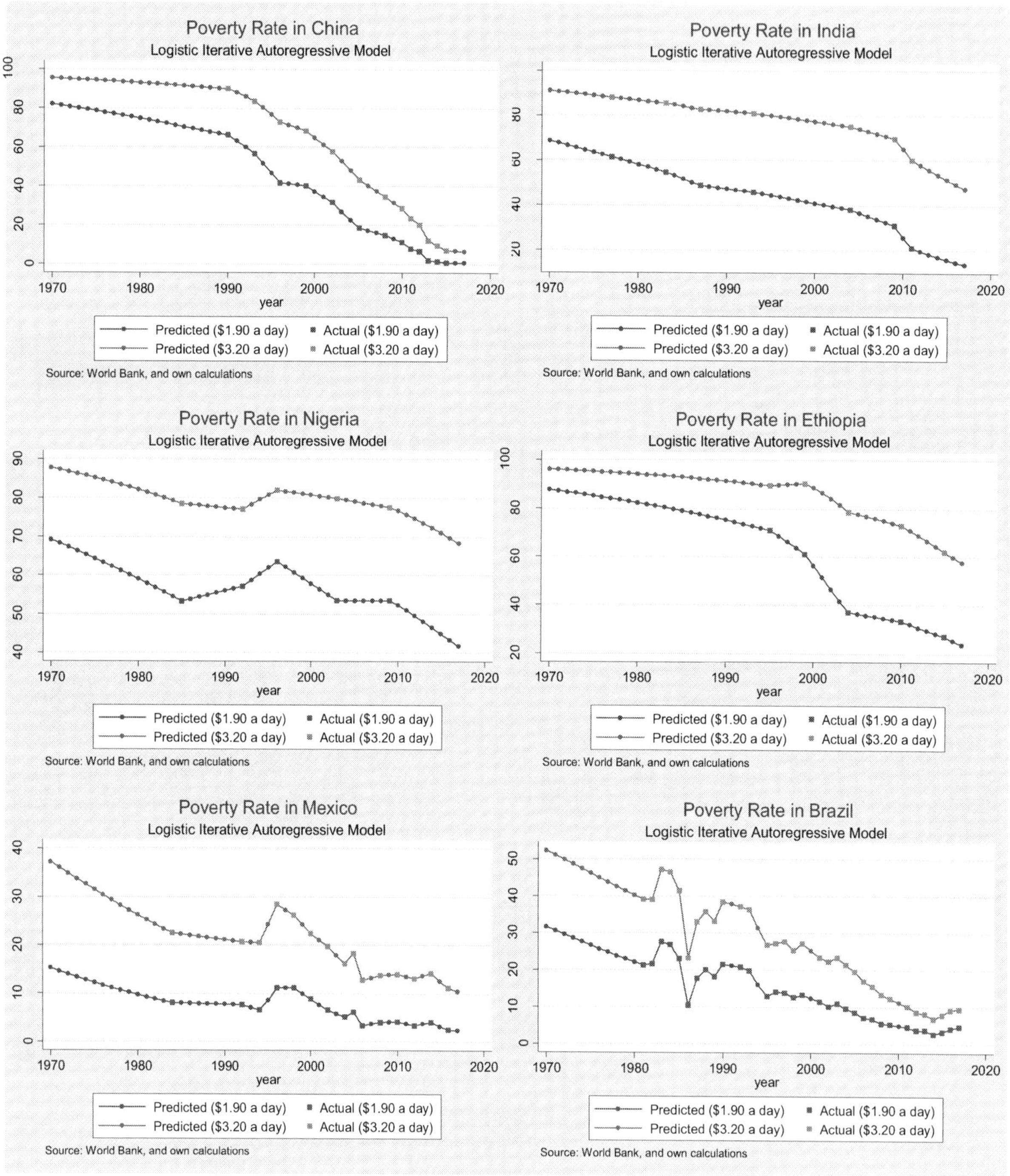

Figure A.2: Predicted and actual poverty rate ($1.90 and $3.20 a day) for selected countries

APPENDIX B

ALTERNATIVE SPECIFICATIONS – CHAPTER TWO

Table B.1: The impact of geographic disadvantages (GeoDis) over time using seemingly unrelated regressions and after controlling for alternative confounders (extension of Table 2.8)

	(1)	(2)	(3)
	Dependent Variable is Growth of Per Capita GDP (15-Year Periods)		
Log Initial Per Capita GDP		-0.54***	-0.14
		(-6.52)	(-1.60)
Log Initial Population		0.11***	0.13***
		(2.63)	(3.13)
Change in the Prime Working Age 25-59 Share		0.17***	0.19***
(During the Period)		(9.35)	(10.29)
Dummy Middle Eastern Oil Exporters		-1.90***	-2.21***
		(-4.79)	(-4.78)
Change in EFW During the Period			0.26***
			(3.33)
1975-1990	-0.57**	-0.82***	-0.83**
	(-2.02)	(-3.12)	(-2.35)
1980-1995	-0.95***	-1.39***	-1.54***
	(-3.37)	(-5.21)	(-4.56)
1985-2000	-0.19	-0.70***	-1.13***
	(-0.67)	(-2.61)	(-3.30)
1990-2005	0.43	-0.16	-0.74**
	(1.53)	(-0.58)	(-2.19)
1995-2010	1.09***	0.45	-0.20
	(3.86)	(1.63)	(-0.62)
2000-2015	1.00***	0.47*	0.05
	(3.54)	(1.73)	(0.14)
GeoDis Main Effect (or effect during 1970-1985)	-0.81***	-0.82***	-0.82***
	(-4.30)	(-4.51)	(-2.94)
1975-1990 × GeoDis	0.10	0.20	0.02
	(0.39)	(0.80)	(0.05)
1980-1995 × GeoDis	0.03	0.10	0.30
	(0.12)	(0.42)	(0.95)
1985-2000 × GeoDis	-0.22	-0.21	-0.11
	(-0.83)	(-0.87)	(-0.34)
1990-2005 × GeoDis	0.08	-0.02	0.24
	(0.32)	(-0.09)	(0.76)
1995-2010 × GeoDis	0.71***	0.44*	0.63**
	(2.69)	(1.81)	(1.98)
2000-2015 × GeoDis	1.19***	0.76***	1.04***
	(4.49)	(3.09)	(3.29)
Intercept	1.52***	5.82***	2.36***
	(7.62)	(8.07)	(2.89)
Observations	945	945	669
R-squared	0.17	0.29	0.35

Notes: All equations were estimated using Seemingly Unrelated Regressors (SUR). z-statistics in parentheses. *** p<0.01, ** p<0.05, * p<0.1

Table B.2: Geographic disadvantages, trade, poverty, and under-5 mortality rates, after controlling for population (similar to columns 1-4 of Table 2.11)

	(1)	(2)	(3)	(4)
	International Trade (% of GDP)		International Trade (dollars per capita)	
Year Effect				
1975	7.21**	8.07*	835.91	810.49
	(2.14)	(1.77)	(0.94)	(0.84)
1980	12.22***	13.38***	1,518.79*	1,487.70
	(3.76)	(3.28)	(1.77)	(1.63)
1985	11.89***	10.77***	1,532.17*	1,545.26
	(3.55)	(2.70)	(1.73)	(1.64)
1990	14.54***	13.77***	2,010.18**	2,059.50**
	(3.99)	(3.16)	(2.27)	(2.20)
1995	20.80***	20.67***	2,831.98***	2,928.70***
	(5.27)	(4.35)	(3.11)	(3.12)
2000	28.31***	27.83***	4,019.39***	4,178.28***
	(7.45)	(6.06)	(3.86)	(4.10)
2005	35.85***	35.16***	5,371.57***	5,647.33***
	(7.74)	(6.90)	(4.47)	(4.96)
2010	38.47***	38.02***	6,311.41***	6,728.34***
	(7.52)	(7.24)	(4.99)	(5.74)
2015	39.06***	38.93***	6,976.91***	7,557.53***
	(7.16)	(7.02)	(5.10)	(6.32)
GeoDis Effect		-7.12***		-1,529.10***
		(-3.43)		(-3.11)
Interactions:				
1975×GeoDis		1.14		-510.89
		(0.32)		(-0.75)
1980×GeoDis		1.74		-1,048.07
		(0.56)		(-1.52)
1985×GeoDis		-1.86		-1,292.08*
		(-0.63)		(-1.83)
1990×GeoDis		-0.95		-1,820.97**
		(-0.24)		(-2.36)
1995×GeoDis		-0.04		-2,544.72***
		(-0.01)		(-3.21)
2000×GeoDis		-0.58		-3,846.19***
		(-0.13)		(-3.99)
2005×GeoDis		-1.47		-5,050.92***
		(-0.28)		(-4.59)
2010×GeoDis		-2.28		-5,456.44***
		(-0.43)		(-4.71)
2015×GeoDis		-2.30		-5,807.22***
		(-0.42)		(-4.66)
Log population	-14.11***	-13.68***	-1,910.07***	-2,004.18***
	(-12.31)	(-11.54)	(-12.54)	(-14.06)
Intercept	81.07***	74.71***	10,489.52***	10,735.13***
	(15.24)	(13.54)	(11.33)	(11.69)
Observations	1,346	1,346	1,346	1,346
R-squared	0.35	0.38	0.14	0.31

Notes: t-ratios in parentheses. *** $p<0.01$, ** $p<0.05$, * $p<0.1$.

APPENDIX C

ALTERNATIVE SPECIFICATIONS – CHAPTER THREE

Table C.1: Descriptive statistics for the base sample of 135 countries (extension of Table 3.3)

Panel A: Average 1985-2015	N	Simple Mean	Median	Standard Deviation	Min.	Max.
EFW	112	6.28	6.27	0.99	4.29	8.93
Area 2 (EFW)	108	5.15	4.96	1.72	1.98	8.57
Rule of Law (WGI)	135	0.03	-0.15	0.99	-1.71	1.98
Democracy (Polity IV)	126	2.92	4.07	5.92	-10.00	10.00
Executive Constraints (Polity IV)	121	4.78	5.00	1.80	1.00	7.00
Political Rights (FH)	135	3.55	3.71	1.93	1.00	7.00
Civil Liberties (FH)	135	3.54	3.71	1.65	1.00	6.86
Political Freedom (FH)	135	4.46	4.36	1.77	1.14	7.00
Democracy (ANRR)	134	0.58	0.67	0.41	0.00	1.00
Strong Democracy	126	0.29	0.00	0.41	0.00	1.00
Panel B: Time-Invariant Variables						
Malaria Ecology	135	6.80	6.90	0.93	2.96	8.97
Distance to Major Markets	135	5.30	5.16	1.63	1.85	8.88
Coastal Population	135	0.05	-0.15	1.00	-2.03	2.06
Geographic Disadvantage	127	4.66	7.00	5.89	-10.00	10.00
Migratory Distance	124	5.33	6.00	1.82	1.00	7.00
Genetic Diversity	135	3.33	3.00	2.07	1.00	7.00
Ethno-Linguistic Fractionalization	135	3.27	3.00	1.76	1.00	7.00
Absolute value of Latitude	135	4.70	5.00	1.88	1.00	7.00

Table C.2: Changes in economic and political institutions, and changes in poverty rates for the subsample of developing economies (extension of columns 7 and 8 of tables 3.7, 3.8, and 3.9, but for developing economies)

	(1)	(2)	(3)	(4)	(5)	(6)
	Dependent Variable is the Change in Poverty Rate (15-Year Periods)					
EFW 5-years prior to the beginning of the period	-3.16***	-2.72***			-3.44***	-3.07***
	(-2.94)	(-3.36)			(-3.02)	(-3.58)
Change in EFW 5-years prior to the period	-0.05	-1.99**			0.24	-2.18**
	(-0.03)	(-2.10)			(0.16)	(-2.15)
Change in EFW first 5-years of the period	-0.45	-1.12			-1.18	-1.44
	(-0.30)	(-1.19)			(-0.73)	(-1.44)
Change in EFW second 5-years of the period	-2.41*	-0.65			-2.18	-0.94
	(-1.82)	(-0.66)			(-1.50)	(-0.90)
Democracy, 5-years prior to the beginning of the period			0.33**	0.30***	0.23	0.14
			(2.30)	(2.89)	(1.41)	(1.17)
Change in Democracy 5-years prior to the period			0.16	0.46***	0.18	0.22
			(0.81)	(3.46)	(0.85)	(1.52)
Change in Democracy first 5-years of the period			0.15	0.53***	0.16	0.36**
			(0.78)	(3.86)	(0.69)	(2.28)
Change in Democracy second 5-years of the period			0.41**	0.50***	0.37	0.38**
			(2.14)	(3.34)	(1.61)	(2.37)
Initial Poverty Rate	-0.39***	-0.39***	-0.37***	-0.39***	-0.39***	-0.39***
	(-10.20)	(-13.92)	(-10.20)	(-15.02)	(-9.88)	(-13.65)
Log Initial Population	-1.18***	-1.16***	-0.26	-0.32	-1.04**	-1.14***
	(-2.70)	(-3.70)	(-0.62)	(-1.06)	(-2.01)	(-3.09)
Geographic Disadvantage Index	2.64***	2.66***	3.10***	3.14***	2.53**	2.51***
	(2.79)	(3.91)	(3.15)	(4.44)	(2.49)	(3.48)
Change in Prime Age Population	-0.34	-0.46***	-0.45**	-0.66***	-0.32	-0.46***
	(-1.62)	(-2.95)	(-2.38)	(-4.53)	(-1.41)	(-2.75)
Net fuel Exports. Average	-0.11	-0.08	0.02	0.05	-0.10	-0.07
	(-1.59)	(-1.53)	(0.38)	(1.13)	(-1.32)	(-1.25)
Dummy for ME Oil Exporters	6.71	6.18**	6.94*	7.10**	9.86**	8.02**
	(1.62)	(2.11)	(1.74)	(2.46)	(2.01)	(2.28)
War on Soil	6.65	11.18**	19.33***	20.44***	7.83	11.48**
	(1.09)	(2.22)	(3.60)	(4.86)	(1.24)	(2.23)
Dummy for the periods						
2000-2015	-2.40	-0.96	-5.63***	-4.28***	-2.57	-0.04
	(-1.36)	(-0.60)	(-3.69)	(-2.93)	(-1.30)	(-0.02)
1990-2005		0.16		-1.96		-0.31
		(-0.32)		(-1.40)		(-0.20)
1995-2010		-0.34		-2.76*		0.28
		(-0.22)		(-1.89)		(0.17)
Intercept	25.12***	22.68***	4.94**	5.22***	25.47***	23.28***
	(3.79)	(4.45)	(2.42)	(3.20)	(3.65)	(4.35)
Observations	159.00	323.00	190.00	379.00	150.00	304.00
R-squared	0.48	0.46	0.48	0.50	0.48	0.46

Notes: z-stat in parentheses. * p<0.1 ** p<0.05 *** p<0.01. Estimation by Seemingly Unrelated Regressions (SUR).

Table C.3: Changes in economic freedom and executive constraints, and changes in poverty rates for the subsample of developing economies (extension of columns 7 and 8 of tables 3.7, 3.8, and 3.9, but for developing economies)

	(1)	(2)	(3)	(4)	(5)	(6)
	Dependent Variable is the Change in Poverty Rate (15-Year Periods)					
EFW 5-years prior to the beginning of the period	-3.16***	-2.72***			-2.84**	-2.20**
	(-2.94)	(-3.36)			(-2.35)	(-2.49)
Change in EFW 5-years prior to the period	-0.05	-1.99**			-0.17	-1.65
	(-0.03)	(-2.10)			(-0.11)	(-1.54)
Change in EFW first 5-years of the period	-0.45	-1.12			-0.30	-0.85
	(-0.30)	(-1.19)			(-0.18)	(-0.81)
Change in EFW second 5-years of the period	-2.41*	-0.65			-1.73	-0.22
	(-1.82)	(-0.66)			(-1.05)	(-0.20)
Executive Constraints, 5-years prior to the period			0.89*	0.79**	0.40	0.21
			(1.86)	(2.26)	(0.76)	(0.55)
Change in Exec. Const., 5-years prior to the period			0.47	1.12**	0.39	0.47
			(0.77)	(2.55)	(0.62)	(1.04)
Change in Exec. Constr. First 5-years of the period			0.92	1.42***	0.80	0.91*
			(1.37)	(3.12)	(1.12)	(1.88)
Change in Exec. Constr. Second 5-years of the period			1.02	1.33***	0.74	1.03**
			(1.60)	(2.81)	(1.01)	(2.08)
Initial Poverty Rate	-0.39***	-0.39***	-0.36***	-0.39***	-0.38***	-0.39***
	(-10.20)	(-13.92)	(-9.13)	(-13.85)	(-8.68)	(-12.52)
Log Initial Population	-1.18***	-1.16***	-0.46	-0.41	-1.20**	-1.20***
	(-2.70)	(-3.70)	(-1.03)	(-1.28)	(-2.22)	(-3.15)
Geographic Disadvantage Index	2.64***	2.66***	2.37**	2.46***	2.07*	2.00***
	(2.79)	(3.91)	(2.26)	(3.35)	(1.92)	(2.67)
Change in Prime Age Population	-0.34	-0.46***	-0.53***	-0.74***	-0.42*	-0.57***
	(-1.62)	(-2.95)	(-2.68)	(-4.86)	(-1.77)	(-3.23)
Net fuel Exports. Average	-0.11	-0.08	0.07	0.11**	-0.03	0.01
	(-1.59)	(-1.53)	(0.96)	(2.04)	(-0.44)	(0.10)
Dummy for ME Oil Exporters	6.71	6.18**	4.19	3.68	6.16	4.30
	(1.62)	(2.11)	(1.04)	(1.24)	(1.30)	(1.24)
War on Soil	6.65	11.18**	18.13***	19.18***	-0.63	-0.45
	(1.09)	(2.22)	(2.80)	(3.62)	(-0.07)	(-0.05)
Dummy for the periods						
2000-2015	-2.40	-0.96	-6.14***	-5.27***	-2.61	-1.33
	(-1.36)	(-0.60)	(-3.94)	(-3.56)	(-1.26)	(-0.75)
1990-2005		-0.46		-2.59*		-1.18
		(-0.32)		(-1.80)		(-0.74)
1995-2010		-0.34		-3.47**		-0.93
		(-0.22)		(-2.33)		(-0.54)
Intercept	25.12***	22.68***	2.63	3.93	21.72***	19.35***
	(3.79)	(4.45)	(0.83)	(1.60)	(2.93)	(3.48)
Observations	159.00	323.00	172.00	342.00	136.00	277.00
R-squared	0.48	0.46	0.50	0.53	0.49	0.49

Notes: z-stat in parentheses. * p<0.1 ** p<0.05 *** p<0.01. Estimation by Seemingly Unrelated Regressions (SUR).

Table C.4: Changes in economic freedom and democracy (ANRR), and changes in poverty rates for the subsample of developing economies (extension of columns 7 and 8 of tables 3.7, 3.8, and 3.9, but for developing economies)

	(1)	(2)	(3)	(4)	(5)	(6)
	Dependent Variable is the Change in Poverty Rate (15-Year Periods)					
EFW 5-years prior to the beginning of the period	-3.16***	-2.72***			-3.17***	-2.86***
	(-2.94)	(-3.36)			(-2.92)	(-3.51)
Change in EFW 5-years prior to the period	-0.05	-1.99**			0.07	-2.02**
	(-0.03)	(-2.10)			(0.05)	(-2.12)
Change in EFW first 5-years of the period	-0.45	-1.12			-0.44	-1.16
	(-0.30)	(-1.19)			(-0.29)	(-1.22)
Change in EFW second 5-years of the period	-2.41*	-0.65			-2.30*	-0.79
	(-1.82)	(-0.66)			(-1.68)	(-0.79)
Dem (ANRR), 5-years prior to the period			3.16*	3.28***	0.89	0.62
			(1.82)	(2.58)	(0.46)	(0.45)
Change in Dem (ANRR), 5-years prior to the period			0.83	3.63**	-0.59	0.12
			(0.35)	(2.34)	(-0.25)	(0.07)
Change in Dem (ANRR). First 5-years of the period			1.18	4.87***	-0.14	1.67
			(0.48)	(3.16)	(-0.05)	(0.96)
Change in Dem (ANRR). Second 5-years of the period			2.34	4.32***	1.28	2.87
			(1.23)	(2.83)	(0.52)	(1.63)
Initial Poverty Rate	-0.39***	-0.39***	-0.37***	-0.41***	-0.39***	-0.39***
	(-10.20)	(-13.92)	(-10.85)	(-16.44)	(-9.94)	(-13.83)
Log Initial Population	-1.18***	-1.16***	-0.44	-0.54**	-1.11**	-1.17***
	(-2.70)	(-3.70)	(-1.18)	(-2.07)	(-2.44)	(-3.65)
Geographic Disadvantage Index	2.64***	2.66***	3.06***	3.36***	2.62***	2.62***
	(2.79)	(3.91)	(3.31)	(5.12)	(2.69)	(3.82)
Change in Prime Age Population	-0.34	-0.46***	-0.46***	-0.62***	-0.34	-0.46***
	(-1.62)	(-2.95)	(-2.67)	(-4.68)	(-1.63)	(-2.95)
Net fuel Exports. Average	-0.11	-0.08	0.02	0.05	-0.11	-0.07
	(-1.59)	(-1.53)	(0.41)	(1.16)	(-1.52)	(-1.40)
Dummy for ME Oil Exporters	6.71	6.18**	4.29	4.37*	7.26*	6.55**
	(1.62)	(2.11)	(1.25)	(1.79)	(1.68)	(2.17)
War on Soil	6.65	11.18**	18.75***	21.02***	7.21	11.81**
	(1.09)	(2.22)	(3.57)	(5.09)	(1.17)	(2.33)
Dummy for the periods						
2000-2015	-2.40	-0.96	-5.45***	-4.68***	-2.47	-0.46
	(-1.36)	(-0.60)	(-3.90)	(-3.47)	(-1.32)	(-0.28)
1990-2005		0.46		-2.21*		-0.32
		(-0.32)		(-1.68)		(0.22)
1995-2010		-0.34		-2.89**		0.14
		(-0.22)		(-2.14)		(0.09)
Intercept	25.12***	22.68***	4.84**	5.69***	24.54***	22.74***
	(3.79)	(4.45)	(2.38)	(3.47)	(3.67)	(4.44)
Observations	159.00	323.00	204.00	412.00	158.00	322.00
R-squared	0.48	0.46	0.48	0.51	0.48	0.46

Notes: z-stat in parentheses. * p<0.1 ** p<0.05 *** p<0.01. Estimation by Seemingly Unrelated Regressions (SUR). Democracy (ANRR) is the dichotomous measure of democracy as used by Acemoglu et al. (2019).

Table C.5: Changes in economic and political freedom, and changes in poverty rates for the subsample of developing economies (extension of columns 7 and 8 of tables 3.7, 3.8, and 3.9, but for developing economies)

	(1)	(2)	(3)	(4)	(5)	(6)
	Dependent Variable is the Change in Poverty Rate (15-Year Periods)					
EFW 5-years prior to the beginning of the period	-3.16***	-2.72***			-3.10***	-2.82***
	(-2.94)	(-3.36)			(-2.76)	(-3.34)
Change in EFW 5-years prior to the period	-0.05	-1.99**			-0.01	-2.12**
	(-0.03)	(-2.10)			(-0.01)	(-2.16)
Change in EFW first 5-years of the period	-0.45	-1.12			-0.54	-1.24
	(-0.30)	(-1.19)			(-0.34)	(-1.27)
Change in EFW second 5-years of the period	-2.41*	-0.65			-2.09	-0.65
	(-1.82)	(-0.66)			(-1.54)	(-0.65)
Political Freedom, 5-years prior to the period			0.88*	0.68*	0.34	0.05
			(1.75)	(1.82)	(0.57)	(0.11)
Change in Political Freedom, 5-years prior to the period			-0.87	0.34	-0.71	-0.38
			(-1.13)	(0.69)	(-0.87)	(-0.71)
Change in Political Freedom. First 5-years of the period			0.48	0.79	0.44	0.37
			(0.64)	(1.58)	(0.49)	(0.66)
Change in Pol. Freedom. Second 5-years of the period			1.00	0.89	0.63	0.74
			(1.52)	(1.63)	(0.78)	(1.21)
Initial Poverty Rate	-0.39***	-0.39***	-0.36***	-0.40***	-0.39***	-0.39***
	(-10.20)	(-13.92)	(-10.39)	(-15.44)	(-10.01)	(-13.78)
Log Initial Population	-1.18***	-1.16***	-0.24	-0.39	-0.97**	-1.16***
	(-2.70)	(-3.70)	(-0.63)	(-1.48)	(-2.08)	(-3.54)
Geographic Disadvantage Index	2.64***	2.66***	2.88***	3.21***	2.59***	2.61***
	(2.79)	(3.91)	(3.18)	(4.84)	(2.69)	(3.78)
Change in Prime Age Population	-0.34	-0.46***	-0.45***	-0.64***	-0.34	-0.47***
	(-1.62)	(-2.95)	(-2.61)	(-4.78)	(-1.61)	(-2.97)
Net fuel Exports. Average	-0.11	-0.08	0.03	0.04	-0.10	-0.08
	(-1.59)	(-1.53)	(0.46)	(0.88)	(-1.46)	(-1.48)
Dummy for ME Oil Exporters	6.71	6.18**	4.41	4.17*	7.45*	6.10**
	(1.62)	(2.11)	(1.28)	(1.68)	(1.70)	(1.97)
War on Soil	6.65	11.18**	19.09***	20.19***	7.66	11.08**
	(1.09)	(2.22)	(3.64)	(4.80)	(1.22)	(2.17)
Dummy for the periods						
2000-2015	-2.40	-0.96	-4.89***	-4.84***	-2.26	-0.61
	(-1.36)	(-0.60)	(-3.68)	(-3.63)	(-1.27)	(-0.38)
1990-2005		-0.46		-1.98		-0.37
		(-0.32)		(-1.51)		(-0.26)
1995-2010		-0.34		-3.11**		-0.29
		(-0.22)		(-2.35)		(-0.19)
Intercept	25.12***	22.68***	2.17	4.81**	22.87***	23.06***
	(3.79)	(4.45)	(0.70)	(2.04)	(3.34)	(4.43)
Observations	159.00	323.00	203.00	410.00	158.00	322.00
R-squared	0.48	0.46	0.49	0.49	0.49	0.46

Notes: z-stat in parentheses. * p<0.1 ** p<0.05 *** p<0.01. Estimation by Seemingly Unrelated Regressions (SUR).

Table C.6: Changes in economic freedom and strong democracy, and changes in poverty rates for the subsample of developing economies (extension of columns 7 and 8 of tables 3.7, 3.8, and 3.9, but for developing economies)

	(1)	(2)	(3)	(4)	(5)	(6)
	Dependent Variable is the Change in Poverty Rate (15-Year Periods)					
EFW 5-years prior to the beginning of the period	-3.16***	-2.72***			-3.18***	-2.73***
	(-2.94)	(-3.36)			(-2.81)	(-3.18)
Change in EFW 5-years prior to the period	-0.05	-1.99**			0.28	-1.87*
	(-0.03)	(-2.10)			(0.18)	(-1.84)
Change in EFW first 5-years of the period	-0.45	-1.12			-0.58	-0.98
	(-0.30)	(-1.19)			(-0.36)	(-0.97)
Change in EFW second 5-years of the period	-2.41*	-0.65			-2.20	-0.50
	(-1.82)	(-0.66)			(-1.56)	(-0.48)
Strong Democracy, 5-years prior to the period			1.46	-0.59	1.11	0.41
			(0.56)	(-0.31)	(0.42)	(0.21)
Change in Strong Democracy, 5-years prior to the period			-1.46	-2.17	-2.27	-2.44
			(-0.50)	(-1.04)	(-0.78)	(-1.18)
Change in Strong Democracy. First 5-years of the period			-1.99	-1.54	-2.79	-2.21
			(-0.72)	(-0.78)	(-0.97)	(-1.11)
Change in Strong. Dem. Second 5-years of the period			-2.49	-1.87	-1.02	-1.42
			(-0.81)	(-0.94)	(-0.28)	(-0.69)
Initial Poverty Rate	-0.39***	-0.39***	-0.38***	-0.42***	-0.40***	-0.40***
	(-10.20)	(-13.92)	(-10.14)	(-15.28)	(-9.66)	(-13.29)
Log Initial Population	-1.18***	-1.16***	-0.33	-0.35	-1.09**	-1.07***
	(-2.70)	(-3.70)	(-0.76)	(-1.10)	(-2.07)	(-2.83)
Geographic Disadvantage Index	2.64***	2.66***	3.21***	3.23***	2.84***	2.78***
	(2.79)	(3.91)	(3.24)	(4.47)	(2.82)	(3.82)
Change in Prime Age Population	-0.34	-0.46***	-0.47**	-0.71***	-0.33	-0.49***
	(-1.62)	(-2.95)	(-2.44)	(-4.70)	(-1.42)	(-2.87)
Net fuel Exports. Average	-0.11	-0.08	-0.01	-0.00	-0.12*	-0.09
	(-1.59)	(-1.53)	(-0.12)	(-0.00)	(-1.66)	(-1.62)
Dummy for ME Oil Exporters	6.71	6.18**	4.07	3.79	7.80*	6.77**
	(1.62)	(2.11)	(1.07)	(1.35)	(1.69)	(2.04)
War on Soil	6.65	11.18**	17.40***	18.48***	6.79	11.23**
	(1.09)	(2.22)	(3.24)	(4.31)	(1.09)	(2.17)
Dummy for the periods						
2000-2015	-2.40	-0.96	-5.18***	-4.86***	-2.48	-0.75
	(1.36)	(-0.60)	(-3.70)	(-3.46)	(1.32)	(-0.45)
1990-2005		-0.46		-1.77		-0.48
		(-0.32)		(-1.26)		(-0.31)
1995-2010		-0.34		-2.93**		-0.21
		(-0.22)		(-2.06)		(-0.13)
Intercept	25.12***	22.68***	6.15***	8.58***	25.04***	22.73***
	(3.79)	(4.45)	(2.89)	(4.97)	(3.63)	(4.25)
Observations	159.00	323.00	190.00	379.00	150.00	304.00
R-squared	0.48	0.46	0.47	0.47	0.48	0.46

Notes: z-stat in parentheses. * $p<0.1$ ** $p<0.05$ *** $p<0.01$. Estimation by Seemingly Unrelated Regressions (SUR).

Table C.7: Changes in political institutions, growth of per capita GDP, and changes in poverty rates (similar to table 3.8 but using executive constraints as the measure of democracy)

	(1)	(2)	(3)	(4)	(5)	(6)	(7)	(8)
					Panel analysis, 15-year periods			
	Period 1985-2000		Period 2000-2015		No Overlap	Overlap	No Overlap	Overlap
	Dependent Variable (Columns 1-6) Annual Growth Rate of Per capita GDP (15-Year Period)						Dep. Var. (Cols 7-8) Change in Poverty Rate (15-Year Period)	
Log Initial Per Capita GDP	-0.13	-0.57**	-0.73***	-0.61**	-0.62***	-0.52***		
	(-0.57)	(-2.11)	(-4.45)	(-2.51)	(-3.92)	(-4.71)		
Executive Constraints, 5-years prior the period	0.35***	0.17	0.14	-0.01	0.13	0.09	0.75*	0.71**
	(3.19)	(1.02)	(1.30)	(-0.07)	(1.51)	(1.57)	(1.83)	(2.35)
Change in Executive Constraints, 5-years prior the period	0.34***	0.18	0.22	0.11	0.15	0.10	0.42	1.09***
	(3.08)	(1.34)	(1.30)	(0.64)	(1.37)	(1.35)	(0.75)	(2.75)
Change in Exec. Constr. First 5-years of the period	0.08	-0.11	0.32	0.26	-0.02	-0.01	0.95	1.41***
	(0.42)	(-0.51)	(1.03)	(0.90)	(-0.16)	(-0.15)	(1.55)	(3.40)
Change in Exec. Constr. Second 5-years of the period	0.10	-0.03	-0.11	-0.16	-0.14	-0.01	1.04*	1.35***
	(0.51)	(-0.18)	(-0.52)	(-0.88)	(-1.27)	(-0.10)	(1.81)	(3.13)
Log Initial Population		0.12		0.26**	0.18**	0.14***	-0.43	-0.42
		(1.13)		(2.37)	(2.41)	(2.79)	(-1.15)	(-1.56)
Geographic Disadvantage Index		-0.49		-0.30	-0.37**	-0.41***	2.17**	2.39***
		(-1.65)		(-1.42)	(-2.27)	(-3.71)	(2.55)	(4.00)
Change in Prime Age Population		0.19***		0.11***	0.15***	0.14***	-0.54***	-0.64***
		(3.39)		(2.79)	(5.53)	(7.06)	(-3.85)	(-6.06)
Net fuel Exports. Average		-0.02		-0.01	-0.02	-0.01	0.06	0.10**
		(-0.93)		(-0.65)	(-1.42)	(-1.16)	(1.02)	(2.09)
Dummy for ME Oil Exporters		-0.32		-2.06**	-1.07	-1.36**	4.29	3.60
		(-0.26)		(-2.12)	(-1.42)	(-2.55)	(1.18)	(1.35)
War on Soil		-2.31***		-6.37***	-4.21***	-2.90***	17.92***	19.12***
		(-4.54)		(-12.39)	(-3.66)	(-3.17)	(3.03)	(3.96)
Dummy for the periods								
2000-2015					0.54**	0.63***	-5.31***	-4.92***
					(2.27)	(2.79)	(-4.35)	(-4.14)
1990-2005						0.26		-2.24*
						(1.15)		(-1.89)
1995-2010						0.55**		-3.28***
						(2.43)		(-2.73)
Initial Poverty Rate							-0.35***	-0.38***
							(-10.15)	(-15.26)
Intercept	1.13	4.67**	7.93***	6.53***	5.34***	4.70***	2.44	3.14
	(0.59)	(2.10)	(5.44)	(3.10)	(4.10)	(5.22)	(0.85)	(1.43)
Observations	106.00	97.00	114.00	112.00	209.00	416.00	209.00	416.00
R-squared	0.11	0.41	0.20	0.41	0.38	0.30	0.54	0.56

Notes: Robust t statistics in parentheses. * $p<0.1$ ** $p<0.05$ *** $p<0.01$. Seemingly Unrelated Regressions (SUR) used in panel analysis (Columns 5-8).

Table C.8: Changes in political institutions, growth of per capita GDP, and changes in poverty rates (similar to table 3.8 but using Acemoglu et al. (2019), Dem (ANRR), as the measure of democracy)

	(1)	(2)	(3)	(4)	(5)	(6)	(7)	(8)
					Panel analysis, 15-year periods			
	Period 1985-2000		Period 2000-2015		No Overlap	Overlap	No Overlap	Overlap
	Dependent Variable (Columns 1-6) Annual Growth Rate of Per capita GDP (15-Year Period)						Dep. Var. (Cols 7-8) Change in Poverty Rate (15-Year Period)	
Log Initial Per Capita GDP	-0.03	-0.64**	-0.64***	-0.66***	-0.61***	-0.56***		
	(-0.13)	(-2.30)	(-4.88)	(-3.23)	(-4.38)	(-5.61)		
Dem (ANRR), 5-years prior the period	1.93***	1.31**	0.57	0.35	0.84***	0.47**	2.75*	3.08***
	(3.76)	(2.18)	(1.35)	(0.76)	(2.65)	(2.08)	(1.81)	(2.74)
Change in Dem (ANRR), 5-years prior the period	1.08**	0.56	1.08*	0.50	0.50	0.61**	0.67	3.59**
	(2.51)	(1.00)	(1.77)	(0.73)	(1.12)	(2.16)	(0.31)	(2.54)
Change in Dem (ANRR). First 5-years of the period	0.89	0.52	1.02	0.83	0.44	-0.06	1.02	4.81***
	(1.04)	(0.67)	(0.93)	(0.76)	(0.96)	(-0.20)	(0.46)	(3.41)
Change in Dem (ANRR). Second 5-years of the period	0.09	-0.74	0.43	0.25	-0.68*	-0.47*	2.48	4.41***
	(0.14)	(-1.32)	(0.63)	(0.38)	(-1.90)	(-1.69)	(1.42)	(3.15)
Log Initial Population		0.05		0.20**	0.13**	0.12***	-0.38	-0.48**
		(0.50)		(2.30)	(2.07)	(2.70)	(-1.26)	(-2.23)
Geographic Disadvantage Index		-0.30		-0.30	-0.29*	-0.42***	2.70***	3.07***
		(-1.28)		(-1.51)	(-1.86)	(-3.91)	(3.53)	(5.65)
Change in Prime Age Population		0.18***		0.11***	0.15***	0.13***	-0.50***	-0.58***
		(3.52)		(2.86)	(5.68)	(6.91)	(-3.88)	(-5.96)
Net fuel Exports. Average		-0.01		0.01	-0.01	0.00	0.02	0.05
		(-0.41)		(0.39)	(-0.51)	(0.09)	(0.45)	(1.30)
Dummy for ME Oil Exporters		-0.14		-2.48***	-1.23*	-1.43***	4.47	4.29*
		(-0.16)		(-2.74)	(-1.85)	(-3.12)	(1.44)	(1.94)
War on Soil		-2.36***		-6.13***	-3.68***	-3.13***	18.61***	20.97***
		(-4.58)		(-14.89)	(-3.71)	(-4.12)	(3.87)	(5.53)
Dummy for the periods								
2000-2015					0.51**	0.61***	-4.72***	-4.31***
					(2.21)	(2.79)	(-4.25)	(-3.93)
1990-2005						0.34		-1.90*
						(1.54)		(-1.75)
1995-2010						0.56**		-2.69**
						(2.54)		(-2.44)
Initial Poverty Rate							-0.37***	-0.40***
							(-12.10)	(-18.16)
Intercept	0.68	5.58**	7.40***	6.90***	5.54***	5.30***	4.48**	4.90***
	(0.34)	(2.31)	(5.98)	(3.56)	(4.46)	(6.02)	(2.51)	(3.45)
Observations	131.00	117.00	134.00	129.00	246.00	496.00	246.00	496.00
R-squared	0.41	0.55	0.20	0.47	0.35	0.28	0.52	0.54

Notes: Robust t statistics in parentheses. * $p<0.1$ ** $p<0.05$ *** $p<0.01$. Seemingly Unrelated Regressions (SUR) used in panel analysis (Columns 5-8).

Table C.9: Changes in political institutions, growth of per capita GDP, and changes in poverty rates (similar to table 3.8 but using political freedom from Freedom House as the measure of democracy)

	(1)	(2)	(3)	(4)	(5)	(6)	(7)	(8)
					Panel analysis, 15-year periods			
	Period 1985-2000		Period 2000-2015		No Overlap	Overlap	No Overlap	Overlap
	Dependent Variable (Columns 1-6) Annual Growth Rate of Per capita GDP (15-Year Period)						Dep. Var. (Cols 7-8) Change in Poverty Rate (15-Year Period)	
Log Initial Per Capita GDP	-0.11	-0.60**	-0.62***	-0.64***	-0.65***	-0.61***		
	(-0.52)	(-2.24)	(-4.27)	(-2.95)	(-4.20)	(-5.58)		
Political Freedom, 5-years prior the period	0.52***	0.41***	0.09	0.03	0.24***	0.18***	0.66	0.52*
	(4.29)	(2.66)	(0.75)	(0.23)	(2.71)	(2.79)	(1.64)	(1.73)
Change in Political Freedom, 5-years prior the period	0.49***	0.42**	0.57***	0.35	0.39***	0.25***	-0.97	0.28
	(3.01)	(2.33)	(2.89)	(1.57)	(2.79)	(2.96)	(-1.40)	(0.63)
Change in Political Freedom. First 5-years of the period	0.20	0.14	0.64*	0.70**	0.18	0.18**	0.45	0.76*
	(0.91)	(0.58)	(1.92)	(2.15)	(1.26)	(2.04)	(0.66)	(1.66)
Change in Pol. Freedom. Second 5-years of the period	0.23	0.14	0.13	0.55*	0.08	0.18*	0.93	0.85*
	(1.48)	(0.91)	(0.38)	(1.83)	(0.67)	(1.88)	(1.59)	(1.74)
Log Initial Population		0.09		0.17**	0.15**	0.14***	-0.25	-0.39*
		(0.79)		(2.00)	(2.45)	(3.23)	(-0.82)	(-1.78)
Geographic Disadvantage Index		-0.27		-0.32*	-0.32**	-0.45***	2.64***	3.00***
		(-1.13)		(-1.71)	(-2.12)	(-4.33)	(3.49)	(5.40)
Change in Prime Age Population		0.18***		0.10**	0.15***	0.13***	-0.45***	-0.58***
		(3.48)		(2.46)	(5.89)	(7.14)	(-3.39)	(-5.65)
Net fuel Exports. Average		-0.01		0.01	-0.00	0.00	0.02	0.03
		(-0.27)		(0.46)	(-0.33)	(0.60)	(0.43)	(0.91)
Dummy for ME Oil Exporters		0.06		-2.78***	-1.10	-1.26***	4.39	3.90*
		(0.07)		(-3.32)	(-1.64)	(-2.76)	(1.41)	(1.73)
War on Soil		-1.78***		-6.36***	-3.36***	-2.83***	18.77***	20.01***
		(-3.26)		(-11.24)	(-3.45)	(-3.81)	(3.91)	(5.19)
Dummy for the periods								
2000-2015					0.64***	0.73***	-4.30***	-4.46***
					(2.99)	(3.48)	(-4.04)	(-4.10)
1990-2005						0.36*		-1.73
						(1.72)		(-1.59)
1995-2010						0.64***		-2.90***
						(3.07)		(-2.66)
Initial Poverty Rate							-0.35***	-0.39***
							(-11.37)	(-16.77)
Intercept	0.13	3.93*	6.94***	6.80***	5.04***	5.04***	2.37	4.43**
	(0.08)	(1.91)	(5.75)	(3.65)	(4.15)	(5.88)	(0.86)	(2.10)
Observations	131.00	117.00	135.00	130.00	247.00	498.00	245.00	494.00
R-squared	0.16	0.38	0.22	0.42	0.34	0.28	0.52	0.52

Notes: Robust t statistics in parentheses. * $p<0.1$ ** $p<0.05$ *** $p<0.01$. Seemingly Unrelated Regressions (SUR) used in panel analysis (Columns 5-8).

Table C.10: Changes in political institutions, growth of per capita GDP, and changes in poverty rates (similar to table 3.8 but using strong democracy as the measure of political institutions)

	(1)	(2)	(3)	(4)	(5)	(6)	(7)	(8)
					Panel analysis, 15-year periods			
	Period 1985-2000		Period 2000-2015		No Overlap	Overlap	No Overlap	Overlap
	Dependent Variable (Columns 1-6) Annual Growth Rate of Per capita GDP (15-Year Period)						Dep. Var. (Cols 7-8) Change in Poverty Rate (15-Year Period)	
Log Initial Per Capita GDP	0.01	-0.94***	-0.68***	-0.70**	-0.86***	-0.85***		
	(0.03)	(-3.26)	(-3.74)	(-2.36)	(-5.08)	(-7.18)		
Strong Democracy, 5-years prior the period	1.52**	2.29***	0.33	0.28	1.41***	1.43***	1.06	-0.51
	(2.28)	(3.59)	(0.75)	(0.47)	(3.47)	(4.96)	(0.59)	(-0.38)
Change in Strong Democracy, 5-years prior the period	2.28***	3.04***	1.52***	0.88	1.82***	1.75***	-1.35	-1.97
	(3.26)	(3.28)	(2.81)	(1.41)	(3.61)	(5.14)	(-0.53)	(-1.09)
Change in Strong Democracy. First 5-years of the period	1.18*	1.42**	1.64**	1.15	1.18**	1.28***	-2.01	-1.44
	(1.66)	(2.08)	(2.09)	(1.39)	(2.44)	(3.87)	(-0.81)	(-0.81)
Change in Strong. Dem. Second 5-years of the period	0.69	1.12**	2.34**	1.93*	1.15**	0.88***	-2.57	-1.82
	(0.99)	(2.21)	(2.43)	(1.82)	(2.17)	(2.67)	(-0.92)	(-1.00)
Log Initial Population		0.15		0.18	0.16**	0.13***	-0.27	-0.30
		(1.50)		(1.65)	(2.38)	(2.80)	(-0.76)	(-1.15)
Geographic Disadvantage Index		-0.38*		-0.32	-0.39**	-0.43***	2.80***	2.94***
		(-1.73)		(-1.37)	(-2.55)	(-4.11)	(3.39)	(4.87)
Change in Prime Age Population		0.21***		0.11**	0.16***	0.16***	-0.51***	-0.67***
		(4.35)		(2.59)	(5.97)	(7.77)	(-3.47)	(-5.82)
Net fuel Exports. Average		0.00		0.00	-0.00	0.00	-0.00	0.00
		(0.05)		(0.17)	(-0.27)	(0.38)	(-0.04)	(0.10)
Dummy for ME Oil Exporters		0.29		-2.54**	-1.12	-1.19**	4.19	3.64
		(0.31)		(-2.48)	(-1.60)	(-2.46)	(1.23)	(1.45)
War on Soil		-2.29***		-6.24***	-3.79***	-3.14***	17.29***	18.46***
		(-5.52)		(-18.44)	(-4.06)	(-4.46)	(3.52)	(4.71)
Dummy for the periods								
2000-2015					0.80***	0.81***	-4.64***	-4.64***
					(3.76)	(3.96)	(-4.13)	(-4.06)
1990-2005						0.33		-1.60
						(1.59)		(-1.38)
1995-2010						0.68***		-2.84**
						(3.24)		(-2.45)
Initial Poverty Rate							-0.37***	-0.41***
							(-11.08)	(-16.62)
Intercept	0.75	7.55***	7.99***	7.42***	7.41***	7.41***	5.81***	7.87***
	(0.32)	(3.26)	(5.16)	(2.86)	(5.26)	(7.54)	(3.05)	(5.16)
Observations	122.00	109.00	126.00	121.00	230.00	459.00	230.00	459.00
R-squared	0.10	0.47	0.19	0.38	0.39	0.34	0.50	0.51

Notes: Robust t statistics in parentheses. * $p<0.1$ ** $p<0.05$ *** $p<0.01$. Seemingly Unrelated Regressions (SUR) used in panel analysis (Columns 5-8).

Table C.11: Changes in economic and political institutions, growth of per capita GDP, and changes in poverty rates (similar to table 3.9 but using executive constraints as the measure of democracy)

	(1)	(2)	(3)	(4)	(5)	(6)	(7)	(8)
					Panel Analysis 15-year periods			
	Period 1985-2000		Period 2000-2015		No Overlap	Overlap	No Overlap	Overlap
	Dependent Variable (Columns 1-6) Annual Growth Rate of Per capita GDP (15-Year Period)						Dep. Var. (Cols 7-8) Change in Poverty Rate (15-Year Period)	
Log Initial Per Capita GDP	-0.64**	-0.64**	-0.94***	-0.82***	-0.80***	-0.70***		
	(-2.10)	(-2.32)	(-3.82)	(-2.96)	(-4.48)	(-5.67)		
EFW 5-years prior to the beginning of the period	1.10***	0.67***	0.45	0.91**	0.84***	0.85***	-1.94**	-1.37**
	(4.51)	(2.88)	(1.51)	(2.37)	(4.82)	(7.09)	(-2.23)	(-2.15)
Change in EFW 5-years prior to the period	1.89***	0.99***	0.04	0.73	0.97***	0.99***	0.51	-1.04
	(4.62)	(2.86)	(0.10)	(1.40)	(4.11)	(6.41)	(0.40)	(-1.19)
Change in EFW first 5-years of the period	0.95**	0.68**	1.36***	1.53***	1.02***	1.11***	-0.23	-0.48
	(2.53)	(2.11)	(2.89)	(3.16)	(4.00)	(7.25)	(-0.16)	(-0.54)
Change in EFW second 5-years of the period	1.43***	0.75**	-0.12	0.85	0.81***	0.86***	-1.27	0.05
	(4.25)	(2.62)	(-0.17)	(1.14)	(3.20)	(5.22)	(-0.91)	(0.05)
Executive Constraints, 5-years prior to the period	0.20	0.14	0.09	-0.05	0.07	0.04	0.43	0.29
	(1.49)	(1.12)	(0.67)	(-0.37)	(0.81)	(0.70)	(0.94)	(0.87)
Change in Executive Constraints, 5-years prior to the period	0.19	0.13	0.13	-0.01	0.07	0.10	0.39	0.49
	(1.39)	(0.96)	(0.66)	(-0.07)	(0.74)	(1.42)	(0.69)	(1.20)
Change in Exec. Constr. First 5-years of the period	0.11	-0.00	0.11	-0.02	0.01	0.00	0.75	0.91**
	(0.60)	(-0.00)	(0.33)	(-0.05)	(0.07)	(0.04)	(1.18)	(2.09)
Change in Exec. Constr. Second 5-years of the period	0.12	0.12	-0.27	-0.33	-0.08	0.02	0.88	1.08**
	(0.60)	(0.79)	(-1.19)	(-1.47)	(-0.65)	(0.23)	(1.36)	(2.45)
Log Initial Population		0.24**		0.34***	0.28***	0.26***	-0.85**	-0.89***
		(2.07)		(2.83)	(3.74)	(5.15)	(-2.08)	(-3.02)
Geographic Disadvantage Index		-0.43		-0.18	-0.30**	-0.29***	1.69**	1.69***
		(-1.59)		(-0.80)	(-1.98)	(-2.85)	(1.97)	(2.81)
Change in Prime Age Population		0.17***		0.11**	0.14***	0.13***	-0.57***	-0.64***
		(3.38)		(2.14)	(4.77)	(6.71)	(-3.69)	(-5.55)
Net fuel Exports. Average		-0.02		0.03	0.01	0.01*	0.00	0.03
		(-1.11)		(1.29)	(0.63)	(1.65)	(0.00)	(0.65)
Dummy for ME Oil Exporters		-1.47		-4.06***	-2.79***	-2.82***	5.66	3.89
		(-1.48)		(-2.98)	(-3.60)	(-5.30)	(1.36)	(1.28)
War on Soil				-6.08***	-5.57***	-5.77***	-0.60	0.09
				(-10.89)	(-3.96)	(-4.31)	(-0.08)	(0.01)
Dummy for the periods								
2000-2015					0.12	0.20	-3.09**	-2.19
					(0.42)	(0.85)	(-2.06)	(-1.64)
1990-2005						-0.20		-1.11
						(-0.94)		(-0.89)
1995-2010						0.01		-1.38
						(0.05)		(-1.05)
Initial Poverty Rate							-0.38***	-0.38***
							(-9.94)	(-14.02)
Intercept	-0.96	0.72	6.93***	2.19	1.56	0.72	16.75***	14.14***
	(-0.43)	(0.32)	(2.82)	(0.68)	(1.14)	(0.78)	(2.92)	(3.29)
Observations	83.00	77.00	98.00	96.00	173.00	351.00	173.00	351.00
R-squared	0.40	0.61	0.24	0.51	0.51	0.46	0.52	0.52

Notes: Robust t statistics in parentheses. * p<0.1 ** p<0.05 *** p<0.01. Seemingly Unrelated Regressions (SUR) used in panel analysis (Columns 5-8).

Table C.12: Changes in economic and political institutions, growth of per capita GDP, and changes in poverty rates (similar to table 3.9 but using Acemoglu et al. (2019), Dem (ANRR), as the measure of democracy)

	(1)	(2)	(3)	(4)	(5)	(6)	(7)	(8)
					Panel Analysis 15-year periods			
	Period 1985-2000		Period 2000-2015		No Overlap	Overlap	No Overlap	Overlap
	Dependent Variable (Columns 1-6) Annual Growth Rate of Per capita GDP (15-Year Period)						Dep. Var. (Cols 7-8) Change in Poverty Rate (15-Year Period)	
Log Initial Per Capita GDP	-0.61**	-0.64***	-0.83***	-0.80***	-0.72***	-0.65***		
	(-2.45)	(-2.65)	(-3.79)	(-3.14)	(-4.29)	(-5.46)		
EFW 5-years prior to the beginning of the period	1.22***	0.73***	0.50	0.82**	0.80***	0.80***	-2.09***	-1.66***
	(4.60)	(3.56)	(1.62)	(2.24)	(4.84)	(6.84)	(-2.63)	(-2.86)
Change in EFW 5-years prior to the period	1.95***	1.34***	0.15	0.65	1.09***	0.95***	0.86	-1.19
	(5.15)	(4.14)	(0.35)	(1.37)	(4.90)	(6.53)	(0.75)	(-1.52)
Change in EFW first 5-years of the period	1.07***	0.59**	1.19**	1.38***	0.79***	1.01***	-0.32	-0.61
	(2.79)	(2.07)	(2.44)	(3.02)	(3.27)	(6.93)	(-0.25)	(-0.76)
Change in EFW second 5-years of the period	1.39***	0.79***	0.12	0.65	0.71***	0.75***	-1.79	-0.36
	(4.96)	(3.13)	(0.21)	(1.05)	(3.31)	(4.93)	(-1.55)	(-0.42)
Dem (ANRR), 5-years prior to the period	1.16**	0.86*	0.44	0.11	0.50	0.28	1.24	1.19
	(2.31)	(1.82)	(0.87)	(0.25)	(1.57)	(1.26)	(0.73)	(0.96)
Change in Dem (ANRR), 5-years prior to the period	0.44	0.27	1.07*	0.35	0.22	0.37	-0.71	0.15
	(0.80)	(0.50)	(1.82)	(0.55)	(0.55)	(1.35)	(-0.33)	(0.10)
Change in Dem (ANRR). First 5-years of the period	0.51	0.43	1.20	0.78	0.42	0.10	-0.22	1.59
	(0.62)	(0.61)	(0.94)	(0.74)	(0.95)	(0.37)	(-0.09)	(1.02)
Change in Dem (ANRR). Second 5-years of the period	0.45	0.03	0.47	0.09	-0.18	-0.16	1.55	2.78*
	(0.68)	(0.06)	(0.59)	(0.10)	(-0.44)	(-0.55)	(0.70)	(1.76)
Log Initial Population		0.16		0.28***	0.22***	0.22***	-0.67**	-0.71***
		(1.66)		(2.69)	(3.46)	(5.11)	(-2.01)	(-3.03)
Geographic Disadvantage Index		-0.30		-0.19	-0.26*	-0.28***	2.09***	2.09***
		(-1.31)		(-0.86)	(-1.72)	(-2.77)	(2.68)	(3.78)
Change in Prime Age Population		0.13***		0.10**	0.13***	0.12***	-0.53***	-0.61***
		(2.83)		(2.53)	(4.67)	(6.33)	(-3.76)	(-5.75)
Net fuel Exports. Average		-0.01		0.02	0.00	0.01	-0.07	-0.03
		(-0.36)		(1.29)	(0.30)	(0.96)	(-1.11)	(-0.70)
Dummy for ME Oil Exporters		-1.04		-3.79***	-2.22***	-1.99***	6.83*	5.98**
		(-1.13)		(-3.06)	(-3.06)	(-4.11)	(1.79)	(2.24)
War on Soil		-1.09*		-5.79***	-3.33***	-3.00***	7.53	12.17***
		(-1.77)		(-11.90)	(-3.19)	(-3.65)	(1.35)	(2.66)
Dummy for the periods								
2000-2015					-0.14	0.01	-3.13**	-1.74
					(-0.54)	(0.03)	(-2.29)	(-1.40)
1990-2005						-0.20		-0.52
						(-0.96)		(-0.45)
1995-2010						-0.16		-0.65
						(-0.74)		(-0.53)
Initial Poverty Rate							-0.39***	-0.38***
							(-11.15)	(-15.20)
Intercept	-1.59	1.03	5.63***	2.38	1.57	0.94	18.67***	15.95***
	(-0.77)	(0.51)	(2.65)	(0.88)	(1.22)	(1.05)	(3.57)	(4.02)
Observations	100.00	93.00	111.00	107.00	200.00	406.00	200.00	406.00
R-squared	0.43	0.57	0.23	0.48	0.46	0.42	0.50	0.49

Notes: Robust t statistics in parentheses. * $p<0.1$ ** $p<0.05$ *** $p<0.01$. Seemingly Unrelated Regressions (SUR) used in panel analysis (Columns 5-8).

Table C.13: Changes in economic and political institutions, growth of per capita GDP, and changes in poverty rates (similar to table 3.9 but using political freedom from Freedom House as the measure of democracy)

	(1)	(2)	(3)	(4)	(5)	(6)	(7)	(8)
					Panel Analysis 15-year periods			
	Period 1985-2000		Period 2000-2015		No Overlap	Overlap	No Overlap	Overlap
	Dependent Variable (Columns 1-6) Annual Growth Rate of Per capita GDP (15-Year Period)						Dep. Var. (Cols 7-8) Change in Poverty Rate (15-Year Period)	
Log Initial Per Capita GDP	-0.73***	-0.72***	-0.84***	-0.77***	-0.73***	-0.69***		
	(-3.06)	(-2.66)	(-3.60)	(-2.92)	(-4.15)	(-5.56)		
EFW 5-years prior to the beginning of the period	1.15***	0.64***	0.53*	0.81**	0.76***	0.76***	-2.27***	-1.82***
	(4.83)	(3.25)	(1.87)	(2.51)	(4.75)	(6.67)	(-2.66)	(-2.85)
Change in EFW 5-years prior to the period	1.91***	1.32***	0.10	0.63	1.09***	0.91***	0.55	-1.43*
	(4.99)	(4.18)	(0.23)	(1.44)	(4.93)	(6.30)	(0.47)	(-1.75)
Change in EFW first 5-years of the period	0.89**	0.43	0.99**	1.10**	0.69***	0.96***	-0.51	-0.83
	(2.17)	(1.35)	(2.07)	(2.30)	(2.77)	(6.61)	(-0.38)	(-0.99)
Change in EFW second 5-years of the period	1.37***	0.80***	0.02	0.54	0.74***	0.70***	-1.67	-0.31
	(5.37)	(3.13)	(0.04)	(0.91)	(3.50)	(4.71)	(-1.46)	(-0.36)
Political Freedom, 5-years prior to the period	0.35**	0.33**	0.04	-0.06	0.11	0.11	0.51	0.34
	(2.37)	(2.13)	(0.28)	(-0.40)	(1.15)	(1.54)	(1.00)	(0.90)
Change in Political Freedom, 5-years prior to the period	0.24	0.29	0.49**	0.20	0.22	0.19**	-0.80	-0.26
	(1.33)	(1.50)	(2.49)	(1.00)	(1.64)	(2.24)	(-1.10)	(-0.55)
Change in Political Freedom. First 5-years of the period	0.27	0.31	0.56	0.51	0.19	0.18**	0.53	0.44
	(1.16)	(1.37)	(1.45)	(1.54)	(1.27)	(2.03)	(0.67)	(0.86)
Change in Pol. Freedom. Second 5-years of the period	0.02	0.17	0.05	0.45	0.16	0.18*	0.83	0.80
	(0.12)	(1.17)	(0.13)	(1.39)	(1.19)	(1.87)	(1.15)	(1.45)
Log Initial Population		0.19*		0.21**	0.22***	0.23***	-0.56*	-0.69***
		(1.92)		(2.14)	(3.48)	(5.32)	(-1.65)	(-2.90)
Geographic Disadvantage Index		-0.29		-0.21	-0.31**	-0.33***	2.15***	2.15***
		(-1.21)		(-1.00)	(-2.11)	(-3.23)	(2.78)	(3.83)
Change in Prime Age Population		0.14***		0.10**	0.13***	0.12***	-0.48***	-0.59***
		(3.23)		(2.26)	(4.84)	(6.60)	(-3.28)	(-5.41)
Net fuel Exports. Average		-0.00		0.02	0.00	0.01	-0.07	-0.04
		(-0.01)		(1.35)	(0.36)	(1.23)	(-1.14)	(-0.82)
Dummy for ME Oil Exporters		-0.55		-4.31***	-2.33***	-1.92***	7.29*	5.92**
		(-0.58)		(-3.88)	(-3.12)	(-3.91)	(1.88)	(2.16)
War on Soil		-0.59		-6.15***	-3.23***	-2.88***	8.22	11.84**
		(-1.02)		(-8.77)	(-3.07)	(-3.52)	(1.46)	(2.57)
Dummy for the periods								
2000-2015					-0.01	0.11	-2.67**	-1.67
					(-0.04)	(0.51)	(-1.99)	(-1.35)
1990-2005						-0.18		-0.51
						(-0.90)		(-0.45)
1995-2010						-0.10		-0.93
						(-0.48)		(-0.78)
Initial Poverty Rate							-0.38***	-0.38***
							(-11.18)	(-15.11)
Intercept	-1.03	1.06	5.58**	2.71	1.48	1.05	17.53***	16.17***
	(-0.59)	(0.53)	(2.62)	(1.08)	(1.16)	(1.19)	(3.35)	(4.06)
Observations	101.00	94.00	112.00	108.00	202.00	410.00	200.00	406.00
R-squared	0.44	0.58	0.26	0.51	0.34	0.28	0.52	0.52

Notes: Robust t statistics in parentheses. * p<0.1 ** p<0.05 *** p<0.01. Seemingly Unrelated Regressions (SUR) used in panel analysis (Columns 5-8).

Table C.14: Changes in economic and political institutions, growth of per capita GDP, and changes in poverty rates (similar to table 3.9 but using strong democracy as the measure of political institutions)

	(1)	(2)	(3)	(4)	(5)	(6)	(7)	(8)
					Panel Analysis 15-year periods			
	Period 1985-2000		Period 2000-2015		No Overlap	Overlap	No Overlap	Overlap
	Dependent Variable (Columns 1-6) Annual Growth Rate of Per capita GDP (15-Year Period)						Dep. Var. (Cols 7-8) Change in Poverty Rate (15-Year Period)	
Log Initial Per Capita GDP	-0.57	-0.80**	-0.94***	-0.78**	-0.87***	-0.85***		
	(-1.56)	(-2.57)	(-3.35)	(-2.48)	(-4.62)	(-6.48)		
EFW 5-years prior to the beginning of the period	1.34***	0.64***	0.58	0.89**	0.81***	0.80***	-2.44***	-1.99***
	(4.71)	(2.82)	(1.64)	(2.17)	(4.86)	(6.75)	(-2.74)	(-2.96)
Change in EFW 5-years prior to the period	2.06***	1.17***	0.11	0.68	0.97***	0.93***	0.71	-1.36
	(5.01)	(3.56)	(0.23)	(1.19)	(4.29)	(6.45)	(0.56)	(-1.58)
Change in EFW first 5-years of the period	1.35***	0.70**	1.43***	1.54***	0.99***	0.96***	-0.58	-0.67
	(2.88)	(2.22)	(2.78)	(3.04)	(4.02)	(6.68)	(-0.42)	(-0.77)
Change in EFW second 5-years of the period	1.48***	0.64**	0.18	0.96	0.65***	0.71***	-1.85	-0.25
	(5.26)	(2.56)	(0.24)	(1.33)	(3.02)	(4.74)	(-1.52)	(-0.27)
Strong Democracy, 5-years prior to the period	0.06	0.98	0.38	0.13	0.57	0.67**	2.35	2.08
	(0.07)	(1.57)	(0.68)	(0.21)	(1.41)	(2.42)	(1.13)	(1.37)
Change in Strong Democracy, 5-years prior to the period	0.78	1.90**	1.67***	1.11*	1.28***	1.27***	-1.69	-1.49
	(0.97)	(2.02)	(3.36)	(1.92)	(2.79)	(4.03)	(-0.67)	(-0.83)
Change in Strong Democracy. First 5-years of the period	-0.25	0.43	1.19	0.63	0.66	0.82***	-2.42	-1.80
	(-0.33)	(0.68)	(1.43)	(0.77)	(1.40)	(2.63)	(-0.94)	(-1.01)
Change in Strong. Dem. Second 5-years of the period	-0.17	0.49	2.02**	1.88*	1.09*	0.65**	-0.98	-1.30
	(-0.29)	(0.72)	(2.01)	(1.84)	(1.88)	(2.07)	(-0.30)	(-0.70)
Log Initial Population		0.20*		0.31**	0.24***	0.23***	-0.69*	-0.65**
		(1.76)		(2.63)	(3.47)	(5.07)	(-1.77)	(-2.33)
Geographic Disadvantage Index		-0.35*		-0.11	-0.29**	-0.30***	2.38***	2.36***
		(-1.70)		(-0.47)	(-1.97)	(-2.99)	(2.91)	(3.99)
Change in Prime Age Population		0.17***		0.12***	0.14***	0.14***	-0.47***	-0.57***
		(4.12)		(2.72)	(4.95)	(6.92)	(-2.86)	(-4.66)
Net fuel Exports. Average		-0.00		0.02	0.01	0.01	-0.09	-0.06
		(-0.14)		(1.32)	(0.49)	(1.42)	(-1.42)	(-1.25)
Dummy for ME Oil Exporters		-1.24		-3.91***	-2.66***	-2.44***	7.84*	6.79**
		(-1.13)		(-2.88)	(-3.57)	(-4.88)	(1.93)	(2.32)
War on Soil		-1.24**		-5.73***	-3.45***	-3.04***	7.01	11.48**
		(-2.30)		(-16.41)	(-3.46)	(-3.93)	(1.24)	(2.47)
Dummy for the periods								
2000-2015					0.09	0.13	-2.73*	-1.47
					(0.35)	(0.61)	(-1.88)	(-1.12)
1990-2005						-0.18		-0.53
						(-0.87)		(-0.44)
1995-2010						-0.03		-0.64
						(-0.16)		(-0.50)
Initial Poverty Rate							-0.39***	-0.38***
							(-10.70)	(-14.56)
Intercept	-2.17	2.80	6.29**	1.62	2.58*	2.41**	20.59***	17.76***
	(-0.73)	(1.26)	(2.08)	(0.42)	(1.71)	(2.30)	(3.70)	(4.15)
Observations	95.00	88.00	106.00	102.00	190.00	384.00	190.00	384.00
R-squared	0.41	0.62	0.24	0.51	0.51	0.48	0.51	0.49

Notes: Robust t statistics in parentheses. * $p<0.1$ ** $p<0.05$ *** $p<0.01$. Seemingly Unrelated Regressions (SUR) used in panel analysis (Columns 5-8).

Table C.15: Institutions and instrumental variables. Falsification tests (similar to table 3.10)

Panel A: Economic Institutions and Migratory Distance from Addis Ababa, Ethiopia

	(1)	(2)	(3)	(4)	(5)	(6)	(7)
	Per capita GDP			Economic Freedom		Legal System	
Migratory Distance	0.27***	0.11*	0.08	0.22***	0.12**	0.36***	0.12*
	(4.59)	(1.76)	(1.36)	(4.29)	(2.34)	(4.17)	(1.68)
Migratory Distance (Squared)	-0.01***	-0.00	-0.00	-0.01***	-0.00**	-0.01***	-0.01**
	(-4.15)	(-1.49)	(-0.74)	(-3.97)	(-2.29)	(-4.31)	(-2.34)
2015 EFW		0.71***					
		(4.92)					
2015 Area 2 (EFW)			0.54***				
			(12.08)				
2015 Per Capita GDP					0.39***		0.90***
					(8.91)		(11.22)
Intercept	7.98***	3.84***	5.90***	5.85***	2.77***	3.90***	-3.29***
	(27.87)	(4.34)	(20.85)	(24.76)	(6.70)	(10.26)	(-4.42)
Observations	135.00	135.00	135.00	135.00	135.00	135.00	135.00
R-squared	0.12	0.36	0.54	0.12	0.36	0.12	0.54

Panel B: Average Political Institutions (1985-2015) and Settler Mortality Rates (AJR 2003)

	(1)	(2)	(3)	(4)	(5)	(6)	(7)
	Per capita GDP			polm30		xcm30	
Log Settler Mort. Rate	-0.66***	-0.52***	-0.49***	-2.09***	-1.04**	-0.75***	-0.42***
	(-7.46)	(-4.69)	(-3.96)	(-5.12)	(-2.19)	(-5.84)	(-2.73)
polm30		0.06**					
		(2.43)					
xcm30			0.19**				
			(2.25)				
2015 Per Capita GDP					1.64***		0.52**
					(2.93)		(2.61)
Intercept	11.86***	11.04***	10.20***	12.42***	-6.87	8.11***	1.97
	(28.22)	(18.72)	(10.91)	(5.92)	(-1.06)	(12.23)	(0.86)
Observations	73.00	69.00	67.00	69.00	69.00	67.00	67.00
R-squared	0.48	0.52	0.54	0.25	0.32	0.33	0.39

Panel C: Average Political Institutions (1985-2015) and Early Disease Environment (Auer 2013)

	(1)	(2)	(3)	(4)	(5)	(6)	(7)
	Per capita GDP			polm30	polm30	xcm30	xcm30
Colony dummy × EDE	-1.00***	-0.86***	-0.74***	-2.92***	-1.55*	-1.06***	-0.53**
	(-9.22)	(-7.09)	(-5.81)	(-5.96)	(-1.86)	(-6.98)	(-2.29)
polm30		0.05**					
		(2.32)					
xcm30			0.21***				
			(3.32)				
2015 Per Capita GDP					1.38**		0.55***
					(2.33)		(3.25)
Intercept	9.43***	9.24***	8.39***	3.87***	-9.10*	5.12***	-0.05
	(99.96)	(66.89)	(23.27)	(6.99)	(-1.68)	(31.31)	(-0.03)
Observations	122.00	120.00	117.00	120.00	120.00	117.00	117.00
R-squared	0.38	0.42	0.44	0.15	0.20	0.21	0.30

Note: t-statistics in parentheses. * p<0.1 ** p<0.05 *** p<0.01.

Table C.16: Institutions and instrumental variables. Falsification tests (similar to tables 3.10 and C.15)

Panel A: Economic Institutions and Migratory Distance from Addis Ababa, Ethiopia

	(1)	(2)	(3)	(4)	(5)	(6)	(7)
	Per capita GDP			efm30		a2m30	
Migratory Distance	0.27***	0.02	0.06	0.31***	0.13***	0.42***	0.09
	(4.59)	(0.30)	(1.32)	(5.32)	(2.83)	(4.14)	(1.31)
Migratory Distance (Squared)	-0.01***	-0.00	-0.00	-0.01***	-0.00***	-0.02***	-0.00*
	(-4.15)	(-0.24)	(-0.82)	(-4.82)	(-2.65)	(-4.16)	(-1.91)
efm30		0.96***					
		(10.38)					
a2m30			0.55***				
			(17.89)				
2015 Per Capita GDP					0.56***		1.14***
					(12.76)		(12.01)
Intercept	7.98***	3.21***	6.18***	4.93***	0.53	3.51***	-5.75***
	(27.87)	(5.89)	(22.75)	(20.81)	(1.32)	(8.52)	(-6.74)
Observations	135.00	112.00	108.00	112.00	112.00	108.00	108.00
R-squared	0.12	0.60	0.68	0.22	0.64	0.13	0.68

Panel B: Strong Democracy (1985-2015), Executive Const. at Independence, and Settler Mortality Rates (AJR 2003)

	(1)	(2)	(3)	(4)	(5)	(6)	(7)
	Per capita GDP			SDem30		xcon_0	
Log Settler Mort. Rate	-0.66***	-0.47***	-0.62***	-0.13***	-0.03	-0.84***	-0.75**
	(-7.46)	(-4.73)	(-6.17)	(-3.90)	(-0.83)	(-4.10)	(-2.45)
SDem30		1.25***					
		(4.84)					
xcon_0			0.02				
			(0.44)				
2015 Per Capita GDP					0.17***		0.13
					(4.48)		(0.43)
Intercept	11.86***	10.71***	11.56***	0.83***	-1.15***	7.37***	5.88
	(28.22)	(20.19)	(19.59)	(4.43)	(-2.88)	(7.32)	(1.56)
Observations	73.00	69.00	69.00	69.00	69.00	69.00	69.00
R-squared	0.48	0.58	0.48	0.23	0.39	0.23	0.23

Panel C: Strong Democracy, Executive Const. at Independence, and Early Disease Environment (Auer 2013)

	(1)	(2)	(3)	(4)	(5)	(6)	(7)
	Per capita GDP			SDem30		xcon_0	
Colony dummy × EDE	-1.00***	-0.67***	-0.98***	-0.22***	-0.02	-0.34	-0.15
	(-9.22)	(-6.11)	(-8.83)	(-6.28)	(-0.33)	(-1.41)	(-0.50)
SDem30		1.46***					
		(8.72)					
xcon_0			0.04				
			(0.98)				
2015 Per Capita GDP					0.21***		0.19
					(6.23)		(0.97)
Intercept	9.43***	8.90***	9.28***	0.36***	-1.61***	3.32***	1.50
	(99.96)	(73.74)	(52.53)	(8.57)	(-5.35)	(14.70)	(0.81)
Observations	122.00	120.00	120.00	120.00	120.00	120.00	120.00
R-squared	0.38	0.57	0.38	0.17	0.43	0.02	0.02

Note: t-statistics in parentheses. * $p<0.1$ ** $p<0.05$ *** $p<0.01$.

Table C.17: Institutions and instrumental variables. Identification condition falsification tests (similar to tables 3.10, C.15, and C.16)

Panel A: Risk of Epropriation (1985-1995), Social Infrastructure, and Predicted Genetic Diversity

	(1)	(2)	(3)	(4)	(5)	(6)	(7)
	Per capita GDP			Exp.Risk 1985-1995		socinf	
Genetic Diversity	185.26***	14.52	16.84	291.67***	103.83**	59.43***	25.58***
	(4.06)	(0.49)	(0.45)	(4.08)	(2.23)	(6.31)	(3.64)
Genetic Diversity (Squared)	-140.28***	-13.57	-14.95	-215.95***	-73.97**	-44.26***	-18.71***
	(-4.15)	(-0.61)	(-0.54)	(-4.08)	(-2.13)	(-6.36)	(-3.57)
Exp.Risk 1985-1995		0.58***					
		(18.28)					
Social Infrastructure			3.66***				
			(13.11)				
2015 Per Capita GDP					1.03***		0.14***
					(10.35)		(12.51)
Intercept	-51.16***	1.73	3.03	-90.33***	-38.55**	-19.24***	-9.51***
	(-3.36)	(0.18)	(0.24)	(-3.78)	(-2.55)	(-6.11)	(-4.15)
Observations	135.00	107.00	112.00	107.00	107.00	112.00	112.00
R-squared	0.12	0.64	0.61	0.10	0.63	0.21	0.63

Panel B: Risk of Epropriation (1985-1995), Social Infrastructure, and Migratory Distance from East Africa

	(1)	(2)	(3)	(4)	(5)	(6)	(7)
	Per capita GDP			Exp.Risk 1985-1995		socinf	
Migratory Distance	0.27***	0.05	0.05	0.36***	0.09	0.08***	0.03***
	(4.59)	(1.34)	(1.12)	(3.97)	(1.48)	(6.52)	(3.06)
Migratory Distance (Squared)	-0.01***	-0.00	-0.00	-0.01***	-0.00**	-0.00***	-0.00***
	(-4.15)	(-0.61)	(-0.54)	(-4.08)	(-2.13)	(-6.36)	(-3.57)
Exp.Risk 1985-1995		0.58***					
		(18.28)					
Social Infrastructure			3.66***				
			(13.11)				
2015 Per Capita GDP					1.03***		0.14***
					(10.35)		(12.51)
Intercept	7.98***	4.79***	7.07***	5.77***	-2.58***	0.18***	-0.94***
	(27.87)	(15.81)	(29.84)	(14.42)	(-3.03)	(4.02)	(-10.59)
Observations	135.00	107.00	112.00	107.00	107.00	112.00	112.00
R-squared	0.12	0.64	0.61	0.10	0.63	0.21	0.63

Note: t-statistics in parentheses. * p<0.1 ** p<0.05 *** p<0.01. Exp.Risk is the average risk of expropriation during 1985-1995 as used by Acemoglu et al. (2001). Socif is the index of social infrastructure of Hall and Jones (1999). The identification condition between migratory distance and predicted genetic diversity implies that the maximizing value of the likelihood is invariant to the choice between these two sets of instruments. In other words, the statistical information in panels A and B is the same.

APPENDIX D

ALTERNATIVE SPECIFICATIONS – CHAPTER FOUR

Table D.1: School attainment, economic institutions, and per capita GDP. Instrumental variable analysis (similar to Table 4.5 but using years of schooling in 1960 as an instrumental variable)

Panel A: Second Stage Results

	(1)	(2)	(3)	(4)
	Dep Var: Log of Per Capita GDP in 2015			
Economic Freedom Index, 1985-2015	0.97***	0.65**	0.65***	0.68***
	(3.35)	(2.52)	(2.64)	(2.58)
Mean Years of Schooling, 1980-2010	0.09	0.10*	0.06	0.05
	(1.11)	(1.67)	(0.88)	(0.71)
Standardized Geographic Disadvantage Index		-0.29***	-0.25**	-0.23*
		(-3.02)	(-2.54)	(-1.80)
Absolute Value of Latitude			0.01***	0.01***
			(2.98)	(2.71)
Ethnolinguistic Fractionalization				-0.10
				(-0.27)
Intercept	2.90**	4.70***	4.67***	4.58***
	(2.20)	(3.66)	(3.81)	(3.63)
Observations	106.00	106.00	106.00	106.00
R-squared	0.64	0.74	0.75	0.74
p-value (OIR Test)	0.15	0.16	0.14	0.31
F(Weak Id. Kleibergen-Paap)	1.54	1.49	1.48	1.12

Instruments used: Migratory Distance interacted with continents and Years of Schooling in 1960

Table D.1 – Continued

Panel B. First Stages and Falsifications Tests

	(1) Econ. Freedom (EFW) 1980-2010	(2) Years of Schooling 1980-2010	(3) Econ. Freedom (EFW) 1980-2010	(4) Log Per Capita GDP 2015	(5) Years of Schooling 1980-2010	(6) Log Per Capita GDP 2015
Geographic Disadvantage Index	-0.21*	-0.37**	-0.06	-0.26**	-0.11	-0.22**
	(-1.89)	(-2.54)	(-0.55)	(-2.23)	(-0.83)	(-2.06)
Absolute Value of Latitude	-0.00	0.01	-0.01	0.02**	-0.00	0.01*
	(-0.03)	(0.70)	(-0.78)	(2.08)	(-0.48)	(1.90)
Ethnolinguistic Fractionalization	0.23	0.31	0.17	0.04	0.21	0.03
	(0.62)	(0.55)	(0.53)	(0.10)	(0.45)	(0.08)
Migratory Distance × Africa	0.07	-0.22*	0.06	-0.03	-0.22**	0.08
	(0.87)	(-1.98)	(0.98)	(-0.39)	(-2.44)	(1.18)
Migratory Distance × Europe	0.11	-0.02	0.09	0.01	-0.07	0.07
	(1.42)	(-0.31)	(1.28)	(0.16)	(-0.99)	(1.08)
Migratory Distance × Asia	0.09**	-0.00	0.06*	0.03	-0.05	0.07**
	(2.18)	(-0.01)	(1.91)	(0.84)	(-1.22)	(2.03)
Migratory Distance × Americas	0.02	-0.02	0.01	0.00	-0.03	0.02
	(1.05)	(-0.89)	(0.77)	(0.31)	(-1.56)	(1.49)
Migratory Distance × Oceania	0.05**	0.01	0.04**	-0.01	0.00	0.01
	(2.10)	(0.21)	(2.10)	(-0.63)	(0.02)	(0.26)
Years of School Attained, 1960	0.20***	0.89***	0.12***	0.09*	0.76***	-0.14**
	(4.02)	(13.91)	(2.64)	(1.94)	(12.75)	(-2.08)
Log Per Capita GDP, 2015			0.41***		0.74***	
			(4.22)		(6.35)	
Econ. Freedom (EFW), 1980-2010				0.46***		
				(4.41)		
Years of Schooling (YS), 1980-2010						0.37***
						(5.78)
Intercept	4.89***	3.39***	1.58*	5.79***	-2.55***	6.78***
	(15.58)	(7.11)	(1.85)	(10.32)	(-2.64)	(20.35)
Observations	106.00	106.00	106.00	106.00	106.00	106.00
R-squared	0.57	0.88	0.65	0.75	0.91	0.77
F-test (joint sig. of excluded IVs)	2.15	193.61	2.19	0.89	162.46	4.31
p-value (F-test)	0.07	0.00	0.06	0.49	0.00	0.04

Robust t statistics in parentheses. * p<0.1 ** p<0.05 *** p<0.01

Table D.2: School attainment, economic institutions, and per capita GDP. Instrumental variable analysis (similar to Table 4.5 but using British, Scandinavian, and Germanic legal origins as an instrumental variable)

Panel A: Second Stage Results

	(1)	(2)	(3)	(4)
	Dep Var: Log of Per Capita GDP in 2015			
Economic Freedom Index, 1985-2015	0.67***	0.46**	0.53***	0.54***
	(3.87)	(2.39)	(2.63)	(2.60)
Mean Years of Schooling, 1980-2010	0.18***	0.13***	0.06	0.05
	(3.53)	(2.58)	(0.91)	(0.91)
Standardized Geographic Disadvantage Index		-0.34***	-0.29***	-0.27**
		(-3.54)	(-3.15)	(-2.26)
Absolute Value of Latitude			0.02***	0.02***
			(2.92)	(2.80)
Ethnolinguistic Fractionalization				-0.09
				(-0.24)
Intercept	4.17***	5.70***	5.38***	5.33***
	(5.00)	(5.81)	(5.30)	(5.20)
Observations	104.00	104.00	104.00	104.00
R-squared	0.72	0.76	0.75	0.75
p-value (OIR Test)	0.04	0.31	0.39	0.39
F(Weak Id. Kleibergen-Paap)	1.66	1.54	1.55	1.21

Instruments used: Migratory Distance interacted with continents and British, Scandinavian, and Germanic legal origins

Table D.2 – Continued

Panel B. First Stages and Falsifications Tests

	(1) Econ. Freedom (EFW) 1980-2010	(2) Years of Schooling 1980-2010	(3) Econ. Freedom (EFW) 1980-2010	(4) Log Per Capita GDP 2015	(5) Years of Schooling 1980-2010	(6) Log Per Capita GDP 2015
Geographic Disadvantage Index	-0.23**	-0.67**	-0.05	-0.26**	-0.19	-0.20*
	(-1.99)	(-2.46)	(-0.44)	(-2.12)	(-0.87)	(-1.76)
Absolute Value of Latitude	0.01	0.05***	-0.00	0.02***	0.02	0.01*
	(1.44)	(3.22)	(-0.05)	(2.76)	(1.39)	(1.86)
Ethnolinguistic Fractionalization	0.18	0.95	0.06	0.15	0.64	-0.02
	(0.38)	(1.11)	(0.16)	(0.37)	(0.87)	(-0.05)
Migratory Distance × Africa	0.09	-0.17	0.09	-0.04	-0.18	0.06
	(1.16)	(-0.99)	(1.28)	(-0.56)	(-1.25)	(0.80)
Migratory Distance × Europe	0.21***	0.31*	0.15**	0.02	0.14	0.05
	(2.77)	(1.96)	(2.43)	(0.30)	(0.91)	(0.66)
Migratory Distance × Asia	0.12**	0.02	0.08**	0.02	-0.08	0.08**
	(2.62)	(0.29)	(2.37)	(0.52)	(-0.99)	(2.02)
Migratory Distance × Americas	0.04***	0.09***	0.03**	0.01	0.05*	0.01
	(3.06)	(3.26)	(2.06)	(0.62)	(1.71)	(0.51)
Migratory Distance × Oceania	0.09***	0.22***	0.06***	0.00	0.15***	-0.01
	(4.09)	(3.35)	(4.32)	(0.14)	(3.19)	(-0.49)
British Legal Origin	0.52***	1.52***	0.41***	-0.06	1.25***	-0.22
	(2.89)	(4.15)	(2.88)	(-0.35)	(3.96)	(-1.13)
Scandinavian Legal Origin	-0.05	0.47	0.09	-0.26	0.81	-0.42**
	(-0.18)	(0.67)	(0.38)	(-1.29)	(1.39)	(-2.20)
Germanic Legal Origin	-0.00	2.22***	-0.06	0.12	2.07***	-0.52**
	(-0.01)	(4.33)	(-0.20)	(0.78)	(4.40)	(-2.23)
Log Per Capita GDP, 2015			0.47***		1.23***	
			(5.16)		(6.57)	
Econ. Freedom (EFW), 1980-2010				0.56***		
				(5.72)		
Years of Schooling (YS), 1980-2010						0.29***
						(7.12)
Intercept	4.67***	2.84***	1.00	5.28***	-6.87***	7.06***
	(13.64)	(4.58)	(1.21)	(9.63)	(-4.88)	(21.23)
Observations	104.00	104.00	104.00	104.00	104.00	104.00
R-squared	0.54	0.71	0.66	0.73	0.81	0.77
F-test (joint sig. of excluded IVs)	4.66	13.52	4.57	0.54	10.03	2.33
p-value (F-test)	0.00	0.00	0.00	0.75	0.00	0.08

Robust t statistics in parentheses. * p<0.1 ** p<0.05 *** p<0.01

Table D.3: Changes in school attainment and growth. A virtuous cycle (similar to Table 4.6 but using education of the female population)

	(1)	(2)	(3)	(4)	(5)
	Secondary School Completed (Age 15-24) Corresponds to the Female Population (Columns 5 to 8)				
Panel A: Dependent Variable is the Annual Growth Rate, During 15-Year Periods					
Log Initial Per Capita GDP	-0.16	-0.78***	-0.21**	-0.34***	-0.54***
	(-0.61)	(-4.04)	(-1.99)	(-3.43)	(-4.69)
Sec. School Completion Rate, 15-Year Prior to the Period	0.05*	0.06***	0.05***	0.05***	0.03***
	(1.94)	(3.36)	(5.59)	(5.87)	(3.35)
Change in Secondary Completion Rate (Previous 15 Years)	0.08**	0.03*	0.06***	0.04***	0.04***
	(2.55)	(1.93)	(6.11)	(3.75)	(4.23)
Change in the Prime Working Age 25-59 Share, During the 15 years				0.26***	0.22***
				(10.20)	(8.78)
Initial EFW					0.84***
					(7.80)
Change in EFW, During the Period					0.71***
					(6.61)
Intercept	1.78	7.97***	2.32***	2.74***	-0.60
	(0.88)	(5.31)	(2.75)	(3.58)	(-0.72)
Panel B: Dependent Variable is the Change in Secondary School Completion Rate, During 15-Year Periods					
Initial Secondary School Completion Rate	0.06	-0.52***	-0.29***	-0.30***	-0.37***
	(0.66)	(-5.97)	(-7.84)	(-7.90)	(-8.08)
Log Per Capita GDP, 15-Year Before the Beginning of the Period	-1.71	5.55***	2.50***	2.41***	2.75***
	(-1.43)	(4.62)	(4.57)	(4.39)	(3.94)
Annual Growth Rate (Previous 15 Years)	1.83***	0.56	0.79***	0.90***	0.82***
	(4.23)	(1.21)	(4.08)	(4.54)	(3.15)
Intercept	16.71*	-27.52***	-9.66**	-9.11**	-9.95*
	(1.86)	(-2.91)	(-2.28)	(-2.15)	(-1.81)
Observations	114.00	114.00	570.00	570.00	402.00
R-squared 1 (Growth Equation)	0.10	0.13	0.11	0.27	0.43
R-squared 2 (Change in Human Capital Equation)	0.20	0.25	0.11	0.11	0.15
Periods Included:	1975-1990	1995-2010	1975-1990 1980-1995 1985-2000 1990-2005 1995-2010	1975-1990 1980-1995 1985-2000 1990-2005 1995-2010	1980-1995 1985-2000 1990-2005 1995-2010

All equations, by column, were estimated simultaneously. * $p<0.1$ ** $p<0.05$ *** $p<0.01$"

Table D.4: Determinants of PISA reading scores, country-level analysis (extension to Table 4.10)

	(1)	(2)	(3)	(4)	(5)	(6)
	Dependent Variable: PISA Score, Reading					
	Average	Top 95%	Average	Top 95%	Average	Top 95%
Years of Schooling, Pop. Age 30-49, 2010	11.52***	12.67***	10.37***	11.25***	10.50***	11.66***
	(3.42)	(4.42)	(3.13)	(3.78)	(3.39)	(4.11)
Family Size, 2010	-45.07**	-52.33**	-46.68**	-54.87**	-49.43**	-63.71***
	(-2.29)	(-2.61)	(-2.33)	(-2.60)	(-2.62)	(-3.56)
Log Per Capita GDP, 2010	15.05	18.46**	3.32	10.65		
	(1.40)	(2.22)	(0.28)	(1.10)		
EFW Summary Rating, 2000-2015			16.77***	13.12**	18.31***	18.08***
			(3.10)	(2.01)	(3.28)	(3.08)
Intercept	216.32**	322.87***	226.24**	323.74***	248.88***	396.42***
	(2.02)	(3.26)	(2.07)	(3.22)	(4.65)	(6.77)
Observations	66.00	66.00	65.00	65.00	65.00	65.00
R-squared	0.60	0.70	0.64	0.71	0.63	0.70

Robust t statistics in parentheses. * $p<0.1$ ** $p<0.05$ *** $p<0.01$

Table D.5: Determinants of PISA science scores, country-level analysis (extension to Table 4.10)

	(1)	(2)	(3)	(4)	(5)	(6)
	Dependent Variable: PISA Score, Science					
	Average	Top 95%	Average	Top 95%	Average	Top 95%
Years of Schooling, Pop. Age 30-49, 2010	10.15***	12.26***	9.18***	10.95***	9.05***	11.23***
	(3.05)	(4.08)	(2.93)	(3.38)	(2.84)	(3.50)
Family Size, 2010	-64.97***	-75.44***	-66.02***	-77.59***	-63.14***	-83.73***
	(-2.87)	(-3.07)	(-2.91)	(-3.08)	(-3.03)	(-3.99)
Log Per Capita GDP, 2010	10.13	17.16	-3.46	7.39		
	(0.86)	(1.55)	(-0.27)	(0.60)		
EFW Summary Rating, 2000-2015			18.32***	15.03*	16.71***	18.47**
			(3.02)	(1.97)	(2.76)	(2.50)
Intercept	298.30**	358.19***	312.99**	363.29***	289.39***	413.76***
	(2.41)	(2.73)	(2.52)	(2.76)	(4.77)	(6.02)
Observations	66.00	66.00	65.00	65.00	65.00	65.00
R-squared	0.55	0.65	0.60	0.67	0.59	0.66

Robust t statistics in parentheses. * $p<0.1$ ** $p<0.05$ *** $p<0.01$

Table D.6: Determinants of PISA math scores, country-level analysis (extension to Table 4.10)

	(1)	(2)	(3)	(4)	(5)	(6)
	Dependent Variable: PISA Score, Math					
	Average	Top 95%	Average	Top 95%	Average	Top 95%
Years of Schooling, Pop. Age 30-49, 2010	11.68***	11.80***	11.40***	11.18***	11.35***	11.25***
	(2.95)	(3.39)	(3.20)	(3.16)	(3.24)	(3.18)
Family Size, 2010	-79.48***	-96.95***	-78.90***	-97.42***	-77.64***	-98.93***
	(-3.30)	(-3.66)	(-3.26)	(-3.60)	(-3.40)	(-4.20)
Log Per Capita GDP, 2010	12.53	12.71	-1.52	1.83		
	(1.00)	(1.12)	(-0.12)	(0.15)		
EFW Summary Rating, 2000-2015			16.74***	14.18**	16.03**	15.04**
			(2.71)	(2.16)	(2.44)	(2.23)
Intercept	262.18**	414.50***	283.85**	427.70***	273.48***	440.17***
	(2.07)	(3.15)	(2.22)	(3.22)	(4.03)	(6.09)
Observations	66.00	66.00	65.00	65.00	65.00	65.00
R-squared	0.62	0.67	0.66	0.69	0.66	0.69

Robust t statistics in parentheses. * $p<0.1$ ** $p<0.05$ *** $p<0.01$

REFERENCES

Abrigo, Michael R. M., and Inessa Love. 2016. *Estimation of Panel Vector Autoregression in Stata: A Package of Programs*. University of Hawaii at Manoa, Department of Economics. https://ideas.repec.org/p/hai/wpaper/201602.html.

Acemoglu, Daron, and Simon Johnson. 2005. "Unbundling Institutions." *Journal of Political Economy* 113(5): 949–95.

Acemoglu, Daron, Simon Johnson, and James A. Robinson. 2001. "The Colonial Origins of Comparative Development: An Empirical Investigation." *American Economic Review* 91(5): 1369–1401.

Acemoglu, Daron, Simon Johnson, and James A. Robinson. 2005. "Chapter 6 Institutions as a Fundamental Cause of Long-Run Growth." In *Handbook of Economic Growth*, eds. Philippe Aghion and Steven N. Durlauf. Elsevier, 385–472. http://www.sciencedirect.com/science/article/pii/S1574068405010063.

Acemoglu, Daron, Suresh Naidu, Pascual Restrepo, and James A. Robinson. 2018. "Democracy Does Cause Growth." *Journal of Political Economy* 127(1): 47–100.

Acemoglu, Daron, and James A. Robinson. 2012. *Why Nations Fail: The Origins of Power, Prosperity, and Poverty*. Crown Publishers.

Albouy, David Y. 2012. "The Colonial Origins of Comparative Development: An Empirical Investigation: Comment." *American Economic Review* 102(6): 3059–76.

Angrist, Joshua, and Jörn-Steffen Pischke. *Mostly Harmless Econometrics. An Empiricist's Companion*. Princeton University Press.

Ashraf, Quamrul, and Oded Galor. 2013. "The 'Out of Africa' Hypothesis, Human Genetic Diversity, and Comparative Economic Development." *American Economic Review* 103(1): 1–46.

Auer, Raphael A. 2013. "Geography, Institutions, and the Making of Comparative Development." *Journal of Economic Growth* 18(2): 179–215.

Barro, Robert J. 1991. "Economic Growth in a Cross Section of Countries." *The Quarterly Journal of Economics* 106(2): 407–43.

Barro, Robert J., and Jong-Wha Lee. 2010. *A New Data Set of Educational Attainment in the World, 1950-2010. NBER Working Paper No. 15902*. National Bureau of Economic Research.

Becker, Gary. 1960. *An Economic Analysis of Fertility*. National Bureau of Economic Research, Inc. NBER Chapters. https://econpapers.repec.org/bookchap/nbrnberch/2387.htm.

Bennett, Daniel, Hugo Faria, James Gwartney, and Daniel Morales. 2016. *Economic Institutions and Comparative Economic Development: A Post-Colonial Perspective*. University of Miami, Department of Economics. Working Paper. https://econpapers.repec.org/paper/miawpaper/2016-07.htm.

Bennett, Daniel L. et al. 2017. *Evidence on Economic versus Political Institutions as Determinants of Development*. University of Miami, Department of Economics. https://ideas.repec.org/p/mia/wpaper/2017-04.html.

Berggren, Niclas. 2003. "The Benefits of Economic Freedom: A Survey." *The Independent Review* 8(2): 193–211.

Bjørnskov, Christian, and Nicolai J. Foss. 2008. "Economic Freedom and Entrepreneurial Activity: Some Cross-Country Evidence." *Public Choice* 134(3): 307–28.

Blaug, Mark. 1966. "Literacy and Economic Development." *The School Review* 74(4): 393–418.

Boix, Carles, Michael Miller, and Sebastian Rosato. 2013. "A Complete Data Set of Political Regimes, 1800–2007." *Comparative Political Studies* 46(12): 1523–54.

Bolt, Jutta, Robert Inklaar, Herman de Jong, and Jan Luiten van Zanden. 2018. "Maddison Project Database." https://www.rug.nl/ggdc/historicaldevelopment/maddison/releases/maddison-project-database-2018.

Bolt, Jutta, Robert Inklaar, Herman de Jong, and Jan Luiten van Zanden. 2018. "Rebasing 'Maddison': The Shape of Long-Run Economic Development." *VoxEU.org*. https://voxeu.org/article/rebasing-maddison.

Brice, Brandon. 2018. "Violent Conflict and Institutional Change." Doctoral Dissertation. Florida State University.

Cheibub, José Antonio, Jennifer Gandhi, and James Raymond Vreeland. 2010. "Democracy and Dictatorship Revisited." *Public Choice* 143(1): 67–101.

Connors, Joseph, and Hugo Montesinos. 2018. "A Weakly Balanced Data Set of Poverty in the Developing World, 1970-2015." https://sites.google.com/view/hugomoises/research.

Cragg, John G., and Stephen G. Donald. 1993. "Testing Identifiability and Specification in Instrumental Variable Models." *Econometric Theory* 9(2): 222–40.

Curtin, Philip D. 1995. *African History: From Earliest Times to Independence.* London; New York: Longman.

Dawson, John W. 1998. "Institutions, Investment, and Growth: New Cross-Country and Panel Data Evidence." *Economic Inquiry* 36(4): 603–19.

Deaton, Angus, and Bettina Aten. 2017. "Trying to Understand the PPPs in ICP 2011: Why Are the Results So Different?" *American Economic Journal: Macroeconomics* 9(1): 243–64.

Diamond, Jared M. 1997. *Guns, Germs, and Steel: The Fates of Human Societies.* 1st edition. New York: W. W. Norton & Company.

Easterly, William, and Ross Levine. 2003. "Tropics, Germs, and Crops: How Endowments Influence Economic Development." *Journal of Monetary Economics* 50(1): 3–39.

Eckstein, Harry, and Ted Robert Gurr. 1975. *Patterns of Authority: A Structural Basis for Political Inquiry.* Wiley.

Engerman, Stanley L, and Kenneth L Sokoloff. 2002. *Factor Endowments, Inequality, and Paths of Development Among New World Economics.* National Bureau of Economic Research. Working Paper. http://www.nber.org/papers/w9259.

Engerman, Stanley L, and Kenneth L Sokoloff. 2005. *Colonialism, Inequality, and Long-Run Paths of Development.* National Bureau of Economic Research. Working Paper. http://www.nber.org/papers/w11057.

Engerman, Stanley L., and Kenneth L. Sokoloff. 2012. *Economic Development in the Americas Since 1500: Endowments and Institutions.* Cambridge University Press.

Faría, Hugo J. et al. 2013. "Does Corruption Cause Encumbered Business Regulations? An IV Approach." *Applied Economics* 45(1): 65–83.

Faria, Hugo J., and Hugo M. Montesinos. 2009. "Does Economic Freedom Cause Prosperity? An IV Approach." *Public Choice* 141(1): 103–27.

Faria, Hugo J., Hugo M. Montesinos-Yufa, and Daniel R. Morales. 2014. "Should the Modernization Hypothesis Survive Acemoglu, Johnson, Robinson, and Yared? Some More Evidence." *Econ Journal Watch* 11(1): 17.

Faria, Hugo J., Hugo M. Montesinos-Yufa, Daniel R. Morales, and Carlos E. Navarro. 2016. "Unbundling the Roles of Human Capital and Institutions in Economic Development." *European Journal of Political Economy* 45: 108–28.

Faria, Hugo J., Daniel R. Morales, Natasha Pineda, and Hugo M. Montesinos. 2012. "Can Capitalism Restrain Public Perceived Corruption? Some Evidence." *Journal of Institutional Economics* 8(4): 511–35.

Feenstra, Robert C., Robert Inklaar, and Marcel P. Timmer. 2015. "The Next Generation of the Penn World Table." www.ggdc.net/pwt.

Freedom House. 2019. "Methodology: Freedom in the World, Technical Report, Freedom House." https://freedomhouse.org/report/methodology-freedom-world-2019.

Gallup, John Luke, Jeffrey D. Sachs, and Andrew D. Mellinger. 1999. "Geography and Economic Development." *International Regional Science Review* 22(2): 179–232.

Ganzeboom, Harry B. G., Paul M. De Graaf, and Donald J. Treiman. 1992. "A Standard International Socio-Economic Index of Occupational Status." *Social Science Research* 21(1): 1–56.

Ganzeboom, Harry B. G., and Donald J. Treiman. 2003. "Three Internationally Standardised Measures for Comparative Research on Occupational Status." In *Advances in Cross-National Comparison: A European Working Book for Demographic and Socio-Economic Variables*, eds. Jürgen H. P. Hoffmeyer-Zlotnik and Christof Wolf. Boston, MA: Springer US, 159–93. https://doi.org/10.1007/978-1-4419-9186-7_9.

Glaeser, Edward L., and Janet E. Kohlhase. 2004. "Cities, Regions and the Decline of Transport Costs*." *Papers in Regional Science*. https://rsaiconnect.onlinelibrary.wiley.com/doi/abs/10.1007/s10110-003-0183-x.

Glaeser, Edward L., Rafael La Porta, Florencio Lopez-de-Silanes, and Andrei Shleifer. 2004. "Do Institutions Cause Growth?" *Journal of Economic Growth* 9(3): 271–303.

Griliches, Zvi. 1977. "Estimating the Returns to Schooling: Some Econometric Problems." *Econometrica* 45(1): 1–22.

Gwartney, James. 2009. "Institutions, Economic Freedom, and Cross-Country Differences in Performance." *Southern Economic Journal* 75(4): 937–56.

Gwartney, James D., Randall G. Holcombe, and Robert A. Lawson. 2006. "Institutions and the Impact of Investment on Growth." *Kyklos* 59(2): 255–73.

Gwartney, James D., and Hugo M. Montesinos. 2018. "Cato Journal: Former Centrally Planned Economies 25 Years after the Fall of Communism." *Cato Institute*. https://www.cato.org/cato-journal/winter-2018/former-centrally-planned-economies-25-years-after-fall-communism.

Gwartney, James, Robert Lawson, Joshua Hall, and Ryan Murphy. 2018. *Economic Freedom of the World: 2018 Annual Report.* https://www.fraserinstitute.org/studies/economic-freedom-of-the-world-2018-annual-report.

Gwartney, James, Hugo Montesinos, and Joseph Connors. 2018. "The Rise and Fall of Worldwide Income Inequality, 1820-2035." https://sites.google.com/view/hugomoises/research.

Haan, Jakob De, Susanna Lundström, and Jan-Egbert Sturm. 2006. "Market-Oriented Institutions and Policies and Economic Growth: A Critical Survey." *Journal of Economic Surveys* 20(2): 157–91.

Hall, Joshua C., Russell S. Sobel, and George R. Crowley. 2010. "Institutions, Capital, and Growth." *Southern Economic Journal* 77(2): 385–405.

Hall, Robert E., and Charles I. Jones. 1999. "Why Do Some Countries Produce So Much More Output Per Worker than Others?" *The Quarterly Journal of Economics* 114(1): 83–116.

Hammond, Alexander C. R. 2019. "Heroes of Progress, Pt. 17: Malcom McLean." *Human Progress.* https://humanprogress.org/article.php?p=1905.

Hanushek, Eric A., and Ludger Woessmann. 2012. "Do Better Schools Lead to More Growth? Cognitive Skills, Economic Outcomes, and Causation." *Journal of Economic Growth* 17(4): 267–321.

Heckelman, Jac C., and Michael D. Stroup. 2000. "Whcich Economic Freedoms Contribute to Growth?" *Kyklos* 53(4): 527–44.

Heckman, James, and Solomon Polachek. 1974. "Empirical Evidence on the Functional Form of the Earnings-Schooling Relationship." *Journal of the American Statistical Association* 69(346): 350–54.

Inklaar, Robert, and D. S. Prasada Rao. 2017. "Cross-Country Income Levels over Time: Did the Developing World Suddenly Become Much Richer?" *American Economic Journal: Macroeconomics* 9(1): 265–90.

Jones, Eric. 1981. *The European Miracle: Environments, Economies and Geopolitics in the History of Europe and Asia.* First Edition.

Jones, Eric. 2003. *The European Miracle: Environments, Economies and Geopolitics in the History of Europe and Asia.* Cambridge University Press (Third Edition).

Kaufmann, Daniel, and Kraay Aart. 2019. *Worldwide Governance Indicators (WGI)*. The World Bank Group.

Keefer, Philip, and Stephen Knack. 1997. "Why Don't Poor Countries Catch up? A Cross-National Test of an Institutional Explanation." *Economic Inquiry* 35(3): 590–602.

Kiszewski, Anthony et al. 2004. "A Global Index Representing The Stability Of Malaria Transmission." *The American Journal of Tropical Medicine and Hygiene* 70(5): 486–98.

Kleibergen, Frank, and Richard Paap. 2006. "Generalized Reduced Rank Tests Using the Singular Value Decomposition." *Journal of Econometrics* 133(1): 97–126.

Knack, Stephen, and Philip Keefer. 1995. "Institutions and Economic Performance: Cross-Country Tests Using Alternative Institutional Measures." *Economics & Politics* 7(3): 207–27.

Krugman, Paul. 1991. "Increasing Returns and Economic Geography." *Journal of Political Economy* 99(3): 483–99.

Laitin, David D., Joachim Moortgat, and Amanda Lea Robinson. 2012. "Geographic Axes and the Persistence of Cultural Diversity." *Proceedings of the National Academy of Sciences* 109(26): 10263–68.

Landes, David S. 1999. *The Wealth and Poverty of Nations: Why Some Are So Rich and Some So Poor.* unknown edition. New York: W. W. Norton & Company.

Lucas, Robert E. 1988. "On the Mechanics of Economic Development." *Journal of Monetary Economics* 22(1): 3–42.

Machiavelli, Niccolo. 1531. *Discourses on Livy*. Reissue edition. Oxford ; New York: Oxford University Press. 2009.

Marshall, Monty, and Ted Robert Gurr. 2016. "Polity IV Project: Country Reports 2010." *Polity IV Project: Political Regime Characteristics and Transitions, 1800-2013.* https://www.systemicpeace.org/polity/polity4.htm.

Mincer, Jacob. 1974. "Schooling, Experience, and Earnings. Human Behavior & Social Institutions No. 2."

Montesquieu, Charles de. 1748. *Montesquieu: The Spirit of the Laws.* eds. Anne M. Cohler, Basia Carolyn Miller, and Harold Samuel Stone. Cambridge ; New York: Cambridge University Press. 1989.

North, Douglass C., and Robert Paul Thomas. 1973. *The Rise of the Western World: A New Economic History*. Cambridge University Press.

Paldam, Martin, and Erich Gundlach. 2008. "Two Views on Institutions and Development: The Grand Transition vs the Primacy of Institutions." *Kyklos* 61(1): 65–100.

Persson, Torsten, and Guido Tabellini. 2006. "Democracy and Development: The Devil in the Details." *American Economic Review* 96(2): 319–24.

PISA. 2015. "PISA 2015 Results (Volume I) - Excellence and Equity in Education - En - OECD." https://www.oecd.org/education/pisa-2015-results-volume-i-9789264266490-en.htm.

PISA Dataset. 2015. *Programme for International Student Assessment (PISA).* The Organization of Economic Co-operation and Development (OECD). https://www.oecd.org/pisa/data/2015database/.

PISA Technical Report. 2015. *2015 Technical Report - Programme for International Student Assessment (PISA).* The Organization of Economic Co-operation and Development. https://www.oecd.org/pisa/data/2015-technical-report/

Pomeranz, Kenneth. 2000. "The Great Divergence." *Princeton University Press.* https://press.princeton.edu/titles/6823.html.

Putterman, Louis, and David N. Weil. 2010. "Post-1500 Population Flows and The Long-Run Determinants of Economic Growth and Inequality." *The Quarterly Journal of Economics* 125(4): 1627–82.

Rode, Martin, and James D. Gwartney. 2012. "Does Democratization Facilitate Economic Liberalization?" *European Journal of Political Economy* 28(4): 607–19.

Rodrik, Dani. 2000. "Institutions for High-Quality Growth: What They Are and How to Acquire Them." *Studies in Comparative International Development* 35(3): 3–31.

Rodrik, Dani, Arvind Subramanian, and Francesco Trebbi. 2004. "Institutions Rule: The Primacy of Institutions Over Geography and Integration in Economic Development." *Journal of Economic Growth* 9(2): 131–65.

Romer, Paul M. 1989. *Human Capital And Growth: Theory and Evidence.* National Bureau of Economic Research. Working Paper. http://www.nber.org/papers/w3173.

Sachs, Jeffrey D. 2003. *Institutions Don't Rule: Direct Effects of Geography on Per Capita Income.* National Bureau of Economic Research. Working Paper. http://www.nber.org/papers/w9490.

Sachs, Jeffrey D. 2012. "Government, Geography, and Growth: The True Drivers of Economic Development" eds. DARON ACEMOGLU and JAMES ROBINSON. *Foreign Affairs* 91(5): 142–50.

Sarkees, Meredith Reid, and Frank Wayman. 2010. *Resort to War: 1816 - 2007*. Washington DC: CQ Press. http://cow.dss.ucdavis.edu/data-sets/COW-war.

Schultz, Theodore W. 1961. "Investment in Human Capital." *The American Economic Review* 51(1): 1–17.

Smith, Adam. 1776. *The Wealth of Nations*. Cedar Lake Classics. 2019.

Solow, Robert M. 1956. "A Contribution to the Theory of Economic Growth." *The Quarterly Journal of Economics* 70(1): 65–94.

Stock, James H., and Jonathan H. Wright. 2000. "GMM with Weak Identification." *Econometrica* 68(5): 1055–96.

Stock, James H., and Motohiro Yogo. 2005. *Testing for Weak Instruments in Linear IV Regression*. Rochester, NY: Social Science Research Network. SSRN Scholarly Paper. https://papers.ssrn.com/abstract=1734933.

World Bank. 2018. "World Development Report 2018: Learning to Realize Education's Promise." *World Bank*. https://www.worldbank.org/en/publication/wdr2018.

World Bank. 2019. "World Development Indicators."

"World Population Prospects: The 2017 Revision. United Nations Department of Economic and Social Affairs." 2017. https://www.un.org/development/desa/publications/world-population-prospects-the-2017-revision.html.

BIOGRAPHICAL SKETCH

Hugo M. Montesinos-Yufa holds a Ph.D. in Engineering with a concentration in Statistics from Universidad Simon Bolivar (USB) and a Ph.D. in Economics from Florida State University. He served as a professor in the Department of Scientific Computing and Statistics at USB and as a professor at the Center of Finance at the Instituto de Estudios Superiores de Administración (IESA), both located in Caracas, Venezuela. He served as the Director of the Center for Statistics and Mathematical Software at USB before leaving Venezuela to pursue his Ph.D. in Economics at Florida State University. He served as a professor at Ursinus College from 2019 to 2026. He is currently an applied engineer, statistician, and economist specializing in institutional analysis.

FREE DIGITAL COMPANION

FOR SCHOLARS & RESEARCHERS

www.hugomontesinos.com/WealthData

This volume contains detailed econometric models and regression tables that are designed to be studied in high resolution.

Scan the code above to download the free **Empirical Architecture Research Pack**, which includes:

- High-Resolution PDF of all Tables & Figures.
- The Complete Poverty Dataset.
- Replication Data for Researchers.

Made in the USA
Monee, IL
12 November 2026

da7b44c1-8edc-413d-9524-d61def5b37c9R01